Velvet Retro

Worlds of Memory

Editors:
Jeffrey Olick, University of Virginia
Aline Sierp, Maastricht University
Jenny Wüstenberg, York University

Published in collaboration with the Memory Studies Association

This book series publishes innovative and rigorous scholarship in the interdisciplinary and global field of memory studies. Memory studies includes all inquiries into the ways we – both individually and collectively – are shaped by the past. How do we represent the past to ourselves and to others? How do those representations shape our actions and understandings, whether explicitly or unconsciously? The 'memory' we study encompasses the near-infinitude of practices and processes humans use to engage with the past, the incredible variety of representations they produce and the range of individuals and institutions involved in doing so.

Guided by the mandate of the Memory Studies Association to provide a forum for conversations among subfields, regions, and research traditions, Worlds of Memory focuses on cutting-edge research that pushes the boundaries of the field and can provide insights for memory scholars outside of a particular specialization. In the process, it seeks to make memory studies more accessible, diverse, and open to novel approaches.

Volume 2
Velvet Retro
Postsocialist Nostalgia and the Politics of Heroism in Czech Popular Culture
Veronika Pehe

Volume 1
When Will We Talk about Hitler?
German Students and the Nazi Past
Alexandra Oeser

Velvet Retro

Postsocialist Nostalgia and the Politics of Heroism in Czech Popular Culture

Veronika Pehe

berghahn
NEW YORK • OXFORD
www.berghahnbooks.com

First published in 2020 by
Berghahn Books
www.berghahnbooks.com

© 2020, 2024 Veronika Pehe
First paperback edition published in 2024

All rights reserved. Except for the quotation of short passages
for the purposes of criticism and review, no part of this book
may be reproduced in any form or by any means, electronic or
mechanical, including photocopying, recording, or any information
storage and retrieval system now known or to be invented,
without written permission of the publisher.

Library of Congress Cataloging-in-Publication Data
Names: Pehe, Veronika, author.
Title: Velvet retro : postsocialist nostalgia and the politics of heroism
in Czech popular culture / Veronika Pehe.
Description: New York : Berghahn, 2020. | Series: Worlds of memory ; volume
2 | Includes bibliographical references and index.
Identifiers: LCCN 2019043782 (print) | LCCN 2019043783 (ebook) | ISBN
9781789206289 (hardback) | ISBN 9781789206296 (ebook)
Subjects: LCSH: Czech Republic--Politics and government--1993- | Collective
memory--Czech Republic. | Popular culture--Political aspects--Czech
Republic. | Czechoslovakia--History--Velvet Revolution, 1989. | National
characteristics, Czech.
Classification: LCC DB2244.7 .P44 2020 (print) | LCC DB2244.7 (ebook) |
DDC 943.7105--dc23
LC record available at https://lccn.loc.gov/2019043782
LC ebook record available at https://lccn.loc.gov/2019043783

British Library Cataloguing in Publication Data
A catalogue record for this book is available from the British Library

ISBN 978-1-78920-628-9 hardback
ISBN 978-1-80539-140-1 paperback
ISBN 978-1-80539-409-9 epub
ISBN 978-1-78920-629-6 web pdf

https://doi.org/10.3167/9781789206289

For Sławek

Contents

List of Figures	viii
Acknowledgements	ix
List of Abbreviations	xi

Introduction
Returning to the Past … 1

Chapter 1
Painting the Past Black and White: Czech Anticommunism after 1989 … 27

Chapter 2
The Past as Comedy: Representing Socialism in the 1990s … 46

Chapter 3
The Late 1990s: Contesting the Past through Popular Culture … 64

Chapter 4
Petty Heroism: Nostalgia for Resistance … 84

Chapter 5
The Politics and Aesthetics of Retro … 101

Chapter 6
Changing Memory Landscapes in the 2000s … 123

Conclusion
Socialism Remembered … 154

Bibliography … 163
Index … 173

Figures

0.1	The door of Café Kaaba, Prague	2
0.2	Promotional postcard for the Museum of Communism, Prague	10
2.1	*Šakalí léta* (*Jackal Years*), Jan Hřebejk (director, screenwriter) and Petr Jarchovský (screenwriter), 1993	55
2.2	*Kolja* (*Kolya*), Jan Svěrák (director) and Zdeněk Svěrák (screenwriter), 1996	57
3.1	*Pelíšky* (*Cosy Dens*), Jan Hřebejk (director) and Petr Jarchovský (screenwriter), 1999	77
5.1	Botas store, Prague. The sign in the window reads 'Traditional Czech Product'	105
5.2	*Rebelové* (*The Rebels*), Filip Renč (director, screenwriter) and Zdeněk Zelenka (screenwriter), 2001	109
6.1	*Ve stínu* (*In the Shadow*), David Ondříček (director, screenwriter) and Marek Epstein, Misha Votruba (screenwriters), 2012	139

Acknowledgements

It is perhaps no surprise that biographical reasons led me to first take interest in this book's topic. I was always fascinated by the story of my parents' rather dramatic escape from behind the Iron Curtain in the boot of a kind stranger's car. I am therefore first and foremost thankful to my mother and father for sharing their stories with me. I understood their reasons for leaving Czechoslovakia, but I was also curious about the society they left behind. What was it like for those – the vast majority – who stayed? From this question, it did not take long to become captivated with other stories that have been told about the period between 1948 and 1989 in Czechoslovakia – whether in novels, films or TV series. I first started to investigate this topic as a graduate student at University College London. My supervisors at the School of Slavonic and East European Studies, Peter Zusi and Kristin Roth-Ey, were an invaluable source of inspiration and sound advice while guiding me through my doctoral research.

Writing this book would not have been possible without the kind help and support of a number of friends and colleagues. I am particularly grateful to Pavel Kolář and Peter Bugge for reading my work so thoroughly and the comments, criticism and constructive feedback they offered. Many of this book's themes have developed out of my article 'The Colours of Socialism: Visual Nostalgia and Retro Aesthetics in Czech Film and Television', published in 2015 in a special issue of *Canadian Slavonic Papers* on 'Nostalgia, Culture, and Identity in Central and Eastern Europe', edited by Anna Louyest and Graham H. Roberts. I would like to thank the editors for their input. Some parts of that article are also incorporated into the analysis in Chapter 5. Special thanks are also due to those who at various stages read parts of the manuscript, provided advice, inspired me with their ideas or looked up hard-to-find pieces of information: Muriel Blaive, Rosamund Johnston, Chad Bryant, Andrei Sorescu, Sune Bechmann Pedersen, Felix Jeschke, Jack Reilly, Ilya Afanasyev, the Yale Working Group on Globalization and Culture and also my father, Jiří Pehe, to name just a few.

The institutional support and funding I received were also essential during my research and writing, and I am particularly grateful to the Arts and Humanities Research Council for generously supporting my research, as well as the UCL Doctoral School, which enabled me to spend a semester at Yale University, and the Institute for Human Sciences in Vienna, where I spent a productive six months. During the writing stages, I found a welcoming institutional home at the European University Institute in Florence and most recently at the Institute of Contemporary History of the Czech Academy of Sciences in Prague. It is at my current institution that I have been particularly lucky to have kind and understanding colleagues. I am especially thankful to Miroslav Vaněk and Michal Kopeček for their support that allowed me to combine the early months of motherhood and work – something that still cannot be taken for granted in academia. The final stages of this book were written just as my son was born and so finally, my biggest thanks go to my partner and my mother. It is only due to their help and encouragement that I had the privilege of the time and space to concentrate on writing. Without them, this book would never have happened.

Abbreviations

ABS	Archiv bezpečnostních složek	Security Services Archive
ČSSD	Česká strana sociálně demokratická	Czech Social Democratic Party
KPV	Konfederace politických vězňů	Confederation of Political Prisoners
KSČ	Komunistická strana Československa	Communist Party of Czechoslovakia
KSČM	Komunistická strana Čech a Moravy	Communist Party of Bohemia and Moravia
ODS	Občanská demokratická strana	Civic Democratic Party
OF	Občanské fórum	Civic Forum
Stasi	Staatssicherheitsdienst	State Security Service (German Democratic Republic)
StB	Státní bezpečnost	State Security (Czechoslovakia)
ÚSTR	Ústav pro studium totalitních režimů	Institute for the Study of Totalitarian Regimes

INTRODUCTION

Returning to the Past

On a tree-lined street in Prague's upmarket district of Vinohrady, Café Kaaba invites customers to drink a coffee in an interior decorated in 'Brussels Style', the late 1950s and early 1960s wave of design that followed the success of the Czechoslovak Pavilion at the World's Fair in Brussels in 1958. Before entering, Kaaba proudly informs customers of its attitude towards the state socialist past on its door.[1] On a sticker with a crossed-out red circle, where one would often find the symbol of a dog to indicate that pets are not welcome, Kaaba features a crossed-out hammer and sickle. A second sticker displays crossed-out cherries, the symbol of the Communist Party of Bohemia and Moravia (KSČM), in a clear message that communists are not allowed inside (Figure 0.1). The socialist-era design on show in the café is to be enjoyed not for the political era that gave rise to it, but as one of the many available styles that the free market offers. Though the interior of the café is pleasant, the disclaimer on the door suggests that this should not stimulate nostalgia for how things were in the past. Instead, it turns to an alternative line of Czech history, which sees a continuity of national culture irrespective of political regimes. The message implies a hypothetical projection of the achievements of socialism – its design – without its politics: a state socialism without communists.

Such a paradoxical attitude is emblematic of the Czech relationship to state socialism evident in many post-1989 cultural representations of the past and also holds a firm place in public discourse, conducted in the media by politicians, journalists and other commentators, as well as both state and

Figure 0.1 The door of Café Kaaba, Prague. Photo by Prokop Jelínek.

nonstate institutions. The negotiation of this relationship, like elsewhere in the former Eastern Bloc, was one of the pressing issues that Czechoslovakia and, since 1993, the Czech Republic had to deal with after the collapse of the communist regime in the events known as the 'Velvet Revolution' of November 1989 and the end of the Cold War. Throughout the region, reckoning with the legacies of the rule of communist parties (under the guise of a variety of names) has had implications for legislation and the organization of the new political order after 1989 or 1991. Salvaging or condemning aspects of the previous regime has impacted the formation of collective and national identities, and various state and nonstate groups have used the past to legitimate their political aims. While many of these aspects have been addressed by political scientists, the way in which a society understands its own past is not a matter for politicians and legislative measures alone; it is through culture that particular narratives about the past are kept alive and help to structure understandings of the present. This book offers an in-depth analysis of the Czech cultural memory of state socialism. It takes retrospective representations – literature, film and television series – that arose after 1989 as a major component of the collective cultural memory of the state socialist period of 1948–89 in the Czech Republic and sets them in conversation with public debates in the first twenty-five years after the demise of the previous regime.

The time period of a quarter of a century, which this book investigates, is not chosen by chance. For the first twenty-five years after the collapse of the previous regime, concerns with how to evaluate the period of Communist Party rule remained a 'hot' memory issue. Was the regime totalitarian?[2] Who is to be held responsible for its implementation and longevity? Was resistance against it legitimate? Such questions continued to stir commentators in the media, historians and cultural producers. Discussions intensified particularly around 17 November each year, the anniversary of the beginning of the Velvet Revolution of 1989. This date also commemorates Nazi violence against students in 1939, later observed as International Students' Day. It was this anniversary that spurred Czechoslovak students in 1989 to hold a peaceful demonstration, which went on to spark a much wider wave of protests that eventually peacefully brought down the ruling regime, earning the revolution the epithet 'velvet' (in Slovakia, the same events are referred to as the 'gentle' revolution). Today, 17 November is observed as the Day of Struggle for Freedom and Democracy and is a national holiday in both the Czech Republic and Slovakia.

Traditionally, the anniversary was an occasion for students, together with the former student leaders of 1989, to gather in the university district of Albertov in Prague and at Národní třída, the street where police forces brutally beat up demonstrators in 1989. They celebrated the ideals and values that the protestors had demanded and that the new order promised to deliver: democracy, freedom, plurality, openness, a return to Europe. The media would use the occasion to reflect upon the successes and failures of the Czech *Vergangenheitsbewältigung* or coming to terms with the past, and to reinvigorate discussions about the continued legacies of the previous regime within society and their effects on political culture. Although minor protests would take place, in general, the anniversary was an occasion for celebrating the new democracy.

But 17 November 2014 looked different. Commemorating twenty-five years since the Velvet Revolution was marked by current political tensions when protestors threw eggs at President Miloš Zeman, whom they saw as repudiating the liberal values of the postsocialist democratic order.[3] A year later, the traditional gathering of students and citizens at Albertov was blocked by the police because the space had been booked out earlier by the civic initiative Block Against Islam (*Blok proti islámu*) – with President Zeman as special guest.[4] The celebrations of the Velvet Revolution were suddenly no longer framed by turning back to the past, but by pressing issues of the present, specifically social tensions brought about by a number of European-wide crises, among them the arrival of large numbers of refugees from Syria and other war-torn countries into Europe that year, which the President's gathering directly addressed.

The issues these anniversaries brought to the fore were thus referenced less by the country's authoritarian past and more by present international political developments, marking a general departure from the preoccupation with the communist regime that had loomed large over the first decades of postsocialism. When I first became interested in the topic of cultural memory back in 2011 and started the initial research that would eventually develop into this book, it seemed that I was very much investigating ongoing and current processes. Czech Television was still airing its nostalgic soap opera *Tell Me a Story* (*Vyprávěj*, dir. Biser Arichtev, 2009–13) that brought an attractive, colourful picture of state socialism to the small screen. In the media, battles were raging over the direction that memory politics should take at the recently established Institute for the Study of Totalitarian Regimes. In other words, the memory of the socialist past, together with a contention with its problematic aspects – such as uncovering former collaborators of the communist secret police or State Security (Státní bezpečnost (StB)) – was still very much present in the public discourse. This era symbolically came to a close not only with the shift in accent during commemorations of the Velvet Revolution, but also with the political rise of billionaire Andrej Babiš, whose pre-1989 Communist Party membership and alleged secret police collaboration gained media attention and sparked a lawsuit, but had no effect on his immense popularity with voters.[5] Babiš went on to become finance minister in a coalition government with the Social and Christian Democrats in 2014; in 2017, he won the parliamentary elections and became Prime Minister.

With this in mind, it is possible to say that the constant negotiation of the memory of state socialism, whether on the political or cultural level, that had marked the first twenty-five years after 1989 appears to be one of the defining features that allow us to describe this period as 'postsocialist' in the Czech Republic – a condition that is increasingly becoming part of the past rather than the present. Indeed, throughout the whole East-Central European region, postsocialism is being historicized from the perspectives of economic, social and intellectual history, with a number of volumes now dedicated to the wider history of Europe after 1989, as well as several monographs investigating the 1990s specifically in the Czech Republic.[6] The field of cultural production has so far played a less prominent role in this growing new direction of historical research; through tracing the Czech post-1989 relationship to the socialist past, this book presents not just a national case study, but also offers a different take on the history of postsocialism through the lens of cultural memory. The story that I present here is a roughly chronological one: I argue that the lapse of time since the Velvet Revolution of 1989 has brought about a progressively more polarized view on the period, but within this polarization, a plurality of memory is beginning to emerge.

This book sets out to problematize some of the established paradigms that have dominated the study of the memory of the state socialist regimes in East-Central Europe. Among these, the idea of nostalgia – a longing for something lost – has played a prominent role. But as we will see, Czech representations of socialism complicate the idea of a positive, sentimental attachment to the past. I propose 'retro' as a more fruitful designation that captures a dynamic of simultaneous political rejection of the past and aesthetic indulgence combined with ironic appreciation. Yet this is not just a story of Czech particularism. Retro serves to conceptualize a set of complex memory processes that have previously been, somewhat unfairly, thrown into the same bag with nostalgia by scholars of the region. And while attending to the details of the Czech case challenges and nuances more established nostalgic narratives, at the same time, we will see that some of the cultural processes of consuming the past and appreciating it aesthetically are not necessarily linked to the experience of socialism as such. The broader relevance of this book is thus a contribution to understanding how representations and their circulation in the public sphere act as one of the major structuring forces of collective memory; its specificity lies in uncovering the different political agendas to which this memory is harnessed.

The following chapters focus on examples of popular culture – works targeting a wide audience, usually with a commercial aim, which constitute mainstream cultural production and have gained media attention. A canon of literature, film and television production portraying the times before the Velvet Revolution of 1989 has intervened in the way in which Czech state socialism has been remembered, but these cultural phenomena have received limited scholarly attention.[7] Although the Czech post-1989 relationship to the socialist past already has an outstanding study dedicated to it in Françoise Mayer's *Les Tchèques et leur communisme* (*The Czechs and Their Communism*),[8] popular culture receives only cursory mention. Instead, Mayer focuses on other contributors to public discourse, such as former dissidents, political prisoners and communists. Moreover, since the book's publication in 2004, much has changed in the dynamics of Czech memory. This volume thus attempts to bring this story up to date.

Existing studies of specific features of cultural memory have also lacked consideration of the whole post-1989 period, yet the discourse about the socialist past has undergone substantial development during the twenty-five years in question. These cultural reactions to the past deserve attention not only because they form a significant component of the collective memory of the socialist period; the formation of this memory also comprises an important aspect of the wider processes of the systemic transformation from state socialism to liberal democracy. While my analysis aims at capturing cultural narratives that arose in the new political and social circumstances of the systemic transformation, at the same time, it also takes into account that culture industries and the inherited expectations and modes of reception of the socialist era did not disappear overnight; a consideration of cultural continuities is thus also one of the themes picked up in the course of the chapters that follow.

This book explores mainly representations that in some way refer to the pre-1989 past, though some artefacts produced during the socialist period are also included in the analysis where their post-1989 reception triggered a particularly strong debate about the legacies of state socialism. This corpus is by no means exhaustive; I have selected specific works that thematize aspects of the past regime on the basis of their popularity and their impact in the media. The power of some of these representations in shaping the shared images of the past has been massive, to say the least. Films like *Kolya* (*Kolja*, dir. Jan Svěrák, 1996) or *Cosy Dens* (*Pelíšky*, dir. Jan Hřebejk, 1999) were seen by more than one million viewers in cinemas alone (in a country of ten million). Repeats on both public and private television channels have been innumerable. Phrases from the films have become household items. Such representations thus deserve to be treated seriously as memory-making media. For younger generations, they have often served as the first point of access to the socialist past.

Throughout the former Eastern Bloc, narratives about state socialism have to be interpreted against a background of anticommunism. A resolute rejection of the previous regime, which was responsible for a number of terrible crimes, had its necessary and legitimate place in public discourse and to varying degrees also transitional justice legislation throughout the region in the 1990s. The idea of a blanket rejection of all aspects of the socialist past aspired to hegemony after 1989 in Czech postsocialist public discourse through the actions of both politicians and the media. This book analyses how a similar dynamic manifested in the cultural sphere and, indeed, we will see that the Czech cultural memory of socialism differs from some of its neighbours in its actively anticommunist dimension. But anticommunism as one of the prominent grand narratives of the postsocialist era in the Czech Republic suffers from an internal contradiction. On the one hand, by dismissing the past, it divests responsibility and casts the present as a manifestation of obvious progress from the times of state socialism; however, on the other hand, the same anticommunist rejection also leads to the belief that communists still lurk everywhere and public life needs to be purged of them – a convenient political tool that loomed large over the postsocialist public sphere. It thus appears as if the discursive category of 'communists' was suppressed into the background (as in Kaaba's vision of state socialism without communists), yet simultaneously emerged in force after 1989 to jeopardize the new liberal democracy with the communists constant threat of returning matters to the 'old order'.[9]

This book primarily traces the political meanings in cultural narratives about the socialist past. Variations in these political meanings are connected to the genres through which stories about the socialist past are told. James Krapfl demonstrates this effectively in his analysis of the 1989 events in Czechoslovakia in *Revolution with a Human Face*, arguing that narrating the revolutions of that year in different generic plots leads to differing interpretive outcomes.[10] Krapfl draws inspiration from Hayden White's *Metahistory*, which outlines how the same historical events recounted via different 'modes of emplotment' give rise to different meanings.[11] While Krapfl and White are concerned with historical events rather than fictional representations, I loosely adapt the basic insight that, analogously, the choice of literary or cinematic genre is a structuring factor in the interpretation of fictional depictions of the past. For example, retrospectively narrating a period such as Normalization – as the final two decades of state socialism in Czechoslovakia after the 1968 Warsaw Pact invasion are generally known – as either comedy or tragedy generates distinct interpretations, which range from narratives of the nonparticipatory experience of the 'small person', to commentaries on a perceived democratic national identity by casting out 'totalitarian' perpetrators and setting heroes as role models. Indeed, understandings of heroism are key to the overall political interpretation of the past detectable in representations and constitute one of the central themes of the Czech cultural memory of socialism; who can be considered a hero and under what circumstances plays into how aspects of the past are valued. Comedy strives for reconciliation and, as such, presents an egalitarian vision of heroism, in which ordinary characters perform small gestures of resistance. Tragic narratives, on the other hand, tend to paint a starker moral map of the past, with clear heroic role models and villains to match, leaving less room for compromise and more for didactic stories of good and evil.

The choice of genre is also largely dependent on the subject position of the hero – literary or film comedies very often reach for child protagonists, who recount their childhood or teenage years with disarming naivety or with an ironic eye towards the generation of their parents. This device is not limited just to Czech culture in relation to state socialism, though it has received little attention. An early example is the Yugoslav film *Tito and Me* (*Tito i ja*, dir. Goran Marković, 1992), which builds comic situations around the discrepancy between the child protagonist's guileless admiration for Marshall Tito and his parents' opposition to the regime. Michal Viewegh's novel of the same year, *Bliss Was It in Bohemia* (*Báječná léta pod psa*), discussed in Chapter 2, uses the same mechanism to offer a humorous commentary on the political absurdities of late socialism.[12] Much of the production of the German wave of *Ostalgie* – nostalgia for East Germany – are coming-of-age narratives with comic overtones, such as Jana Hensel's *After the Wall* (*Zonenkinder*, 2002). Another prominent example of a humorous story of growing up in the 1970s is Thomas Brussig's *On the Shorter End of Sun Avenue* (*Am kürzeren Ende der Sonnenallee*) and the accompanying film *Sun Alley* (1992). Locating readers' and viewers' sympathies with a child hero leads towards a forgiving view of the past that allows them to laugh away the communist regime's negative aspects. More recently, the Slovak film *The Hostage* (*Rukojemník*, dir. Juraj Nvota, 2014) uses a child protagonist's perspective to turn the regime's repressive apparatus – in this case, its well-guarded border with Austria – into a source of exciting childhood adventure. While much Czech production depicting state socialism is set in such a humorous register, Chapter 6 examines contrasting narratives that employ more 'serious' generic conventions, told from the perspective of an adult hero, who, unlike the cute child or blundering adolescent, challenges the regime, often with tragic consequences.

From Nostalgia to Retro

When discussing the memory of state socialism in the former Eastern Bloc, it is impossible to avoid the notion of nostalgia, which has captured much scholarly attention.[13] I view the phenomenon as longing for an idealized aspect or aspects of the past, with the acknowledgement, in Pam Cook's words, that 'this idealised something can never be retrieved in actuality'.[14] As such, nostalgia is an emotion relating to the past. However, like other emotions, nostalgia is neither totalizing nor systematic. Nostalgia rarely takes the socialist period as a whole as its object, but rather only specific aspects of it, while easily condemning, or simply not addressing others. For instance, a significant object of nostalgia in the Czech context is resistance against the ruling regime between 1948 and 1989. Representations that make use of this trope do not shy away from the more negative aspects of living in an authoritarian regime – they by no means wish to laud the previous political order but generate a nostalgic investment in one specific aspect of the period. The unpleasant features of life under socialism – indeed, a condemnation of the political system – are necessary to this kind of nostalgia: resistant gestures are defined in contradistinction to the regime's oppression.

In this context, one cannot ignore Svetlana Boym's influential study *The Future of Nostalgia*, with its differentiation between restorative and reflective dimensions of the phenomenon: 'restorative nostalgia stresses *nostos* and attempts a transhistorical reconstruction of the lost home. Reflective nostalgia thrives in *algia*, in longing itself, and delays the homecoming – wistfully, ironically, desperately'.[15] In Boym's typology, the former kind of nostalgia lends itself more easily to reactionary nationalist projects, which long for a simple, Manichean conception of good and evil.[16] On the other hand, she evaluates the potential of the reflective strand of nostalgia more optimistically, where 'longing and critical thinking are not opposed to one another, as affective memories do not absolve one from compassion, judgment or critical reflection'.[17] As for the relationship between the two, Boym suggests that the different types of nostalgia may be triggered by the same symbols, but tell different stories about them. However, this book proposes that the two types of nostalgia are not necessarily as opposed as they may initially seem; the two can intermingle in a single artefact and its reception. As the following chapters demonstrate, a wistful longing for a simpler time when it was easy to know which side is the 'right side' and an ironic, distanced appreciation of the aesthetics of the past can comfortably coexist as 'retro', which forms a middle point to Boym's dichotomy.

Retro has received only limited attention in discussions of postsocialist nostalgia.[18] In the literature, cases of stylistic appropriation of artefacts from the socialist past and their refashioning as desirable, quirky, hip or cool in the present are often read as part of such nostalgia. But it seems to me that such a designation suffers a terminological confusion. Mitja Velikonja, in his synthetic study of nostalgic practices across the former Eastern Bloc, distinguishes between first-hand and second-hand nostalgia in a typology similar to Boym's framework of restorative and reflective nostalgia. Yet in what sense is one of the examples Velikonja gives, 'the image of Stalin on an alarm clock with the inscription *Stalminator* — "I will be back"',[19] productively viewed as nostalgia if it does not evince a longing for another era? If there is a rejection of the past at stake, then referring to it as nostalgia is not particularly fitting. Yet it is precisely such a dynamic of refusing the politics of the past while ironically taking pleasure in its aesthetics that constitutes the dominant mode of representing socialism in the Czech context. While some scholars have posited 'postmodern nostalgia' as a suitable term for such a relationship to the past devoid of sentimental longing,[20] my aim is to flesh out 'retro' as a more fitting concept.

To an extent, nostalgia is an inherent feature of remembering youth, which has led some commentators to perceive it as apolitical. Yet it is precisely a political rejection of the past that allows for its aesthetic appreciation or even gives it an air of provocation, which constitutes a political interpretation in its own right. Figure 0.2 shows a postcard sold in the gift shop of the privately owned Museum of Communism in Prague, illustrating this dynamic. In an unmistakable irony, the Museum's exhibition was until 2017 placed in rooms in the Savarin Palace in central Prague, which also houses a casino and a McDonald's outlet. Indeed, the Museum's marketing strategy was well aware of the paradoxical power of this idiosyncratic location. The postcard displays an image of Lenin, while the text reads: 'We're above McDonalds, across from Benetton, viva la imperialism!' The tongue-in-cheek message is ironic towards both socialism and capitalism, but ridiculing the

Figure 0.2 Promotional postcard. © Museum of Communism, Prague.

symbols of socialism sells better: Lenin is overshadowed by slogans confirming capitalism's victory over the politics he represents.

Rather than a subset of nostalgia, the phenomenon described here deserves to be considered on its own terms, given how widespread it is across the former Eastern Bloc and beyond. The term 'retro' is used to designate a memory regime devoid of affect or lived memory, a pick-and-mix attitude capitalizing on the stylistic repertoires of the past, which lends it to various irreverent and ironic iterations, while feasting on the colours, sounds and textures of socialism. While bearing some resemblance to Boym's reflective nostalgia, the latter term is inadequate for two reasons: not only is the emotional dimension associated with nostalgia confusing rather than helpful when discussing such detached appropriations of the past, it is also predicated on a different conception of temporality. And it is to the understanding of the temporal relation between socialism and liberal democracy that the production of political meaning is tied. While nostalgia sees aspects of the present moment as inferior to the past it turns to, retro in the Czech case strives for the end point of the events of 1989 that overthrew the communist regime and ushered in the democratic political order. However, this is not a dynamic characteristic only of the Czech context or indeed postsocialism; an aesthetic fascination with the past narrated from a position of affirming the more enlightened politics of the present can be found across 'Western' representational culture as well. The knowledge of the historical outcome grants retro representations a position of superiority, allowing audiences to appropriate – and ridicule – aspects of the past. In this way, 'velvet retro' acknowledges the fact that this memory regime offers just as much of a commentary on the present as on the past it turns to – it is firmly rooted in the era inaugurated by the Velvet Revolution. And velvet is fitting in another sense too. As we will see, much of the Czech cultural memory of socialism sought not to antagonize, but rather to create a gentle image – to hark back to the Slovak name for the revolution of 1989 – of state socialism.

Most protagonists of the representations discussed in this book, through their ignorance or indifference to politics, cannot be seen as nostalgic for the regime they lived in, but rather for their everyday lives. The locus of nostalgia thus lies not in the political and the public, but in the personal, the private and the familial. In such a reading, nostalgia can be seen as an empowering mechanism. Mayer argues in this vein when she notes that a number of Czech comedies about socialism 'project a non-political vision of history, by which they return the past to all those people "without a story" who were neither communist cadres, nor former prisoners, nor dissidents, who did not particularly engage themselves for or against … and who, after all, constitute the vast – and silent – majority of the population'.[21] In the German context, *Ostalgie* – an amalgam of the German words for nostalgia and east, designating nostalgia for the former German Democratic Republic (GDR) – has been perceived by many commentators as a reaction to the feeling of East Germans that their experience of living in the GDR has been devalued. Nostalgia is thus seen to have a resistant potential; in the eyes of many scholars working on East Germany, it is understood as a memory regime that contributes to a more nuanced understanding of the period.

However, such an interpretation of nostalgia demands revision. We will see that many Czech cultural reflections of the socialist period also turn to everyday experiences, and although they portray instances of – often comic – negotiation with state power, ultimately they are structured in a way that tends to reinforce a binary framework of oppression and resistance. This discursive tendency frames the socialist period in a way that was prevalent in the historiography of the Cold War, which viewed socialist regimes on an axis of a dictatorial regime versus a victimized population, only occasionally complicated by examples of dissent. The corpus of texts and practices I look at does seek to establish some extent of agency for subjects in state socialism through a widespread thematization of resistant gestures that challenge this dichotomy by finding spaces of negotiation in between. But such gestures also produce a narrative of exculpation: responsibility for the regime is always relegated to someone else and not to the positively valued protagonists and actors of the representations and practices in question. In this sense, Czech cultural depictions of socialism are not at odds with the public discourse on the period, which, dominated by anticommunism, elided questions of the public's role in maintaining the communist regime in power and instead cast citizens as controlled by a totalitarian state. Yet, we will see that this dynamic begins to change with the time elapsed since the demise of the previous regime and the eventual pluralization of both the media and political discourse.

The Trouble with the *Ostalgie* Debate

Much has been written on various forms of longing for the former GDR, known as *Ostalgie*. This memory regime describes a captivation with the aesthetics and material and popular culture of socialism that manifests across the former socialist region in literature, film and television, in the popularity of old brands and various other commercial iterations, including the souvenir industry, with its various more or less ironic Lenin and Stalin mementoes. Its perhaps other best-known version has come to be designated as *Yugonostalgia*, referring to nostalgia for the former Yugoslavia. Here, I on the one hand offer a case study that explores the Czech context, which has been largely underrepresented in this burgeoning literature. But, on the other hand, this book is also concerned with a critical assessment of the nostalgia paradigm, which has become so prominent in the study of the memory of state socialism, as an 'exportable' interpretive framework and recognizes that a more complex typology of cultural reactions to the socialist past is necessary.

Unlike Germany, we will see that in the Czech case, there is little evidence for nostalgia for the utopian impulse behind the socialist project or for the values the Communist Party attempted to instil in citizens. Yet neither has the period necessarily been cast as trauma. Instead, what we witness is more akin to a form of amnesia: the dominant narrative of the postsocialist era, as seen in the media, in the discourse of politicians and in cultural production, dismissed the past in order to divest both the population and political elites from responsibility for perpetuating or condoning the previous regime. Simultaneously, a vision of an anticommunist rejection of socialism was retrospectively validated through recurring tropes of personal opposition or what in German has been referred to as the *Nischengesellschaft* – a society that fled to private interests.[22] The dismissal of course applies first and foremost to the injustices committed in this regime's name, while the previous era's achievements are systematically ignored or rhetorically separated from their political context, labelled as arising 'in spite of' the political configuration. It is thus my contention that the object of remembrance in the Czech context is less the period of socialism itself than a narrative of how Czechs successfully lived through it without 'compromising' themselves politically.

Rather than Germany, it would seem that Slovakia would be the most natural point of comparison with the Czech case, given that the Czechs and Slovaks shared one country between 1948 and 1992 and that the socialist past both nations turn to in their memory is a common Czechoslovak one. Yet cultural iterations of postsocialist nostalgia have been scarce in Slovakia, due to a combination of structural, political and cultural reasons. In this book, I argue that while representations of socialism in the Czech Republic tended to predominantly employ the genre conventions of comedy, creating a seemingly lenient picture of the past, they simultaneously carried an underlying anticommunist message. However, the situation in Slovakia was different, not only due to comedy not having as strong a tradition in the Slovak cultural canon, but also because the discourse of anticommunism gained less traction in Slovakia, where the exchange of elites after 1989 was not as complete as in the country's Czech part and the legacy of reform communism continued to enjoy more legitimacy in the immediate aftermath of regime change.[23] Furthermore, film as one of the main mass media of cultural memory did not widely participate in structuring how the socialist past has been remembered in Slovakia, as the country produced only a few feature films in the 1990s, mainly because of the prolonged and unclear privatization of the Koliba film studios in Bratislava and the decimating effect this had on the Slovak film industry.[24] Struggling with a lack of funding, costly costume dramas depicting the socialist past were not a priority for Slovak filmmakers. Such films only started being produced two decades later, after the Slovak film industry's reinvigoration through the founding of the Slovak Audiovisual Fund. By the time Slovak films depicting life under the former regime such as *The Informer* (*Eštébák*, dir. Juraj Nvota, 2012), *Red Captain* (*Rudý kapitán*, dir. Michal Kollár, 2016) and *The Teacher* (*Učiteľka*, dir. Jan Hřebejk, 2016) entered cinemas, the Czech wave of comedy retro nostalgia discussed in the following chapters had subsided. With the exception of the already-mentioned comedy *The Hostage*, these later films, produced as Czecho-Slovak (and in the case of *Red Captain*, also Polish) coproductions, evinced a new trend in both countries that cast the memory of socialism as trauma. Slovak literature displayed a similar move, which will be discussed in more detail in Chapter 6.

The German case thus remains instructive as it has produced the largest body of literature, which has led *Ostalgie* to dominate scholarly work on the topic. Certainly, some of the basic features of the *Ostalgie* discourse apply to the Czech case as well. One is the use of humour and irony as mechanisms for portraying the socialist past, something that the Czech setting shares with its German counterpart, but that is less common in other Eastern European countries.[25] Another important aspect is the role of material culture as a memory trigger – which is often tied to humour – and in particular the commercial exploitation of a past devoid of memory, which opens up questions of who sets the agenda of such ventures and who is being represented. Such comparisons can provide productive springboards, while recognizing that each national context has its historical and political specificities that endow nostalgic practices with different meanings, even if they share the same form.

Ostalgie experienced several waves of popularity: initially, it manifested in the return of GDR-era products onto the market in the 1990s;[26] in 1999, two popular film comedies, *Sun Alley* (*Sonnenallee*, dir. Leander Haußmann, 1999) and *Heroes Like Us* (*Helden Wie Wir*, dir. Sebastian Peterson, 1999), both adapted from literary works by Thomas Brussig, appeared in cinemas and thus paved the way for the mass success of *Good Bye, Lenin!* (dir. Wolfgang Becker) in 2003. These representations have been accompanied by various commercial iterations of the fascination with the GDR: a number of GDR-themed television variety shows in 2003; 'Trabi Safari' tours in Berlin; specialized 'Ossi' shops; the revival of the *Ampelmännchen* pedestrian crossing sign, etc.[27]

However, the major preoccupation in discussions of nostalgia in East Germany has been questions of identity, whether of a specifically East German variety, which *Ostalgie* is seen as forging, or of a unified national kind, to which some perceive *Ostalgie* as posing an obstacle. This then forms the principal difference compared to the Czech Republic. Although the Czechs, especially after splitting from Slovakia in 1993, also grappled with issues of identity, the lack of a 'Western Czechoslovakia' did not foster as strong a comparative identity discourse. This is not to say that any kind of evaluative discourse on the past is also not one that affects identity formation in the present; indeed, the various narratives about the past under scrutiny here often do comment on the idea of a Czech national identity. But the locus of the discussion lies elsewhere: not in the question of how uses of the past contribute to a projection of what it means to be Czech, but in how uses of the past help to create an understanding of how and why Czechs found themselves in the democratic and capitalist present.

Narratives of resistance and overcoming of state socialism imply a return to the 'proper course' of Czech history, with its founding myth of democracy located in the interwar Czechoslovak First Republic, which is widely perceived, in Peter Bugge's summary, as 'the time and place where Czechs were at once most themselves and most European'.[28] Significantly, such narratives conspicuously disregard Slovakia. Although the cultural artefacts discussed in the following chapters all ostensibly turn to a Czechoslovak past, its Slovak part remains strikingly absent, apart from a few outlying examples that feature Slovak-speaking characters. Altogether, this bias is representative of a wider trend of overlooking Slovakia in Czech culture and suggests that the imagined 'golden age' of the First Republic is understood by these representations as an achievement of a distinctly *Czech* democratic spirit.[29]

Returning to Germany, two factors created very different conditions for coming to terms with the past in comparison with other countries of the Eastern Bloc: funding from West Germany that enabled high-quality historical research and effective administration of the archives of the secret police (the Stasi), as well as the historical precedent of having to deal with the legacy of Nazism.[30] While the swift pace of the transformation made the GDR exceptional,[31] it also exacerbated feelings of loss: products from the GDR quickly disappeared off the shelves of shops, a fact that is humorously exploited in *Good Bye, Lenin!*, and the former East German territories were flooded with Western popular and consumer culture.[32]

Indeed, the phenomenon of the success of relaunched East German consumer goods forms the focus of much of the writing on *Ostalgie*. Whereas in the Czech Republic the fascination with socialist brands has been more modest and couched in a narrative of continuity between socialism and postsocialism, in Germany these products became a site of the articulation of an East German *Trotzidentität*[33] or a kind of identity of defiance against what some perceived as West German cultural and economic hegemony. This has been read by some scholars as an empowering gesture for East Germans. Daphne Berdahl, for instance, interprets *Ostalgie* as 'potentially disruptive practices that emanate from the margins to challenge certain nation-building agendas of the new Germany',[34] while Jonathan Bach suggests that 'by refusing the self-evidently superior western goods for the "good old" East German products, it is the easterner who is seeking to use the market symbolically against the West'.[35] Such interpretations tend to come more often from English-speaking scholars. But German critics such as Thomas Abbe, albeit in a more cautious manner, have also pointed to the therapeutic potential of reclaiming Eastern products as a form of self-assurance in a public climate where East German experiences were being diminished.[36] Often, though, GDR product fetishization and other nostalgic cultural forms are seen as an obstacle to a unified German identity, which is usually perceived as the ultimate horizon of interpretation of any debate on the socialist past in Germany.[37]

Ostalgic films have also been read as empowering: Paul Cooke, for example, offers a very positive reading of *Sun Alley*, a tale of a group of teenagers growing up in East Berlin next to the Berlin Wall, when he argues that the film 'is the attempt to give a voice to the experience of ordinary people who lived in the GDR'.[38] Oana Godeanu-Kenworthy's assessment of *Good Bye, Lenin!* is even more optimistic: 'Wolfgang Becker's film represents a powerful statement on the healing potential of a redemptive view of the GDR past … that emphasizes precisely those values that are deemed worthy of salvaging from elimination and of integration into the new collective German identity.'[39] However, such interpretations appear overconfident, not least because box-office successes such as the two films in question are hardly an example of East German grassroots self-representation, but products designed within a complex market environment where West German capital plays an important role and the question of who represents whom for what audience is anything but straightforward.

Nevertheless, one observation is worth dwelling on in more detail in order to highlight an important difference between the Czech and German context, namely the idea that *Ostalgic* representations attempt to recover values of the socialist past that are deemed superior to the values of the present, i.e. they turn back to the utopian impulse behind the socialist project. Much has been written about both *Sun Alley* and *Good Bye, Lenin!* in this regard. The latter film in particular is a story in which the main protagonist Alex rebuilds an idealized version of the GDR: 'The GDR that I created for my mother', he reflects in the film, 'became more and more the GDR which I would have perhaps wished for myself.'[40] An even better example of a nostalgic longing for a more just society can be found in the less discussed film *Kleinruppin Forever* (dir. Carsten Fiebeler, 2004), which explicitly thematizes a desire for those values of socialism that appear absent in capitalism, such as community bonding, genuine solidarity or social security. Using the somewhat contrived device of a chance meeting of identical twins separated at birth who then swap places – one lives in West Germany and the other in the East in the 1980s – the film focuses on the Western twin who comes to reject the values of the achievement-oriented and money-grubbing society he grew up in for a world of a common struggle for justice and true love in the GDR.[41] Such an impulse behind the depiction of the socialist past is hard to detect in the Czech context. Czech representations tend to be wary of any grand narratives, as the discussion of depictions of heroism will show; yet implicitly democracy and freedom (understood largely as the freedom of the market) are valued as the default position from which any retrospective evaluations of the past can be carried out. Unlike Germany, where the memory of National Socialism looms large in the pre-GDR past, Czech representations of socialism can implicitly turn to the interwar First Republic as an object of nostalgia, which Czech postsocialist memory has styled as a cradle of democracy.[42]

A line of argument that comes closer to my focus is the identification of East German products as aesthetically 'camp', which places *Ostalgic* practices within a framework of cultural recycling that acknowledges the products' 'quaintness' or 'backwardness'[43] as a selling point. Such a valuation lends itself to irony and humour: Dominic Boyer points out that *Good Bye, Lenin!*, for instance, builds one of its best jokes on the fact that the main protagonist and his friend are able to easily imitate one of the most advanced technological products of the GDR – the main television news programme – with just a few props.[44] Such a positioning depends on who is performing it. As Jonathan Bach observes, *Ostalgie* can be interpreted as a genuine longing for a gone world on the part of East Germans: 'yet when the subject is the knowingly ironic westerner (or the "sophisticated" easterner) enjoying the retro aura of GDR era design, Ostalgia appears as a (p)ostmodern artifact valued precisely for its lack of emotional attachment to a specific past'.[45] It is such an examination of how facets of the past are either co-opted or discarded to form the ideological fabric of the present that lies at the heart of the analysis in this book.

Narrating Memory

My examination of representations of socialism is predicated on the basic insight that narrative gives meaning to the past and that it is the form narratives take that contributes to what they tell us. Therefore, thinking about retrospective representations of the past is not a question of 'how it really was', but a question of memory. Memory is first and foremost individual remembering and the memories that each individual holds are initially, as Aleida Assmann remarks, fragmentary, unformed and restricted. It is 'only through narrativization that they subsequently acquire form and structure'.⁴⁶ Such narrated memories, if they are publicly circulated, can become part of a shared discourse about the past. The circulation of these narratives, which are through various processes the subject of either consensus or contestation in the public sphere, is captured in the metaphor of collective memory.⁴⁷

As Andreas Huyssen observes, 'the past is not simply there in memory, but it must be articulated to become memory'.⁴⁸ In this way, representation – and, in particular, visual representation – often structures the way in which the past is remembered. If we think about how the past is accessible, especially to a younger generation who did not themselves experience socialism, popular culture (and film and television especially) becomes central to the understanding of this metaphorical collective memory. This book is thus concerned with collective cultural memory as opposed to communicative memory, to use Jan Assmann's distinction: it deals with memory that is transmitted by various institutional and cultural media, rather than the oral transmission of lived experience.⁴⁹ Yet what complicates the picture is that in the studied period – the first twenty-five years after 1989 – the memory of the previous regime was very much still part of living, communicative memory of several generations who had experienced it first hand; at the same time, this memory was already being mediated by various means. Such parallel processes in cultural and communicative memory mean that it is difficult to separate the two – lived memories influence mediated representations and these in turn have the power to shape the communicative memory of what audiences 'actually remember'. The phenomenon whereby images are internalized as memories, usually by spectators of visual representations, has been termed 'prosthetic memory' by Alison Landsberg.⁵⁰ How the past is remembered is thus constituted in a wider mediascape, which the breadth of sources that this book draws on tries to capture.

At the same time, institutions also attempt to forge collective memory through active interventions in remembrance practices. In the case of the memory of socialism in the Czech Republic, these efforts manifested themselves, for example, in the various transitional justice laws of the early 1990s – such as the restitution of property confiscated by the communist state – which attempted to 'repair history' in the legal sphere. Another example is the setting up of the state-sponsored Institute for the Study of Totalitarian Regimes, which is discussed in Chapter 6. But a number of nonstate actors also actively tried to shape memory, such as the activities of the Confederation of Political Prisoners (Konfederace politických vězňů (KPV)), which sought to promote the active remembrance of the injustices committed by the communist regime. Such institutional interventions take the form of 'memory politics', which, as Jan Kubik and Michael Bernhard argue, interpret the past for the purposes of the 'reformulation of collective identities and the introduction or reinvigoration of the principles of legitimizing power'.[51] Uses of the past thus have an instrumental side to them, in that they are more often than not tied to a project of negotiating not only collective identities, but also the notion of a single national identity.

However, we must keep in mind that representation and memory are not equivalent. The circulation of images of the past contributes to a public discourse on this past, but that is not ground enough to draw conclusions about the memory of the general population. Cultural producers and those who contribute to media debates are necessarily elite groups with sufficient social capital to be able to set the agenda of public discussion; an analysis of public discourse is always limited to this field and cannot be used to extrapolate conclusions about the memory of the population at large.[52] This is not to say that audiences are passive agents in this process. Although I will show that in the Czech case, cultural production and official memory politics do often reaffirm one another, this is not to construct an argument for a 'culture industry' that manipulates its consumers.[53] Rather, while we need to take into account that popular culture resources are produced by those who hold hegemonic status and thus 'carry the interests of the economically and ideologically dominant',[54] the ability of these resources to generate resistant meanings is equally important. If I argue that representations of socialism are structurally organized in a way that leads to an anticommunist rejection of the past, this is not necessarily the meaning that all consumers will take away, as Chapter 3 will show.

However, it is an acknowledged limitation of the scope of this book that it chooses to focus on fictional images of the past; as such, it looks at cultural memory projects, but is less concerned with how this cultural memory is assimilated in communicative memory amongst the population. To avoid discussing only the reception of the artefacts in question amongst the limited groups of reviewers and journalists, I also take into account reception figures (such as book sales, box office figures and TV ratings) as one of the criteria of popularity on the basis on which examples in this book were chosen.[55] In this sense, I am following Astrid Erll's conceptualization of 'media of cultural memory', which acknowledges that while representations may employ conscious strategies to shape the memory of the past they represent, they also must be received as memory-making media in order to have a real impact on how the past is remembered.[56] Thus, for instance, I do not discuss films with low audience figures and a lack of reviews (or mention them only cursorily), as we can assume they did not widely affect shared ideas about the past either among critics or audiences. For analogous reasons, I have decided to omit documentary films from the discussion, as these also target specialized audiences.

Moreover, how Czech viewers receive representations of the socialist past is a topic that has received scholarly attention, albeit of limited scope. Historian Kamil Činátl offers a persuasive example of how the analysis of internet forums can help to gauge how viewers negotiate resistant meanings in relation to texts such as the Czech Television series *Tell Me a Story*.[57] Irena Reifová, Kateřina Gillarová and Radim Hladík have examined viewers' responses to the same series based on focus groups with audience members.[58] In a further study, Reifová argues that the elite discourses of official memory politics have promoted a memory of discontinuity embodied by radical mnemonic actors (dissidents, political prisoners, party officials) to whom the majority of the population could not relate. She thus reads postsocialist nostalgia as a manifestation of a memory of continuity of 'ordinary people' from below.[59] Such an approach can undoubtedly produce valuable conclusions if close attention to reception experiences is paid; this book is mostly concerned with the textuality of mediations of the socialist past, yet with an effort to avoid the methodological error of extrapolating the wider social uses of particular artefacts from their structure, as Reifová warns.

What is thus at stake in the following chapters is an examination of how memories of the past are harnessed to particular ideological projects. By understanding the processes that construct memory – in whose interest it is to propagate a particular narrative and who it is aimed at – one can begin to unravel the agendas behind different memories, be it, for instance, the legitimation of particular groups in the political arena or the creation of group or national identities. Chapter 1 deals with narratives of anticommunism in both the political and cultural sphere in the 1990s, providing the background necessary to understanding the public relationship to the socialist past and how it has been shaped by memory politics. Chapter 2 maps the cultural landscape of the same decade in relation to portraying socialism and discusses comedy as the principal memory vehicle for representing the past in the immediate aftermath of the demise of state socialism. In Chapter 3, several events that took place around 1999 are taken as a case study for examining the relevance of the concept of nostalgia to the Czech situation. The chapter analyses several controversies around socialist-era popular culture and contrasts the memory of continuity expressed by audiences with the dismissive approach of a cultural elite in the media.

Chapter 4 identifies 'petty heroism' as a central trope in Czech representations of socialism, whereby through the performance of minor gestures of resistance, the mantle of heroism is taken on by 'ordinary' characters, and the population at large is thus seen as collectively taking an exemplary stance of resistance against an authoritarian regime. Chapter 5 then presents the book's main theoretical contribution in elaborating the central concept of retro: it shows that an aesthetic fascination with state socialism is not at odds with rejecting its ideology and practical implementation. I demonstrate that, ultimately, representations of socialism tell a story in which liberal democracy is seen as a natural culmination of Czech history, a process that is, however, not unique to the Czech Republic or indeed the postsocialist space.

Chapter 6 discusses how in the mid 2000s, the Czech public sphere witnessed a discursive shift on both the institutional and representational level, which brought the memory of oppression and heroic resistance under state socialism to the fore. This 'fortification' of heroic memory, I argue, came at a time when the dominant anticommunist discourse of the postsocialist years was increasingly coming under challenge from academic circles and a new generation of media actors. Such a pluralization of both representational culture and public debates has led to the past becoming a site of productive debate and contestation in some cases. Finally, the conclusion summarizes the book's main arguments and offers some thoughts on their wider applicability.

Notes

1. Throughout this book, the terminology used to refer to the period between 1948 and 1989 in Czechoslovakia distinguishes between the ideological project of the Czechoslovak Communist Party (communism, the communist regime and Communist Party rule) and its practical, day-to-day implementation (state socialism).
2. 'Totalitarianism' not only as a discursive category but also as an analytical concept in historiography saw renewed interest in East-Central Europe after the collapse of state socialism (while discussions of this category had been ongoing already prior to that on the other side of the Iron Curtain); see B. Hoenig, 'Možnosti a meze jednoho paradigmatu: Teorie totalitarismu aplikovaná na státní socialismus středovýchodní Evropy', *Soudobé dějiny* 16(4) (2009), 640–52. Key works of the theory of totalitarianism were translated into Czech in the 1990s, e.g. Hannah Arendt's *Origins of Totalitarianism* (published by OIKOYMENH in 1996). However, in the Czech context, the analytical concept is often confused with 'totalita', the more common Czech designation for totalitarianism, which functions as a political and moral shorthand for the communist regime.
3. H. Válková, bse, 'Hodnocení oslav: nadšení z Listopadu trvá, Zeman si za pískot mohl sám' ['Enthusiasm for November (1989) Prevails, the Whistling was Zeman's Own Fault'], *iDnes.cz*, 18 November 2014. Retrieved 15 August 2019 from http://zpravy.idnes.cz/anketa-vyroci-listopad-ohlednuti-dlc-/domaci.aspx?c=A141118_094055_domaci_hv.
4. iDnes.cz, ČTK, 'Policejní blokáda Albertova zneuctila 17. listopad, míní děkan i studenti' ['Police Blockade of Albertov Defiled 17 November, Says Dean and Students'], *iDnes.cz*, 18 November 2015. Retrieved 15 August 2019 from http://zpravy.idnes.cz/dekan-studenti-i-ucitele-ztratili-letos-na-albertove-svobodu-ptn-/domaci.aspx?c=A51118_152653_domaci_zt.

5. For more on Babiš's biography, see T. Pergler, *Babiš: Příběh oligarchy* (Prague: Mladá fronta, 2014).
6. See, for instance, A. Wirsching, *Der Preis der Freiheit: Geschichte Europas in unserer Zeit* (Munich: C.H. Beck, 2012); M. Kopeček and P. Wciślik (eds), *Thinking through Transition: Liberal Democracy, Authoritarian Pasts, and Intellectual History in East Central Europe after 1989* (Budapest: CEU Press, 2015); P. Ther, *Europe since 1989: A History*, trans. Charlotte Hughes-Kreutzmüller (Princeton: Princeton University Press, 2016); A. Gjuričová et al. (eds), *Rozděleni minulostí: Vytváření politických identit v České republice po roce 1989* (Prague: Ústav pro soudobé dějiny, 2012); M. Kopeček and A. Gjuričová (eds), *Kapitoly z dějin české demokracie po roce 1989* (Prague and Litomyšl: Paseka, 2008); L. Kopeček, *Éra nevinnosti: Česká politika 1989–1997* (Brno: Barrister and Principal, 2010); A. Gjuričová and T. Zahradníček, *Návrat parlamentu: Češi a Slováci ve Federálním shromáždění 1989–1992* (Prague: Argo, 2018).
7. Appraisals of cultural responses to the socialist past remain partial in the Czech Republic and have mainly been conducted through the prism of nostalgia. For example, Martin Franc has studied the popularity of socialist-era brands, Andrew Roberts has addressed re-emergent socialist popular culture and Irena Reifová is concerned with nostalgia in television production. A growing literature analyses cinematic portrayals of the past, in particular the work of Kamil Činátl, Radim Hladík and the edited collection *Film a dějiny 4: Normalizace*. See M. Franc, 'Ostalgie v Čechách', in M. Kopeček and A. Gjuričová (eds), *Kapitoly z dějin české demokracie po roce 1989* (Prague and Litomyšl: Paseka, 2008), 193–216; M. Franc, 'Ostalgie v České republice a v SRN', in D. Kunštát and L. Mrklas (eds), *Historická reflexe minulosti aneb 'Ostalgie' v Německu a Česku* (Prague: CEVRO Institut, 2009), 7–14; A. Roberts, 'The Politics and Anti-politics of Nostalgia', *East European Politics and Societies* 16(3) (2002), 764–809; I. Reifová, 'Kryty moci a úkryty před mocí: Normalizační a postkomunistický televizní seriál', in J. Končelík, B. Köpplová and I. Prázová (eds), *Konsolidace vládnutí a podnikání v České Republice a v Evropské unii II. Sociologie, prognostika a správa. Média* (Prague: Matfyz Press, 2002), 354–71; I. Carpentier Reifová, K. Gillarová and R. Hladík, 'The Way We Applauded: How Popular Culture Stimulates Collective Memory of the Socialist Past in Czechoslovakia: The Case of the Television Serial *Vyprávěj* and its Viewers', in A. Imre, T. Havens and K. Lustyik (eds), *Popular Television in Eastern Europe during and since Socialism* (New York: Routledge, 2013), 199–221; K. Činátl, *Naše české minulosti* (Prague: Nakladatelství Lidové noviny, 2014); R. Hladík, 'Traumatické komedie: Politika paměti v českém filmu', *Sociální studia* 1 (2010), 9–26; P. Kopal (ed.), *Film a dějiny 4: Normalizace* (Prague: Casablanca and ÚSTR, 2014).
8. F. Mayer, *Les Tchèques et leur communisme: Mémoire et identités politiques* (Paris: Editions de l'Ecole des hautes études en sciences sociales, 2004).
9. The fear of 'returning to the times before 1989' is a very common rhetorical trope, omnipresent in everyday speech and in the media, as Susanna Trnka summarizes in her ethnographic study 'Forgotten Pasts and Fearful Futures in Czechs' Remembrances of Communism', *Focaal – Journal of Global and Historical Anthropology* 66 (2013), 36–46. The trope often emerges in reaction to steps that are perceived by the speaker as undemocratic or to rhetoric that is seen to be reminiscent of the language of the state socialist era. On the economic level, Ilona Švihlíková remarked in 2015 that the 'argument of "returning before November [1989]" is … used even nowadays against all those who have other than neoliberal ideas about economic policy'; I. Švihlíková, *Jak jsme se stali kolonií* (Prague: Rybka Publishers, 2015), 62.

10. J. Krapfl, *Revolution with a Human Face: Politics, Culture, and Community in Czechoslovakia, 1989–1992* (Ithaca: Cornell University Press, 2013).
11. H. White, *Metahistory: The Historical Imagination in Nineteenth-Century Europe* (Baltimore: Johns Hopkins University Press, 1973).
12. Where possible, I have quoted published translations of books and official English distribution titles of films. All other translations are my own.
13. Several edited volumes have now been devoted either entirely or partially to nostalgia across a range of countries of the former Eastern Bloc. See M. Todorova and Z. Gille (eds), *Post-communist Nostalgia* (New York: Berghahn Books, 2010); M. Todorova (ed.), *Remembering Communism: Genres of Representation* (New York: Social Science Research Council, 2010); A. Dimou, M. Todorova and S. Troebst (eds), *Remembering Communism: Private and Public Recollections of Lived Experience in Southeast Europe* (Budapest: Central European University Press, 2014); O. Angé and D. Berliner (eds), *Anthropology and Nostalgia* (New York: Berghahn Books, 2015).
14. P. Cook, *Screening the Past: Memory and Nostalgia in Cinema* (New York: Routledge, 2005), 4.
15. S. Boym, *The Future of Nostalgia* (New York: Basic Books, 2001), xviii.
16. Ibid., 43.
17. Ibid., 48–50.
18. Retro as a cultural phenomenon (rather than marketing and advertising mechanism) has mainly been discussed in the post-Soviet context. See, for instance, N. Ivanova, 'No(w)stalgia: Retro on the (Post)-Soviet Television Screen', *The Harriman Review* 12(2–3) (1999), 25–32; K.M.F. Platt, 'Russian Empire of Pop: Postsocialist Nostalgia and Soviet Retro at the "New Wave" Competition', *The Russian Review* 72(3) (2013), 447–69; E. Kalinina, *Mediated Post-Soviet Nostalgia* (Huddinge: Södertörn University, 2014).
19. M. Velikonja, 'Lost in Transition: Nostalgia for Socialism in Postsocialist Countries', *East European Politics and Societies* 23(4) (2009), 535–51 (538).
20. The label goes back to Fredric Jameson and has been taken up, for example, by Paul Grainge in *Monochrome Memories: Nostalgia and Style in Retro America* (Westport: Praeger, 2002). See also F. Jameson, *Postmodernism, or, the Cultural Logic of Late Capitalism* (New York: Verso, 1991).
21. Mayer, *Les Tchèques et leur communisme*, 266.
22. The term *Nischengesellschaft* was coined by Günther Gaus in *Wo Deutschland liegt – Eine Ortsbestimmung* (Hamburg: Hoffmann and Campe, 1983); for a more critical discussion of the term's utility, see M. Fulbrook, *Anatomy of a Dictatorship: Inside the GDR, 1949–1989* (Oxford: Oxford University Press, 1995), especially 129–50.
23. For a comparison of Czech and Slovak elites after 1989 and their discourses, see G. Eyal, *The Origins of Postcommunist Elites: From Prague Spring to the Breakup of Czechoslovakia* (Minneapolis: University of Minnesota Press, 2003).
24. For more on Slovak film in the early 1990s, see V. Macek and J. Paštéková, *Dejiny slovenskej kinematografie* (Martin: Osveta, 1997), 487–522.
25. For instance, in Bulgaria, Vania Stoianova notes that comedy is an extremely rare genre in films about state socialism. See V. Stoianova, 'The Communist Period in Postcommunist Bulgarian Cinema', in Todorova and Gille (eds), *Post-communist Nostalgia*, 373–90 (388). Likewise, neighbouring Poland has only seldom experienced comedy as the genre of choice for portraying the period; rather, the dominant trope in various cultural mediations of the socialist past is that of 'absurdity'. See Z. Grębecka, 'Między śmiechem a nostalgią – powroty do komunistycznej przeszłości', in M. Bogusławska and Z. Grębecka

(eds), *Popkomunizm: Doświadczenie komunizmu a kultura popularna* (Cracow: Libron, 2010), 321–43.
26. See D. Berdahl, '"(N)Ostalgie" for the Present: Memory, Longing, and East German Things', *Ethnos* 64(2) (1999), 192–211; M. Blum, 'Remaking the East German Past: Ostalgie, Identity, and Material Culture', *Journal of Popular Culture* 24(3) (2000), 229–53.
27. For a comprehensive overview of the *Ostalgie* phenomenon, see P. Cooke, *Representing East Germany since Unification: From Colonization to Nostalgia* (New York: Berg, 2005).
28. P. Bugge, 'Longing or Belonging? Czech Perceptions of Europe in the Inter-War Years and Today', *Yearbook of European Studies* 11 (1999), 111–29.
29. Czech historiography evinces a similar problem, tending to overlook Slovakia. More sustained attention is only beginning to be paid to the intellectual history of the idea of Czechoslovakism and a shared past. See A. Hudek, M. Kopeček and J. Mervart (eds), *Čechoslovakismus* (Prague: Nakladatelství Lidové noviny, 2019).
30. Cooke, *Representing East Germany*, 27.
31. K. Neller, *DDR-Nostalgie: Dimensionen der Orientierungen der Ostdeutschen gegenüber der ehemaligen DDR, ihre Ursachen und politischen Konnotationen* (Wiesbaden: VS Verlag für Sozialwissenschaften, 2006), 21.
32. For more on consumption practices in relation to GDR products, see Berdahl, '"(N)Ostalgie" for the Present', 192–211.
33. Neller, *DDR-Nostalgie*, 48.
34. Berdahl, '"(N)Ostalgie" for the Present', 193.
35. J. Bach, '"The Taste Remains": Consumption, (N)ostalgia, and the Production of East Germany', *Public Culture* 14(3) (2002), 545–56 (549).
36. T. Abbe, *Ostalgie: Zum Umgang mit der DDR-Vergangenheit in den 1990er Jahren* (Erfurt: Landeszentrale für Politische Bildung 2005), 44.
37. See T. Goll, 'Einführung – Erinnerungskultur und Ostalgie', in T. Goll and T. Leuerer (eds), *Ostalgie als Erinnergungskultur? Symposium zu Leid und Politik in der DDR* (Baden Baden: Nomos, 2004), 9–15; see also Neller, *DDR-Nostalgie*, whose book focuses on the idea that positive relationships towards the GDR might constitute obstacles to the 'inner unity' of Germany (especially 26).
38. P. Cooke, 'Performing "Ostalgie": Leander Haussmann's *Sonnenallee*', *German Life and Letters* 56(2) (2003), 156–67 (160).
39. O. Godeanu-Kenworthy, 'Deconstructing Ostalgia: The National Past between Commodity and Simulacrum in Wolfgang Becker's *Good Bye Lenin!* (2003)', *Journal of European Studies* 41(2) (2011), 161–77 (174).
40. 'Die DDR, die ich für meine Mutter schuf wurde immer mehr die DDR, die ich mir vielleicht gewünscht hätte.' *Good Bye, Lenin!*, 2003.
41. For more on *Kleinruppin Forever*, see A. Enns, 'The Politics of Ostalgie: Postsocialist Nostalgia in Recent German Film', *Screen* 48(4) (2007), 475–91.
42. In his analysis of the press of the 1990s, Stanislav Holubec notes that the First Republic was often posited as a model for democracy building in the post-1989 era and that in this journalistic approach, Czechs were seen as 'reliving' their history after the collapse of state socialism. See S. Holubec, *Ještě nejsme za vodou: Obrazy druhých a historická paměť v období postkomunistické transformace* (Prague: Scriptorium, 2015), 102.
43. Berdahl, '"(N)Ostalgie" for the Present', 194.
44. D. Boyer, 'Ostalgie and the Politics of the Future in Eastern Germany', *Public Culture* 18(2) (2006), 361–81 (376).
45. Bach, '"The Taste Remains"', 546–47.

46. A. Assmann, *Der lange Schatten der Vergangenheit: Erinnerungskultur und Geschichtspolitik* (Munich: C.H. Beck, 2006), 25.
47. Since the 1980s, the disciplines of history and broadly conceived cultural studies have been experiencing a 'memory boom'. Among the most prominent contributions are M. Halbwachs, *On Collective Memory*, ed. and trans. Lewis A. Coser (Chicago: University of Chicago Press, 1992); P. Nora, 'Between Memory and History: Les Lieux de Mémoire', *Representations* 26 (1989), 7–24; A. Assmann, *Der lange Schatten der Vergangenheit: Erinnerungskultur und Geschichtspolitik* (Munich: C.H. Beck, 2006); J. Assmann, 'Collective Memory and Cultural Identity', trans. John Czaplicka, *New German Critique* 65 (1995), 125–33; M. Hirsch, *The Generation of Postmemory: Writing and Visual Culture after the Holocaust* (New York: Columbia University Press, 2012). The state of the field is summarized in A. Erll and A. Nünning (eds), *Cultural Memory Studies: An International and Interdisciplinary Handbook* (Berlin: Walter de Gruyter, 2008).
48. A. Huyssen, *Twilight Memories: Marking Time in a Culture of Amnesia* (New York: Routledge, 1995), 2–3. The memory boom has given rise to a number of recent interdisciplinary edited volumes concerning twentieth-century European memory, and Eastern Europe in particular. See e.g. J. Niżnik (ed.), *Twentieth-Century Wars in European Memory* (Frankfurt am Main: Peter Lang, 2013); U. Blacker, A. Etkind, and J. Fedor (eds), *Memory and Theory in Eastern Europe* (Basingstoke: Palgrave Macmillan, 2013); M. Pakier and J. Wawrzyniak (eds), *Memory and Change in Europe: Eastern Perspectives* (New York: Berghahn Books, 2015).
49. J. Assmann, 'Communicative and Cultural Memory', in A. Erll and A. Nünning (eds), *Cultural Memory Studies: An International and Interdisciplinary Handbook* (Berlin: Walter de Gruyter, 2008), 109–18.
50. A. Landsberg, 'Prosthetic Memory: The Ethics and Politics of Memory in an Age of Mass Culture', in P. Grainge (ed.), *Memory and Popular Film* (Manchester: Manchester University Press, 2003), 144–61.
51. M. Bernhard and J. Kubik, 'A Theory of the Politics of Memory', in M. Bernhard and J. Kubik (eds), *Twenty Years after Communism* (Oxford: Oxford University Press, 2014), 7–30 (8).
52. In his doctoral research, Vincent Post demonstrated that while attitudes towards the socialist past continue to sway the media and political discussion, they do not constitute an equally salient topic for the electorate: 'The preponderance of what we know about Czechs' views regarding the communist past shows that Czech voters are mostly ambivalent about the communist past and do not share the wholesale rejection that characterizes anticommunism.' See V. Post, 'Putting out the Fire, or Fanning the Flames? How Regulating Secret Service Files and Personnel Affects Contestation over the Communist Past' (PhD thesis, Department of Political Science, McGill University, 2015), 104.
53. For more on the culture industry, see T. Adorno and M. Horkheimer, *The Dialectic of Enlightenment*, trans. J. Cumming (London: Verso, 1997).
54. J. Fiske, *Reading the Popular* (Boston: Unwin Hyman, 1989), 2.
55. To determine a work's impact, I looked at reception networks, constituted by a combination of factors. These include the number of press reviews; where relevant, the number and liveliness of internet discussions dedicated to the work in question; print-runs in the case of literature; awards and prizes; ratings in the case of television shows; box-office statistics in the case of films, as well as DVD releases (including 'cheap DVD' releases, i.e. the rerelease of a film on DVD usually sold with tabloid newspapers and magazines for a price significantly lower than the original DVD). All data on box-office ticket sales, unless otherwise stated, is taken from the Czech Union of Film Distributors, which

publishes annual box office rankings on its website (www.ufd.cz). DVD release data is available from the Czech and Slovak Film Database (www.csfd.cz). Where relevant, works that only gained a small audience and scant reviews are mentioned to illustrate how certain visions or interpretations of the past did not gain traction.

56. A. Erll, 'Literature, Film, and the Mediality of Cultural Memory', in A. Erll and A. Nünning (eds), *Cultural Memory Studies: An International and Interdisciplinary Handbook* (Berlin: Walter de Gruyter, 2008), 389–98 (395).
57. An analysis of reception through the internet is of course only possible with the caveat that those who choose to participate in internet debates are a specific group and not representative of reception trends as a whole. See Činátl, *Naše české minulosti*, in particular 127–76.
58. Reifová, Gillarová and Hladík, 'The Way We Applauded', 199–221.
59. I. Reifová, 'The Pleasure of Continuity: Re-reading Postsocialist Nostalgia', *International Journal of Cultural Studies* 21(6) (2018), 587–602.

Chapter 1

PAINTING THE PAST BLACK AND WHITE

Czech Anticommunism after 1989

Anticommunism as 'the defining feature of the emerging Czech political culture'[1] after the regime change of 1989 has attracted ample attention from political scientists and historians alike,[2] and, as such, it is impossible to discuss any forms of memory of the previous regime without reference to it. While this anticommunist line was largely promoted by the new political class and found a solid place in the media, this chapter shows how it was also taken up by cultural actors in the form of representations, art installations and public initiatives. Cultural producers were keen to depict heroes of anticommunist resistance, make statements that would present communism as a Soviet import, and criticize the Communist Party in order to align themselves with specific political causes, helping to shape a public memory in which a wholesale rejection of the country's socialist past became the norm. An examination of the cultural memory of state socialism not only in the Czech Republic thus cannot take place without a consideration of anticommunism as one of the guiding ideological forces of the East-Central European systemic transformations.

Existing accounts across the region largely neglect how cultural workers contributed to a discursive separation from the past. In the case of the Czech Republic, this is particularly striking given that the perceived significance of cultural elites for Czech political discourse has a long tradition and the prominent political role of intellectuals forms one of the founding blocks of Czech national mythology, with the first interwar democratic president, Tomáš Garrigue Masaryk and first postsocialist president, Václav Havel, usually given as examples. In his study of Czech national identity, anthropologist Ladislav Holý argues that 'the Czechs substantiate their image of themselves as an exceptionally cultured and well-educated nation by a specific reading of their history in which they construct a close relationship between culture and politics'.[3] Indeed, the opposition to the Normalization-era regime, in the milieu of both dissent and the underground, was largely constituted by artists and those in cultural and/or intellectual fields.[4] While some of these actors chose to actively enter politics after 1989 – most prominently of course playwright Václav Havel, who became President – others remained outside the party political arena, but their actions and discourse were given coverage in the media. In this chapter, I draw mainly on the printed media as major facilitators of public debates at the time.[5]

Examining the dominant narratives relating to the socialist past in the post-1989 Czech public sphere provides essential groundwork for understanding the political dimensions of the cultural memory of socialism. I argue that in contrast to the widespread nostalgia paradigm, retrospective representations of socialism often helped in consolidating an anticommunist interpretation of the socialist period. The following chapters will show that the nostalgia for socialism witnessed in fictional representations does not in fact reject, but rather interacts with this mainstream anticommunist discourse, especially since anticommunism was a narrative championed equally by a cultural as by a political elite.

In Czechoslovakia the condemnation of the previous forty years of Communist Party rule emerged as a major point on the political agenda in the immediate aftermath of the collapse of the communist regime in November 1989. In comparison to neighbouring countries, Czechoslovakia fairly swiftly introduced a set of legal measures that dealt with the socialist past, including the restitution of property nationalized by the previous regime to private individuals and organizations, the privatization of state enterprises and the vetting of public officials in a process known as lustration. After the country separated into two on 1 January 1993, the Czech Republic also passed the Act on the Illegality of the Communist Regime in the same year, though the Communist Party continued to exist, ostracized by all other parties.[6]

Altogether, these measures served to validate an institutional anticommunism in the Czech Republic, though its force was much less prominent in Slovakia. The paths of the two parts of the country quickly diverged in terms of priorities. Not only was the national question much more prominent in Slovak politics; the Slovak part of the country had experienced less repression in the Normalization era and, as a result, reform communists enjoyed greater legitimacy after 1989. It was the so-called sixty-eighters who dominated electoral lists in the first free elections in Slovakia.[7] As sociologist Gil Eyal summarizes, while in the Czech part of the country, the greatest political gains were to be made through a policy of a radical break with the communist past, in Slovakia, 'the greatest political profits were secured by an opposite political strategy, which emphasized continuity with the communist past, particularly 1968'.[8] The relative lack of instrumental anticommunism as a means of legitimization (though we cannot doubt the authenticity of anticommunism as an ideological stance, especially coming from former political prisoners or dissidents) meant that this discourse did not come to occupy such a position of hegemony in Slovakia. As such, it also did not translate into as significant a force within the cultural sphere. Where relevant, throughout this book I will refer to examples of Slovak representations that support or counter Czech trends; nevertheless, they are not a topic of systematic analysis.

On an Axis of Good and Evil

In 1996, the discussion programme *7 čili sedm dní* (*7, that is Seven Days*), broadcast on the private TV channel Nova, hosted a heated debate. Facing each other were former exile journalist, opposition activist and post-1989 Minister of Culture Pavel Tigrid, and popular actress, former leader of the Artist's Union and Communist Party politician Jiřina Švorcová. In the hour-long programme, Tigrid, speaking from the position of a 'victor' of the revolution, repeatedly accused Švorcová of moral failure for her participation in Communist Party structures. 'Using administrative power, you aided non-freedom and forty years of totalitarianism', Tigrid told Švorcová, adding: 'You harmed so many people.' When Švorcová replied not in the same abstract categories, but with specific facts and events, Tigrid opined with a metaphor referring to her supposedly bad conscience, which he urged her to lay bare in front of television viewers: 'You have disappointed me, you only took out a quarter of your drawer and a few pages from your diary.'[9] Tigrid called for a language of moral purification, performing his anticommunist position not only in political but also in ethical terms.

Tigrid's position typifies a particularly strong discursive trend in postsocialist Czech Republic, namely a view that sees the Communist Party and, by extension, socialism not in political terms, but on an ethical axis of good vs. evil, the former being represented by the current political order. It is such an attitude that gained firm grounding in the Czech relationship towards the socialist past throughout the 1990s and that continued to play a prominent role well into the 2000s and 2010s, though it increasingly came under challenge from various corners, as the later chapters in this volume will show. Tigrid's case also illustrates that anticommunism did not appear overnight with the collapse of the communist regime: as a political and intellectual position, it had its firm place among the cultural elite of the interwar First Republic, among parts of the government in exile during the Second World War, and its tradition continued during communist rule in dissident and exile circles. Already before the communist takeover of power in 1948, Tigrid edited the journal *Obzory* (*Horizons*), which had an anticommunist agenda, and continued these activities during communist rule in exile as the editor-in-chief of the quarterly *Svědectví* (*Testimony*), published initially from New York and later Paris. But it was only after 1989 that anticommunism became widely adopted by all who wished to identify with the new order.

In an essay that provides a particularly perceptive diagnosis of the Czech postsocialist condition, literary critic Miroslav Balaštík argued that an ethical axis was already present in the catchphrase of the Velvet Revolution: 'truth and love will prevail over lies and hatred'. The outcome of the changes of 1989 has been cast as 'truth and love', i.e. unequivocal good, while the socialist past was degraded to the evil of 'lies and hatred'. As a result, Balaštík writes that 'the flat rejection of the communist past simultaneously brought a fetishization of liberal democracy as a system that is good a priori'.[10] This narrative of the historical development from socialism into capitalism is also the implicit assumption around which many representations of the past structure their narratives; furthermore, it also functioned as an effective tool for stifling any critique of the inherent problems of liberal democracy and the free market.

The widespread binary narrative of communism as the embodiment of evil and the inherent goodness of the post-1989 developments was championed by right-wing parties, which swiftly dominated the political scene after the broad coalition of political persuasions in the Civic Forum (Občanské Forum (OF)) – the umbrella movement formed in November 1989 that led the opposition against the communist government – proved ineffectual.[11] The course of the economic transformation was steered by Václav Klaus and his colleagues along neoliberal lines,[12] in a fate resembling many postsocialist countries. Championed by both Western advisors and local economists, as Philipp Ther argues in his post-1989 history of Europe, faith in unbridled market forces offering the best solutions for reform became hegemonic throughout the continent after the collapse of the Iron Curtain, to an extent thanks to postsocialist countries becoming 'experimentation sites for neoliberal policy'.[13] This does not mean that the left was erased from the political map. Aside from the still-existing Communist Party, the second most prominent leftist actor was the Social Democratic Party (ČSSD), which was renewed shortly after the 1989 regime change, though it remained weak throughout the first half of the 1990s, slowly building up its support towards victory in the 1998 parliamentary elections. In the arena of party politics, through a conflation of communism with left-wing politics in general, anticommunist rhetoric was used by newly formed right-wing forces to discredit not only the continued presence of the Communist Party on the political scene, but also the Social Democrats and indeed the left as understood in the broadest possible sense.[14]

However, instrumental anticommunism was not just used as a means of creating a binary opposition of good vs. evil, to which political opponents could be relegated; it was also taken up as the most immediately available token of right-wing credentials in the new political climate. Although the desire of those adopting anticommunist attitudes to perform and enact a genuine reckoning with the past cannot be underestimated, many of the actors from diverse backgrounds entering politics at the time did not have access to the contents of neoliberal ideology in the same way as Klaus and other economic experts, who came from an academic policy-oriented milieu, which had long been conversant with Western economic paradigms.[15] Those who could not master this specialized language could not persuasively build their rhetoric on economic expertise,[16] and so a broad anti-left stance became an efficient gesture of moral exculpation: they may not have been dissidents, but could now retrospectively validate their inner anti-regime attitude.

However, the right-wing consensus was somewhat shaken by an economic recession in 1997. In combination with the revelation of financial scandals associated with Klaus's ruling Civic Democrats (Občanská demokratická strana (ODS)), Czech society experienced a certain level of disenchantment with the course of the economic transformation. Václav Havel famously described this state with the term 'blbá nálada' (a foul or bad mood) in 1997.[17] Klaus's ODS-dominated government collapsed in the same year, and the following year, the Social Democrats won the parliamentary elections, ruling by means of the so-called 'opposition agreement' with their alleged arch-enemy, the discredited ODS.[18] This development led to further disenchantment with politics that manifested itself in the form of several protest initiatives.[19] In these circumstances, the socialist past and the Communist Party were used as a scapegoat for the dissatisfaction with the current state of affairs by the media and public initiatives. With these political changes, the nature of anticommunism also underwent a transformation. Political scientist Ondřej Slačálek argues that the initial period of the 1990s was marked by anticommunism as a distancing mechanism of moral superiority, but also tolerance of the continued presence of the Communists on the political scene (encapsulated in one of the slogans of 1989: 'We are not like them'). But during the first decade of the new millennium, and more specifically around 2003, when communist votes became necessary to elect Václav Klaus as the Czech Republic's President, the discourse of anticommunism became more confrontational towards the KSČM, as well as the legacies of communism, according to Slačálek. In other words, the right-wing consensus of the first postsocialist decade was coming under fire as the communists once again became a serious political player; this led to an escalation of anticommunist rhetoric in public discourse.[20]

Czech anticommunism thus differs from that of its neighbours such as Slovakia and Poland, where, as Jiří Koubek and Martin Polášek observe, 'postcommunists' (i.e. former communists, whether reformed or not) successfully merged with the new elites, which then led to a disillusioned 'anticommunism of the defeated'[21] in what was viewed as a betrayal of the changes of 1989. Of course, certain members of the old regime elites also found their place in the new order in the Czech Republic. Nevertheless, the structure of Czech anticommunism is different from its populist version in neighbouring Poland, for instance; with left-leaning dissidents and reform communists losing their legitimacy, and the existing KSČM systematically not being granted the status of equal partner by other parliamentary parties for a number of years,[22] Czech anticommunism is, in Koubek and Polášek's words, 'an elite ideology. It is a firm and natural part of the cultural hegemony'.[23] This, however, has the effect of creating the preconditions for the creative potential of Czech anticommunism. Indeed, the rhetoric of anticommunism has often been mobilized by artists and public intellectuals, and this has significant implications for the memory of socialism in the country. If we understand collective memory as being to a large extent shaped by popular representations, such as films or television programmes, then this memory in the Czech context necessarily incorporates the political stance of cultural producers who often either consciously or implicitly acknowledged the anticommunist consensus of the cultural elites.

Making Heroes out of Victims

The particular tenor of anticommunist sentiment is often connected to ideas of heroism. In other words, who resisted communist rule, how is such resistance valued and in what ways, if at all, should it be commemorated? One organization that from the early 1990s sought to directly promote a memory of anticommunist resistance was the Confederation of Political Prisoners (Konfederace politických vězňů (KPV)), which brought together those who had been politically persecuted by the previous regime. The KPV sought acknowledgement for the victims of communist injustice, but its militancy in terms of who could claim resistant credentials led to it becoming mired in personal disputes, further aggravated by its unforgiving stance towards lawmakers across the political spectrum, whom it accused of having transferred economic power into the hands of 'former nomenclature Bolsheviks'.[24] The organization viewed politicians as not radical enough in their condemning stance towards the past and therefore as unworthy interlocutors, which prevented the KPV from becoming a serious political actor, largely failing throughout the 1990s and 2000s to achieve material and symbolic gains, such as financial compensation and social and political recognition according to its wishes.[25] While the radical discourse of the KPV thus proved rather ineffectual, when the anticommunist hero was narrativized in the work of writer Jiří Stránský, it proved a more persuasive idea, gaining a wider audience.

Stránský (1931–2019), who came from a patrician family, was persecuted during communist rule for his class origins and spent several years working in uranium mines and labour camps in the 1950s. Later, he was forced to work in manual professions. He made use of his direct experience with the regime's repressive apparatus in a number of screenplays and fictional texts. Set in the Czech-German borderlands, Stránský's novels *A Land Gone Wild* (*Zdivočelá země*, 1991) and *The Auction* (*Aukce*, 1997)[26] were adapted for the television screen in the four-season series *A Land Gone Wild* (*Zdivočelá země*, dir. Hynek Bočan, 1997, 2001, 2008–9, 2012). The narrative ambitiously details the whole socialist period through the story of former RAF pilot Antonín Maděra and his persecution by the communist authorities. The series was described in the press as 'returning memory' to the nation[27] and was generally praised for offering a 'true interpretation of history'.[28] Reviewers saw the main contribution of the edifying project Stránský took upon himself in the presentation of a heroic role model. The hero of the story, Maděra, is a man whose democratic principles are never shaken and who does not break even under the duress of a communist labour camp. Instead, he continues his project of building an island of freedom on his cooperative farm, where he pursues his beloved interest of raising horses, deemed ideologically suspect by the authorities. Stránský's work moderates the uncompromising rhetoric of the KPV by portraying an overwhelmingly positive hero who suffers only from a few minor personality faults, such as a hot temper.

The notion of heroism is an important component of historical memory; as subsequent chapters will demonstrate, different conceptions of heroism play into different narrative modes about the socialist past. As in other cultural traditions, the Czech understanding of heroism has its particular cultural models and precursors. While Slovak or Polish national mythology finds its models of heroism in active and often armed resistance, particularly during the Second World War, Françoise Mayer posits that 'Czech "heroes" are often martyrs (remember Hus, Fučík, Palach), but only rarely fighters (with the exception of Jan Žižka)',[29] and Robert Pynsent traces this 'Czech martyr complex' to the writings of Tomáš Garrigue Masaryk.[30] This reading is corroborated by anthropologist Ladislav Holý in his detailed study of perceptions of Czech national identity. Holý identifies a particular Czech resistance to individual exceptionalism and instead finds a widespread egalitarian ethos, founded on a belief in an equal distribution of intelligence (as opposed to an unequal distribution of hard work). In his exploration of Czech historical myths, Jiří Rak traces this ethos to the historical absence of an aristocracy and relatively weak bourgeoisie in the Bohemian and Moravian social make-up, characteristics that were seized upon by the National Revival of the nineteenth century, which celebrated the 'simple' Czech people as the source of Czech national identity.[31] If there are any heroes to be found in the Czech historical canon that were equally lauded during the National Revival, the interwar First Republic and the period of Communist Party rule, it was the fifteenth-century Hussite religious reform movement. But particularly the Communist Party's efforts to interpret Hus and his followers as proto-communists defending ordinary people against oppressors discredited this heroic narrative to a large extent.[32] Indeed, the early 1990s were marked by an emphasis on lauding the victims of the political repressions of the former regime. An active understanding of heroism is also endorsed rather lukewarmly in Czech representations. 'Hero' can be used as an insult: characters in the popular Czech Television series *Tell Me a Story* set in late socialism, which is the subject of more detailed analysis in Chapter 5, often use the term *hrdina* (hero) pejoratively or ironically to indicate disapproval of actions by which other characters draw too much attention to themselves.

A Land Gone Wild thus presents something of an exception to the general trend amongst the representations discussed in this book, in that it attempts to shift the story of the political prisoners of the communist regime from victimhood to a more genuine heroism. Part of this strategy is to give the protagonist Maděra heroic credentials by making him an RAF pilot in the Second World War, a heroic discourse that was only reinstated after 1989, as its memory had been suppressed by communist authorities. Heroism is introduced through the form of an adventure story – the narrative, particularly when it recounts the immediate aftermath of the War, is modelled on the genre of the Western, with the Bohemian borderlands imagined as an unexplored Wild West, up for grabs by both honest and nefarious characters. Stránský presents dynamic narratives with a sustained arc over several decades, where Maděra is continuously met by new pitfalls, which he manages to resolve in a model manner.

The series had high ratings especially in the first season.[33] Within Czech cultural production of the 1990s, it forms an exception in tackling the topic of resistance against the communist regime in the 1950s. Stránský was practically alone in championing this agenda in both written and visual production; the film *Bumerang* (*Boomerang*, dir. Hynek Bočan, 1996), set in a 1950s labour camp for political prisoners, was also the result of a cooperation between Stránský and director Bočan. In the 2000s, three more films based on Stránský's writings, all portraying the regime's cruel treatment of political prisoners, were made: two television films, *Uniforma* (*The Uniform*, 2002) and *Žabák* (*The Frog*, 2003), both directed by Bočan, and *Kousek nebe* (*A Piece of Sky*, dir. Petr Nikolaev, 2005). However, none of these was a major success with audiences.[34] The notion of 'Third Resistance' – i.e. the idea that anticommunist resistance continued the tradition of so-called First and Second Resistance of the two World Wars – remains fraught. Even after the passing of the Act on Third Resistance in 2011, which gave the concept a legal stamp and offered compensation to those persecuted by the previous regime, prominent resistance cases remained controversial.

The legacy of political prisoners and anticommunist resistance has not been successful in coming to represent models of heroic behaviour during the socialist period. But, despite Václav Havel's efforts, nor did public discourse incorporate the dissident experience into the collective memory of socialism.[35] This was largely due to the failure of many ex-dissidents to become convincing political actors, exemplified in particular by the inefficacy of the Civic Movement (Občanské hnutí), a successor party to the OF gathering many former dissidents, which had depleted itself by the mid 1990s.[36] Instead, subsequent chapters will show that the mantle of heroism has been taken up and transferred to the narrative of 'ordinary people', who in literary, cinematic and other representations of socialism are depicted as the carriers of small, resistant gestures. Such representations on the one hand play into the egalitarian ethos in Czech culture identified by Holý, where few stand out as exceptional figures. On the other hand, such depictions also obscure engagement with the concept of accountability: if everyone is cast as having resisted in some small way, this poses an obstacle to an inquiry into the regime's longevity and consensual aspects.

Artistic Interventions in the Anticommunist Landscape

Artists and cultural workers did not always limit themselves to written, cinematic or television representations of the past, or indeed other fields of artistic activity. Playing into the perceived tradition of cultural workers as political actors, they intervened to shape attitudes towards the past through petitions and initiatives. Perhaps the earliest and most publicized example of an artist who decided to make a public commentary on a particular aspect of the legacy of socialism was sculptor David Černý, at the time a student of the Academy of Arts, Architecture and Design in Prague, who in late April 1991 painted a Soviet tank pink that stood in a square in the fifth district of Prague as a memorial to the liberation of Czechoslovakia by the Red Army at the end of the Second World War.[37] This artistic act stirred up a storm of controversy, angering supporters of the communists (at that time still in the form of the KSČ – the Communist Party of Czechoslovakia) and those who had witnessed the liberation. A commentator for *Rudé právo*, which had been the Party newspaper during communist rule, wrote that 'a happening of pranksters is one thing, but insulting the memorials of those who died to save our lives is another'.[38] Indignation could also be witnessed at the highest levels: the Soviet ambassador viewed the event as a diplomatic insult.[39] The tank was promptly repainted its original colour by the local council. Yet at a time when the spirit of dissent still occasionally manifested in parliamentary politics, it was soon after once again coated in pink by a group of Civic Forum deputies of the Federal Assembly. This was, as one federal deputy explained, to register their protest with the criminal proceedings against Černý for his act of 'vandalism'.[40]

While Černý, speaking to the press at the time, claimed that the gesture was of a pacifist nature,[41] the crux of the matter was that even though the tank was meant to commemorate the liberation of Czechoslovakia, it was inevitably, as the cultural quarterly *Prostor* wrote in its analysis of the event, widely understood as 'a symbol of the occupation of 1968'.[42] A further commentary added that given the fact that 'Tank no. 23', as it was known, was not the first liberating tank to enter Prague, as the memorial claimed, but in fact a wholly different machine, the memorial also served as a reminder of the 'falsification of history'.[43] The tank was used by the communist regime for the purposes of pro-Soviet propaganda in order to cover up the memory of the fact the district of Prague where the tank stood had been liberated not by the Red Army, but by General Vlasov's Russian Liberation Army. The pink coating of the tank was an act that, through protesting against what the memorial stood for, blurred the distinction between anticommunist and anti-Russian sentiment.

Through this rhetorical move of conflation, the action can be seen as one of the early prominent examples of a narrative of externalization, where the communist regime is perceived as a Soviet imposition, which, as Michal Kopeček summarizes, depicts the period as 'an interlude, an aberration from the supposed natural path of national history, an "Asiatic despotism" imported from the "East"'.[44] Indeed, this trope resonated with one of the main slogans and grand narratives of the early postsocialist years – the idea of the 'return to Europe', championed by political elites across the spectrum, feeding into a national myth encapsulated by Milan Kundera in his essay 'The Tragedy of Central Europe', in which he described Czechoslovakia as a 'kidnapped West', forcefully dragged to the East by the Soviet Union.[45]

At the same time, the word 'prank' (in Czech: *recese*), which came up in the press in response to Černý's bold act, captures an ironic dimension of the reception of the communist past in artistic reworkings, where the symbolism of the communist regime can be made light of through aestheticization. Černý's act can be interpreted as following from a tradition of downplaying militarism in Czech culture that harks back to Jaroslav Hašek's seminal First World War novel *The Good Soldier Švejk* (1921–23). Indeed, film comedies that ridiculed the socialist army were one of the first representational means of reckoning with the period of communist rule in the early 1990s.[46] The case of the tank demonstrates that an ironic stance that finds enjoyment in the symbols it ridicules can also be a gesture of the condemnation of the previous regime.

From the beginning of the 2000s, anticommunist rhetoric was taken up by artists and other cultural figures with greater vehemence. This may in part be interpreted as a certain polarization within Czech public discourse around the year 1999, which, as Chapter 3 will demonstrate, witnessed a 'nostalgic turn': while on the one hand, the public enjoyed a successful film comedy set in the 1960s and revelled in the resurgent popularity of Normalization-era singers and television series, on the other hand, commentators in the press worried about these developments. Where Černý's Pink Tank allowed for various interpretations (for instance, pacifist, antimilitaristic), by 2000, the artistic collective Podebal was much more unequivocal in the message of its exhibition *Malík urvi* (literally, rip off the pinkie; in Czech also a play on the words *malý kurvy* – little whores). This installation consisted of large-scale photographic portraits of a number of public figures with a communist or StB past, who continued to play a role in public life at the time of the exhibition. *Malík urvi* reignited the accusatory logic of various 'lustration affairs', setting the exhibition's motivations on par with the highly controversial exposure of various public figures as StB agents in the early 1990s in the so-called 'Cibulka lists', published by anticommunist activist Petr Cibulka in his newspaper *Necenzurované noviny* (*Uncensored News*) in 1992.

While some saw *Malík urvi* as a genuine attempt to come to terms with the past through artistic means,[47] others were offended by the fact that the exhibition once again dug up old lustration affairs in which alleged StB collaborators had been cleared by court.[48] For example, social democratic politician and diplomat Jan Kavan was angered that his reputation was once again being publicly questioned: 'it was total, naked disrespect of the decision of an independent court',[49] he said, referring to the 1996 ruling that had cleared him of all charges. The unforgiving logic of the exhibition treated possible collaboration as a kind of indelible mark, where the verdict of a democratic court could not overrule the initial stigma levied upon Kavan.

The exhibition remained a niche event. Soon, however, numerous artists and activists would start a public campaign in which they criticized the lack of decommunization and demanded that mainstream political parties stop cooperating with the KSČM on any level, inaugurating what Slačálek terms the 'exclusionary' phase of Czech anticommunism, which attempted to eliminate communists from public debate. Initiated by former dissident and writer Petr Placák and David Černý of Pink Tank fame, the 2003 petition 'One Does Not Speak to Communists' was signed by dozens of public figures and eventually garnered several thousand signatures, illustrating particularly clearly the thesis that anticommunism is a discourse that has been championed by the cultural elite in the Czech Republic.[50] Černý managed to secure prominent publicity for the initiative when he designed a T-shirt depicting a raised middle finger and bearing the slogan 'Fuck the KSČM' worn by guitarist Keith Richards during a Rolling Stones concert in Prague in July 2003.[51] Domestic musicians also expressed support for the initiative through a series of concerts in Prague and elsewhere.[52] One popular rock band frontman invoked the aforementioned perceived tradition of cultural opposition to the ruling power when on the occasion of the first concert, he said that 'people who worked in culture used to speak out against communism, this concert is a continuation of that tradition'.[53] The petition reopened the question of banning the KSČM in the media, though politicians were clear that the initiative would not set a new agenda.[54] Where initially even more leftwing commentators interpreted the petition as a genuine civic movement for finally dealing with communist legacies and a real intervention in the political landscape, in retrospect the whole initiative lends itself to being read as yet another instrumental use of anticommunism to discredit particular personalities. 'One Does Not Speak to Communists' in fact targeted Václav Klaus, who had by then not only become President by disregarding his previous anticommunism and was elected into office thanks to the votes of KSČM MPs, but had also invited representatives of the Communist Party for top-level discussions at the presidential residence in Lány.[55]

The discourse around the initiative produced a polarization between 'intellectuals' and 'politicians' that was already familiar from the days of the Normalization-era opposition to the communist regime.[56] As philosopher Václav Bělohradský argues, this dichotomy between 'non-politicians' as 'honest people' and dishonest politicians, which has its roots in the dissident tradition of intellectuals posing a critique to the ruling order outside of the sphere of politics, is a significant feature of Czech political culture adopted by the liberal elites.[57] In this discourse, communists are rhetorically not only banished as 'Other' from the field of politics, but also from the historical record itself.

This trope was perhaps best expressed in the controversy around David Černý's commission for a memorial to the Czech anti-fascist resistance during the Second World War in 2004, which was to stand in a green space in Prague's first district. Despite the fact that Černý's proposal had won an open competition, the memorial was in the end designed by Vladimír

Preclík, due to a remark that Černý made in an interview with the magazine *Nedělní svět* (*Sunday World*), in which he claimed that 'a dead communist [is] a good communist'.[58] The journal did not fail to pick up on the irony that 'David Černý irreconcilably hates communists. Nevertheless, he will soon build hundreds of them a memorial'.[59] The article thus pointed to the fact that many in the antifascist resistance were also communist sympathizers. After Černý's remarks garnered protest from the Czech Union of Freedom Fighters, a Second World War veterans' organization, the councillors of Prague's first district voted to hand over the commission to Preclík.[60] The incident also illustrates that in comparison with the endorsement members of parliament gave to Černý's Pink Tank action in 1991, by this point public discourse had shifted, and in a political culture where the KSČM had firmly established itself as part and parcel of the political scene, garnering stable support of around 15% even fifteen years after 1989, officials were more cautious in openly angering a hardly negligible political force.

Černý nevertheless reacted to the decision by saying that it is proof that 'communists still have a large say in Czech society'.[61] The sculptor's rhetorical effort to discredit communist antifascist resistance is emblematic of a strategy of erasing communism from historical memory, a kind of sanitization of the past, which is reimagined as having taken place without communists – an exclusion of this group from the 'we' of democratic Czech society. This trope rests on the presupposition of equating communism with fascism, which comes up time and again in public debates on the past. After long discussions about a planned 'Institute of National Memory',[62] the stance would eventually be institutionalized through the setting up of the Institute for the Study of Totalitarian Regimes in 2007, the mission of which is to study both the Nazi and communist periods, both designated as 'totalitarian dictatorships'.[63]

Anticommunism's Shifting Object

Throughout the first postsocialist decade and beyond, anticommunism was used as a token of symbolically eliminating the adversary – anyone who did not embrace radical decommunization, and moreover anyone with leftist leanings, could be labelled as calling for a return to the old order, a very common and still-used rhetorical move. It also often fulfilled a role of a smokescreen for a critique of the status quo. As political scientist Lukáš Valeš notes, this became a convenient tool for right-wing political parties, who could use the 'scarecrow' of a return before 1989 to obscure salient social and economic problems, and position themselves as the saviours of democracy.[64]

To some extent, the discourse of anticommunism also suggests a generational story: on the one hand, the most radical anticommunists were the political prisoners of the 1950s, who perceived themselves as the most genuine resistance to the communist regime. The political prisoners found little common ground with the next generation of anticommunist opposition, the dissidents of the 1970s, whom they saw as 'not having known the true face of Bolshevism'.[65] The rhetoric of 'non-political politics' and human rights on the part of the dissident initiative Charter 77 translated into an inclusive and pluralistic vision of democracy for many of its signatories, where even the voices of (ex-)communists could be heard – and, indeed, many Charter activists had been members of the Communist Party before 1968. But yet another group comes into play and shapes post-1989 discourse: the 'second generation' of dissent in the form of children of Charter signatories, representatives of oppositional interest groups and multiplying ecological and student initiatives of the 1980s, some of whom subsequently took up an anticommunist activist position, for instance, in the 'One Does Not Speak to Communists' campaign.

Anticommunism defines itself negatively (as is already apparent from the term itself); it requires an adversary for its very existence, even if the notion of this adversary has to shift to some extent in order to maintain this existence. It is thus by no means a unified strategy, as we saw in the diversity of its manifestations discussed in this chapter. In anticommunist discourse, identification with the status quo happens on the basis of the exclusion of the Other, who can, depending on the particular situation, mean current and former communists, secret police agents and collaborators, or can at other times be externalized completely, where the communist regime is viewed as a Soviet imposition. Hand in hand with the strategy of an all-round rejection of the past comes the levelling of the different historical periods through which state socialism developed, also on the level of official memory politics. For instance, critics of the 1993 Act on the Illegality of the Communist Regime pointed out that this law equated the protagonists of the Prague Spring with those who then eradicated the architects of reform socialism during Normalization.[66] A further extension of this logic is the equation of Nazism and communism under the bracket of 'totalitarianism' – in this way, much of the twentieth century, with the exception of the inter-war First Republic, is relegated to taking up the role of undifferentiated evil.

In his satirical essays on postmodernism, writer Jan Stern notes that of the strategies that serve to legitimate the new political order, 'surely the most remarkable mythological rhetorical figure is the confusion of democracy and capitalism'.[67] A third part to this terminological equation is added by Holý, who notes that 'for most Czechs, democracy is first of all coterminous with freedom'.[68] The triumvirate democracy-capitalism-freedom became interchangeable and naturalized; thus, Karel, the main hero of the soap opera *Tell Me a Story*, which in its fourth season portrays the turmoil of building capitalism in the 1990s, proclaims 'it's pretty great we have freedom and democracy', when what he in fact finds so great is that the free market has allowed him to become an entrepreneur.[69]

Together with politicians who exploited this conflation of the triumvirate of democracy, capitalism and freedom to blame contemporary failures on the socialist past, it was often artists and individuals active in the cultural sphere who championed the discourse of the ethical opposition. Images of the past thus operated to varying degrees with the basic assumption that the present from which narratives of the past are retrospectively retold is necessarily better. Is it then meaningful to speak of nostalgia, if the 'lost home' is relegated to the land of evil? This will be the main question addressed in the following chapters.

Notes

1. M. Kopeček, 'Disent jako minulost, liberalismus jako projekt: Občanské hnutí – Svobodní demokraté v české polistopadové politice', in A. Gjuričová et al. (eds), *Rozděleni minulostí: Vytváření politických identit v České republice po roce 1989* (Prague: Ústav pro soudobé dějiny, 2012), 61–106 (85).
2. Much of this work has emerged from the Institute of Contemporary History of the Czech Academy of Sciences. See, for example, J. Suk, *Labyrintem Revoluce: Aktéři, zápletky a křižovatky jedné politické krize (od listopadu 1989 do června 1990)* (Prague: Prostor, 2003), which is a comprehensive investigation of the consolidation of power of the new elites. See also P. Roubal, 'Anticommunism of the Future: Czech Post-dissident Neoconservatives in Post-communist Transformation', in M. Kopeček and P. Wciślik (eds), *Thinking through Transition: Liberal Democracy, Authoritarian Pasts, and Intellectual History in East Central Europe after 1989* (Budapest: CEU Press, 2015), 171–200. See also the collected volume A. Gjuričová et al. (eds), *Rozděleni minulostí: Vytváření politických identit v České republice po roce 1989* (Prague: Ústav pro soudobé dějiny, 2012). For a political science perspective, see L. Valeš, 'Antikomunismus jako nová politická ideologie?', in P. Kopeček et al. (eds), *Společenskovědní aspekty fenoménu vyrovnání se s minulostí v kontextu výchovy k občanství* (Prague: Nakladatelství Epocha, 2013), 60–81.
3. L. Holý, *The Little Czech and the Great Czech Nation: National Identity and the Post-communist Transformation of Society* (Cambridge: Cambridge University Press, 1996), 83.
4. The cultural milieu of Czechoslovak dissent and underground is explored in detail in J. Bolton, *Worlds of Dissent: Charter 77, The Plastic People of the Universe, and Czech Culture under Communism* (Cambridge, MA: Harvard University Press, 2012).
5. This chapter draws particularly on the three major daily newspapers that have been continuously published since the 1990s. *Lidové noviny* (*People's News*), with roots going back to the 1890s, was renewed as a samizdat organization and initially staffed by dissidents; its association with opposition samizdat publishing brought it considerable prestige in the early 1990s. However, its circulation eventually declined and was overtaken by the other two major dailies: *Mladá fronta Dnes* (*Young Front Today*), originally the newspaper

of the Socialist Union of Youth, which transformed itself into an independent publication after 1989, and *Právo* (*Law*), until 1995 *Rudé právo* (*Red Law*), the official newspaper of the Communist Party of Czechoslovakia, now independent, but maintaining a slightly more left-of-centre profile than its two main competitors. Another source is also the liberal weekly *Respekt* (Respect), which arose from a pre-1989 samizdat publication. The newly founded tabloid press, particularly *Blesk* (*Lightning*), was immensely popular in the 1990s. Blesk even became the biggest-selling daily after its founding in 1992, although by 1995, the dailies *Mladá fronta* and *Právo* sold more copies. The tabloid press, including the publications *Expres* (*Express*) in the early 1990s, and later *Aha!*, swiftly profiled themselves as focused on sensationalist crime stories and celebrity gossip. Apart from *Špígl* (from the German *Spiegel* (Mirror), transcribed phonetically into Czech), published between 1990 and 2001, which pursued political topics in a sensationalist fashion, Czech tabloids gave remarkably little attention to politics, making them a less useful source for this enquiry. For more on the structure of the Czech press in the 1990s, see B. Köpplová and J. Jirák, 'Masová média a česká společnost 90. let 20. století: Průběh a důsledky transformace českých médií', in G. Heiss et al. (eds), *Česko a Rakousko po konci studené války: různými cestami do nové Evropy* (Ústí nad Labem: Albis International, 2008), 207–29.
6. The KSČM formed in 1990, after the KSČ (the Communist Party of Czechoslovakia) transformed itself into the KSČS, the federal Communist Party of Czechoslovakia. After the split of the Slovak communists in 1992, the KSČM continued its existence as a separate entity on the territory of the Czech Republic. For more on the post-1989 fate of the Communist Party, see P. Fiala et al., *Komunismus v České republice* (Brno: Masarykova univerzita, 1999).
7. See S. Szomolányi, *Kľukatá cesta Slovenska k demokracii* (Bratislava: Stimul 1999), 45–48.
8. G. Eyal, *The Origins of Postcommunist Elites: From Prague Spring to the Breakup of Czechoslovakia* (Minneapolis: University of Minnesota Press, 2003), xxix.
9. Pavel Tigrid and Jiřina Švorcová in *7 čili sedm dní* (*7, that is Seven Days*), TV Nova, broadcast 29 September 1996. Retrieved 16 August 2019 from https://www.youtube.com/watch?v=ZTO2FTQaBhM.
10. M. Balaštík, 'Banány přestaly být symbolem' ['Bananas are No Longer a Symbol'], *Lidové noviny*, 17 January 2015, 19–20.
11. For more on the Civic Forum's rise and disintegration, see L. Kopeček, *Éra nevinnosti: Česká politika 1989–1997* (Brno: Barrister and Principal, 2010); and S. Hanley, *The New Right in the New Europe: Czech Transformation and Right-Wing Politics, 1989–2006* (London: Routledge, 2006).
12. Neoliberalism is here understood, following David Harvey, as 'a theory of political and economic practices that proposes that human well-being can best be advanced by liberating individual entrepreneurial freedoms and skills within an institutional framework characterized by strong private property rights, free markets, and free trade'. See D. Harvey, *A Brief History of Neoliberalism* (Oxford: Oxford University Press, 2005), 2–3.
13. P. Ther, *Europe since 1989: A History*, trans. Charlotte Hughes-Kreutzmüller (Princeton: Princeton University Press, 2016), 20.
14. For a detailed analysis of the party-political dimension of anticommunism in the Czech Republic, see J. Koubek and M. Polášek, *Antikomunismus: nekonečný příběh české politiky?* (Prague: Friedrich-Ebert-Stiftung, 2013).
15. As Johanna Bockman and Gil Eyal demonstrate, from the 1960s onwards, academic economic exchange between the Eastern Bloc and Western countries, in particular

the United States, flourished to a much larger degree than is generally assumed. See J. Bockman and G. Eyal, 'Eastern Europe as a Laboratory for Economic Knowledge: The Transnational Roots of Neoliberalism', *American Journal of Sociology* 108(2) (2002), 310–52.
16. Klaus was always keen to demonstrate to the public that he was conversant with English-language economic and political theory, often introducing English terms into his speeches and written texts. See, for instance, V. Klaus, 'Snahy o hledání třetí cesty nekončí' ['Efforts to Find a Third Way Are Not Over'], *Lidové noviny*, 7 March 1994, 1, 3.
17. Havel first used this term in an interview ('Interview s prezidentem V. Havlem') broadcast on the First Channel of Czech Television on 1 April 1997. See L. Kopeček, *Deformace demokracie? Opoziční smlouva a česká politika v letech 1998–2002* (Brno: Barrister and Principal, 2015), 25–27.
18. For a comprehnsive analysis of the 'opposition agreement', see Kopeček, *Deformace demokracie?*
19. The two most significant ones included 'Impuls 99' (Impulse 99), a social initiative organized by several public intellectuals close to Václav Havel calling for the development of civil society, and 'Děkujeme, odejděte' (Thank you, time to go), a declaration initiated by several former student leaders of the 1989 Revolution, expressing dissatisfaction with the opposition agreement and calling for political elites to resign.
20. O. Slačálek, 'Český antikomunismus jako pokus o obnovu hegemonie' ['Czech Anticommunism as an Effort to Restore Hegemenony'], *Britské listy*, 22 June 2009. Retrieved 16 August 2019 from https://legacy.blisty.cz/art/47533.html.
21. Koubek and Polášek, *Antikomunismus*, 9.
22. Even the Social Democratic Party, who are the Communists' most natural partner on the Czech political scene, accepted the 'Bohumín Resolution' in 1995, which prevented them from entering into government with the KSČM.
23. Koubek and Polášek, *Antikomunismus*, 10.
24. P. Levý, 'Konfederace politických vězňů navázala na normalizací zakázaný Klub 231' ['The Confederation of Political Prisoners Picks up the Threads of Club 231 Banned under Normalization'], *Pardubické noviny*, 23 March 2000, 18.
25. Representatives of the KPV repeatedly complained about the lack of transitional justice. For instance, in 1997, a KPV member objected that: 'We have a feeling that the authorities and judges are waiting for all of us to die out. But it will also be the witnesses and perpetrators who die out.' See L. Navara, 'Potrestání zločinů komunismu vázne' ['Punishing the Crimes of Communism at a Standstill'], *Mladá fronta Dnes*, 25 October 1997, 1.
26. J. Stránský, *Zdivočelá země* (Prague: Nakladatelství Lidové noviny, 1991); J. Stránský, *Zdivočelá země. Aukce* (Prague: Knižní klub, 1997).
27. M. Spáčilová, 'Seriál Zdivočelá země je western o naší paměti' ['The Series Zdivočelá země is a Western about Our Memory'], *Mladá fronta Dnes*, 24 February 1997, 11; (rt), 'Zdivočelá země nám vrací paměť ['Zdivočelá země Returns Our Memory to Us'], *Slovo*, 13 March 1997, 3.
28. M. Spáčilová, 'Zdivočelá země vnesla politiku do kovbojských snů' ['Zdivočelá země Brings Politics into Cowboy Dreams'], *Mladá fronta Dnes*, 13 May 1997, 19; V. Just, 'Zdivočelá země – Antinástup z gulagu' ['Zdivočelá země – Anti-*Nástup* (a reference to the 1951 socialist realist novel by Václav Řezáč – *my note*) from the Gulag'], *Lidové noviny*, 15 May 1997, 11.
29. F. Mayer, *Les Tchèques et leur communisme: Mémoire et identités politiques* (Paris: Editions de l'Ecole des hautes études en sciences sociales, 2004), 33.

30. R. Pynsent, *Questions of Identity: Czech and Slovak Ideas of Nationality and Personality* (Budapest: Central European University Press, 1994), in particular 190–210.
31. J. Rak, *Bývali Čechové: české historické mýty a stereotypy* (Jinočany: H and H, 1994), 85.
32. Ibid., 66.
33. The first season of the series (12 episodes) was watched by approximately 2,900,000 viewers above the age of 15. Source: Czech Television diary research [*Deníčkový výzkum ČT*], Czech Television Archive. See also R. Hrdinová, 'Zdivočelá země vítězí nad Dallasem' ['Zdivočelá země Is Winning over Dallas'], *Právo*, 10 April 1997, 10.
34. *Boomerang* was seen by a meagre 18,559 viewers in cinemas. See *Filmová ročenka 1997* (Prague: Národní filmový archiv, 1998), 284. *The Uniform* had a rating of 11.2%, while *The Frog* had only a slightly better rating of 13.1% (source: ATO – Nielsen Admosphere, courtesy of Czech Television). *Piece of Sky* did not make it among the fifty most visited films in cinemas in 2005. All audience figures for Czech films produced after 1998 are taken from the Union of Film Distributors (retrieved 16 August 2019 from http://www.ufd.cz/prehledy-statistiky). For Slovakia, film statistics come from the Union of Film Distributors of the Slovak Republic (retrieved 16 August 2019 from http://www.ufd.sk/archiv).
35. F. Mayer, 'Des musées de l'anticommunisme', in F. Rousseau (ed.), *Les présents des passés douloureux: Musées d'histoire et configurations mémorielles. Essais de muséohistoire* (Paris: Michel Houdiard Editeur, 2012), 304–25 (314).
36. See Kopeček, 'Disent jako minulost, liberalismus jako projekt'.
37. (bč), 'Tank zahalen' ['Tank Covered'], *Rudé právo*, 30 April 1991, 1–2.
38. J. Holý, 'Vandalský happening' ['A Vandalistic Happening'], *Rudé právo*, 29 April 1991, 1–2.
39. J. Sirotek, 'Růžová aféra' ['The Pink Affair'], *Prostor* 6(16) (1991), 16–17.
40. Reported in *Události* (News), Czech Television, broadcast on ČT1 on 9 May 2001.
41. (bč), 'Tank zahalen', 1–2.
42. Sirotek, 'Růžová aféra', 17.
43. Z. Hojda and J. Pokorný, *Pomníky a zapomníky* (Prague and Litomyšl: Paseka, 1996), 224.
44. M. Kopeček, 'In Search of "National Memory": The Politics of History, Nostalgia and the Historiography of Communism in the Czech Republic and East Central Europe', in M. Kopeček (ed.), *Past in the Making: Historical Revisionism in Central Europe after 1989* (Budapest: Central European University Press, 2007), 75-95 (77).
45. M. Kundera, 'The Tragedy of Central Europe', *New York Review of Books*, 6 April 1984, 33-38.
46. *The Tank Battalion* (*Tankový prapor*, dir. V. Olmer, 1991) and *Black Barons* (*Černí baroni*, dir. Z. Sirový, 1992) are discussed in more detail in Chapter 2.
47. T. Marjanovič, quoted in 'Rozbor nevšední výstavy' ['Analysis of an Uncommon Exhibition'], *Dobré ráno s BBC*, broadcast 14 February 2000.
48. P. Rezek, 'Legenda o KSČ a StB' ['Legend about the KSČ and StB'], *Lidové noviny*, 13 January 2000, 19–20.
49. R. Kalenská, 'Jan Kavan: Nejsem žádný KATO' ['Jan Kavan: I Am No KATO'], *Pátek: Magazín Lidových novin*, 24 March 2000, 4–9.
50. E. Tabery, 'Nemluvte s bolševiky' ['Don't Speak to Bolsheviks'], *Respekt*, 23 June 2003, 4.
51. Jhv, 'FUCK THE KSČM', *Mladá fronta Dnes*, 29 July 2003, 7.
52. The first concert took place in Prague on 18 November 2003, followed by a concert on 23 April 2004 in the Moravian town of Frýdek-Místek. Another event entitled 'S komunisty se nemluví II' ('One Does Not Speak to Communists II') took place in Prague on 26 September 2004. See V. Vlasák, 'Muzikanti s komunisty nemluví' ['Musicians Are Not

Speaking to Communists'], *Mladá fronta Dnes*, 15 November 2003, 12; M. Jiroušek, 'Umělci zahrají proti komunistům' ['Artists Will Play against the Communists'], *Mladá fronta Dnes*, 22 April 2004, 11; V. Vlasák, 'Znovu proti komunistům' ['Once Again against the Communists'], *Mladá fronta Dnes*, 10 September 2004, 7.

53. vla, 'Hudebníci proti komunismu' ['Musicians against Communism'], *Mladá fronta Dnes*, 29 October 2003, 10.
54. *Právo*, for instance, reported that 'politicians have doubts about the petition against the communists'; several leading political figures expressed their opinion that the communists can only be marginalized through 'quality political work' and not petitions. See (dan), 'Politici pochybují o petici proti komunistům' ['Politicians Have Doubts about Petition against Communists'], 11 June 2003, 3. See also Tabery, 'Nemluvte s bolševiky', 4.
55. Klaus's decision is criticized in the text of the petition itself. See 'S komunisty se nemluví' ['One Does Not Speak to Communists'], *Babylon* 12(10) (2003), 4. See also čtk, 'Intelektuálové varují před komunisty' ['Intellectuals Warn against Communists'], *Mladá fronta Dnes*, 11 June 2003, 4.
56. A number of articles in the press framed the petition as an initiative of 'intellectuals'. See čtk, 'Intelektuálové varují před komunisty', 4; čtk, 'Petice "S komunisty se nemluví" narazila' ['One Does Not Speak to Communists" Petition Hits a Hard Spot'], *Hospodářské noviny*, 4 July 2003, 3; J. Pehe, 'Kdo mluví a nemluví s komunisty' ['Who Is and Is Not Speaking to Communists'], *Lidové noviny*, 19 November 2003, 11. Not surprisingly, the Communist Party daily *Haló noviny* was also keen to pejoratively dismiss the initiative as the work of intellectuals removed from the people. See D. Strož, 'Proč prý intelektuálové "nemluví" s komunisty' ['Why Intellectuals Are Allegedly "Not Speaking" to Communists'], *Haló noviny*, 14 June 2003, 5.
57. V. Bělohradský, 'Antipolitika v Čechách: Příspěvek ke gramatice kýče', in P. Fiala and F. Mikš (eds), *Česká konzervativní a liberální politika* (Brno: CDK, 2000), 33–59.
58. jhv, 'Černý: Mrtvý komunista, dobrý komunista' ['Černý: A Dead Communist (is) a Good Communist'], *Nedělní svět*, 29 August 2004, 1.
59. Ibid.
60. čtk, 'Radnice Prahy 1 nechce pomník obětem odboje od Davida Černého' ['Prague 1 Council Does Not Want Monument to Victims of Resistance by David Černý'], *Lidové noviny*, 5 October 2004, 8.
61. Ibid.
62. ODS senators began to prepare a legislative proposal for the foundation of such an institute in 2005. See čtk, 'Přístup k spisům StB se má rozšířit' ['Access to StB Files to Be Broadened'], *Právo*, 12 April 2005, 4.
63. See Act 181/2007 Coll. on the Institute for the Study of Totalitarian Regimes and the Security Forces Archive, available on the Institute's website. Retrieved 16 August 2019 from http://www.ustrcr.cz/cs/zakon-c-181-2007-sb.
64. Valeš, 'Antikomunismus jako nová politická ideologie?', 62.
65. P. Pečínka, 'Političtí vězni se cítí opomíjeni' ['Political Prisoners Feel Neglected'], *Rovnost*, 30 October 1999, 4.
66. Z. Jičínský, 'Despekt k pražskému jaru je účelový' ['Disdain for the Prague Spring Is Calculated'], *Právo*, 15 August 1998, 6.
67. J. Stern, *Média, psychoanalýza a jiné perverze* (Prague: Malvern, 2006), 214.
68. Holý, *The Little Czech*, 70.
69. *Vyprávěj*, 2009–13, Season 4, Episode 15.

Chapter 2

THE PAST AS COMEDY

Representing Socialism in the 1990s

No sooner had the communist regime fallen in 1989 than cultural producers began turning to the previous political era as a subject of representation. In the case of the film industry, some of the narratives set in the socialist past that were screened in cinemas in the early 1990s had already begun production before the political changes of 1989.[1] At other times, works that could not be published during state socialism served as inspiration for film production in the new liberal order. Such was the case of two films made in the early 1990s, which set the tone for retrospectively portraying the socialist past in the Czech Republic: *The Tank Battalion* (*Tankový prapor*, dir. Vít Olmer, 1991) and *Black Barons* (*Černí baroni*, dir. Zdeněk Sirový, 1992). This chapter looks primarily at the stylistic repertoires cultural producers reached to when attempting to capture the recent past in the 1990s. In contrast to the anticommunist tone of reckoning in the political arena, writers and filmmakers adopted a wide array of techniques. The traumatic aspects of the previous regime, in particular its repressive apparatus, were mitigated by humour, often aided by seemingly naïve child narrators. Stylistically, they drew on repertoires as diverse as camp and kitsch to harness particular emotions in relation to the past: reconciliation, relief, but also an effort to render the past harmless through stylization or congratulate audiences on how well 'we' collectively survived difficult times.

Both *The Tank Battalion* and *Black Barons* were greatly anticipated and much discussed in the press not only for being adaptations of previously banned popular literary texts (*The Tank Battalion* was based on the eponymous novel by émigré writer Josef Škvorecký, while Miloslav Švandrlík's stories served as a template for *Black Barons*), but also because they were amongst the first pictures in Czechoslovakia to be produced by private production companies, and the former film especially was accompanied by a spectacular 'Western' marketing campaign.[2] This strategy paid off: both were the most-watched films in cinemas in 1991 and 1992, respectively.[3] The films are comedies set in a military environment in the 1950s and view the period benignly, depicting the hardships of service in the army with humorous exaggeration. The choice of genre did not go unnoticed by commentators at a time when politicians were debating how best to distance themselves from the past and deal with its legacies, in particular its repressive apparatus. *Black Barons* elicited some unease from reviewers regarding the humorous portrayal of the Auxiliary Technical Battalions, special units of the Czechoslovak People's Army that conscripted political offenders to carry out hard labour, often in uranium mines. These had received their most famous but also damning portrayal in Milan Kundera's 1967 novel *The Joke* (*Žert*). One reviewer expressed concern that the jovial vision of the 1950s would create an objectionable myth about Czech history.[4] Others had doubts as to whether comedy was a dignified enough vehicle to do justice to conscripts who were forced to carry out hard labour in the harsh conditions of the Battalions.[5]

Nevertheless, most reviews were not taken aback by the humorous overtones of these films. Indeed, their comic nature set a precedent for portraying the socialist past in Czech culture; comedy became the dominant genre in which socialism was recounted until the 'dramatic turn' of the second half of the 2000s, which will be the subject of the final chapter. As James Krapfl suggests, comedy (understood less in the conventional sense as a humorous cultural artefact and more as a mode of emplotment in narrative theory, as developed by Northrop Frye) played a significant role in understandings of the Velvet Revolution of 1989 and the subsequent changes it brought about. Comedy strives for reconciliation; its goal is to include as many protagonists as possible into its final outcome. Krapfl argues that this was the discourse of the OF during the final months of 1989, especially its post-dissident elites, who sought a compromise with the Communist Party via roundtable discussions, which later translated into demands of legal continuity and a conciliatory approach towards transitional justice. Monetarist elites around Klaus, on the other hand, cast the outcome of the regime change as tragedy, which eschews reconciliation and instead lends itself to a more radical programme of change.[6] Seen through Krapfl's framework, the mode of representation preferred by cultural producers in the 1990s resonated more with the former, comic interpretation of the Revolution.

Yet this comic mode presented an obvious choice for writers and filmmakers working within established cultural patterns. As film scholar Radim

Hladík notes, comedic cinematic production about state socialism has been viewed unfavourably by some critics as both distorting of the past and aesthetically lacking as a 'low' genre.[7] However, this choice of genre need not be an occasion for lament, but can rather be read as part of a 'nationally specific tradition of political comedy',[8] which enjoys a high degree of popularity and legitimacy from audiences. Indeed, comedy holds a special status within Czech culture as a source of potential subversion: such a reading has its strongest canonical model in Jaroslav Hašek's novel *The Good Solider Švejk* (1921–23), which recounts the tale of a soldier who obeys orders so literally that he exposes their absurdity. A less than reverent attitude towards authority and simultaneous disdain for heroism characterizes much of Czech comedy.[9] In the 1990s, it allowed cultural producers to adopt a lenient, conciliatory view of the past that appealed to wide audiences.

During socialism, the well-known mechanism of 'reading between the lines'[10] imbued comedy, which often builds jokes around double entendres, with subversive critical potential and granted it popularity. This technique was mastered by the filmmakers of the Czechoslovak New Wave such as Miloš Forman or Ivan Passer, who turned observations on the most banal of everyday experiences into political allusions. Later, a prevalence of what has come to be known as 'kind-hearted' (*laskavý*) humour became a leitmotif of late socialism, associated especially with names like screenwriter and actor Zdeněk Svěrák and director Jiří Menzel. As Paulina Bren demonstrates in her study of Normalization-era television, the socialist state was keen to sponsor light-hearted entertainment and react to popular demand; the immense popularity of such programmes helped to maintain the illusion of a broad social consensus with the Normalization regime.[11] Film comedies and TV series played into the popularity of 'plebeian' humour in Czech culture, which builds its stories around 'small people' and their everyday troubles, keeping within the limits of the private.[12] It is also in this tradition that retrospective comic representations of socialism mostly operate, in a genre often termed 'bittersweet' (*hořkosladká*) comedy by critics. As the previous chapter has shown, while some film and television representations of the 1990s did attempt to engage with the socialist period through less light-hearted modes, these were not always met with popular response.[13] Apart from the aforementioned *A Land Gone Wild*, the only other artefact that enjoyed good viewer ratings was the series *The End of the Long Vacation* (*Konec velkých prázdnin*, dir. Miloslav Luther, 1996), which dealt with the topic of emigration beyond the Iron Curtain.[14]

Significantly, both of the aforementioned army films chose to tackle traumatic topics in Czechoslovak history, which in terms of their content would easily lend themselves to a serious or even tragic depiction very much in the spirit of Jiří Stránský's accounts of active anticommunist resistance. Instead, however, the films set up a narrative structure that suspends trauma; unpleasant aspects of authoritarian rule are glossed over in order to emphasize the comic absurdities of the period, which is cast as farce. The comic mode affords a sense of detachment; it employs what Michael Mulkay calls different 'plausibility requirements'[15] in comparison with the serious mode. Such a mode of slight exaggeration enables representations to focus on the comedy of characterization – both films are full of larger-than-life characters, most memorably perhaps Pavel Landovský's simple-minded Major Terazky in *Black Barons* or Roman Skamene's Major Borovička, also known as the Tiny Devil, in *The Tank Battalion* – while eliding large historical events. The locus of many comedic representations of socialism thus became the private, be it the family, the peer group or a specific subculture, such as that of the Auxiliary Technical Battalions, in this way continuing in the tradition of late socialist entertainment and indeed the longer tradition of comedy as focused on the private sphere. Its compromising rather than conflictual nature allows for happy endings and an ultimately forgiving view of the past: at the end of *Black Barons*, the film's hero, Private Kefalín, departs from his obnoxious and crude superior, Major Terazky, in good humour and bearing no grudges.

Postmodern Stylistics

The foregrounding of private narratives and strong comic characters is also a strategy employed by Michal Viewegh (born 1962) in his novel *Bliss Was It in Bohemia* (*Báječná léta pod psa*).[16] The novel, first published in 1992, appeared in the same year that *Black Barons* premiered in cinemas and went on to gain the status of an enduring classic, going on to be successfully adapted for the screen in 1997 by director Petr Nikolaev.[17] Viewegh has since become the bestselling Czech writer of the post-1989 era, authoring over fifty books, which have altogether sold over one million copies, and *Bliss* alone was republished eight times.[18] The mark the novel left on the public memory of the past is thus not negligible. Focusing on the period of so-called Normalization of the 1970s and 1980s, the novel too plays out as comedy, but in comparison to the films above, it adopts a wistful, at times nostalgic tone for youth gone by.[19] Nostalgia as a mood was not absent from narratives of socialism in the 1990s; cultural producers necessarily turned back to what had been so familiar with a certain sense of loss. But, as we will see, such sentimental longing for the past, especially with the passage of time, rather took second place to another emotion: *Bliss*, which Viewegh published at the age of thirty, was heralded as the voice of a generation that could look back at the period of its youth and adolescence with self-deprecating irony. This ironic approach arose from Viewegh's retrospective narrative strategy, as he recounted late socialism through an older version of the precocious child and later aspiring novelist, Kvido. And it is irony that would also go on to become the key ingredient in the mix of sentiments employed by cultural producers to capture the past.

Viewegh's narrative finds its locus in one of the most frequent tropes employed by retrospective representations of socialism – that of childhood or teenage reminiscence, which lends itself easily to setting up both a wistful mood of longing for youth gone by, as well as a sense of distance crucial for comic portrayals. Already the title of Viewegh's novel expresses the discrepancy between the adult and childhood view. Translated into English as *Bliss Was It in Bohemia*,[20] the original title is a humorous oxymoron. On the one hand, the years of Kvido's childhood and adolescence are filled with pleasant memories – *báječná léta*, or *wonderful years*. On the other hand, they also took place in the difficult period of late socialism – hence *léta pod psa*, or *years that sucked*. The tension between these two positions provides Viewegh with a source of humour, as the juxtaposition of a narrative of the past with a retrospective present view reveals various comic incongruities. Beginning with the demotion of Kvido's father from the progressive economic institute where he works after the political crackdown of the late 1960s, through the family's forced move to a provincial town, the father's inability to secure adequate housing and eventual mental breakdown, Viewegh chronicles how political pressures traumatized the protagonist's family. But though the parents' view, which is aware of how their reality is limited by political pressures, is presented, this trauma is always mediated through the eyes of Kvido, who looks back at the time as primarily that of his largely happy childhood and adolescence.

Virtually all Czech comic representations of socialism employ the structuring device of a child's political innocence to achieve humorous effects or recount the period through the eyes of a rebelling adolescent. Such a narrative position has a long tradition in Czech culture, with important predecessors in Karel Poláček's humoristic novel *There Were Five of Us* (*Bylo nás pět*, first published 1946), in which he reminisces about his childhood in a provincial Bohemian town, but also in Normalization-era film production, in particular the family comedies with immensely popular child actor Tomáš Holý of the late 1970s. The clever, endearing and somewhat canny young boy as narrator and protagonist is thus a recurring trope in Czech culture. More recently, a clear reference to this precursor is present in the Slovak and Czech coproduction *The Hostage* (*Rukojemník*, dir. Juraj Nvota, 2014). The film, which was a success in Slovakia, though it fared worse in the Czech Republic,[21] is based on Peter Pišťanek's eponymous novel, nostalgically recounting the childhood of little Peter, torn between allegiance to his friends and grandparents in socialist Czechoslovakia, and his desire to join his long-absent parents on the other side of the Iron Curtain in Vienna.

Filmmakers outside of the Czechoslovak cultural space have also reached for a similar structuring mechanism. The setting of growing up and experiencing first loves against a backdrop of more or less repressive state socialism is also present, for example, in the Polish film *All That I Love* (*Wszystko, co kocham*, dir. Jacek Borcuch, 2009) or the Russian picture *The House of the Sun* (*Dom Solntsa*, dir. Garik Sukachev, 2010). While not all of these representations are comedies, the coming-of-age narrative facilitates a nostalgic, rose-tinted gaze, which avoids engaging with what it meant to live under a dictatorship through its focus on the inner emotional lives of its protagonists. As Micha, the protagonist of the cult *Ostalgie* film *Sun Alley* (*Sonnenallee*, dir. Leander Haußmann, 1999), summarizes in voiceover commentary: 'It was the nicest time of my life, for I was young and in love.'[22]

While the nostalgia of *Bliss* is invested in the private, the humour of the text arises from the juxtaposition of this private sphere with larger, public events. Structurally, this effect is furthered by the use of a politically innocent child protagonist, who does not necessarily perceive the wider political implications of everyday occurrences. These, however, are known to the adult characters, as well as the reader, who can thus ironically appreciate the young hero's naivety. Thus, for little Kvido, knocking down the portrait of President Husák in a game of skittles at school is an unfortunate accident; for his cautious father, it is a deliberate political provocation on the part of his son. The incongruity of the child and the adult view is a source of comic misunderstanding in this scene.

Viewegh's depiction of Normalization received very positive reviews. At a time when condemnation of the previous regime ruled public debates, the writer's tackling of the socialist period with humour and detachment was welcomed by literary critics. This was the era when various 'mnemonic warriors' were battling over a radical break with the past, mostly in line with the agenda of the increasingly prominent political force of Klaus's ODS. However, not all parts of the cultural establishment felt comfortable with such a stark condemnation of the previous regime. Literary historian Pavel Janáček, for example, remarks that the novel offers not just entertainment, but also 'a feeling of relief that events and attitudes, conventionally circumscribed by a complex of seriousness, have been treated as a *buffonerie*'.[23] To an extent, this echoes the text accompanying the DVD edition of *Black Barons*: 'a proof that even in the 1950s, when smiles were hard to come by, there were still many things to laugh about'.[24] Jiří Tyl goes even further, finding an almost carnivalesque sense of release in being able to laugh at the period: 'Viewegh's liberated laughter is contagious – the opportunity to laugh at all of that is a true asset.'[25] *Bliss* is thus a significant text for the development of the generic repertoires employed to portray socialism by mitigating traumatic memories with humour.

The term 'nostalgia' was not invoked in contemporary reviews of Viewegh's novel; however, Vladimír Novotný entitled his review in the daily *Mladá fronta Dnes* 'Docela báječné retro' ('A Quite Wonderful Retro'). While this was not the first time that the term 'retro' appeared in Czech postsocialist journalistic discourse, its use was rather erratic: it came up, for example, in reviews of Jan Svěrák's 1991 film *The Elementary School* (*Obecná škola*), set in the early postwar years,[26] or in relation to Michelangelo Antonioni's *Blow-Up* (1966).[27] Retro did not therefore bear associations with the socialist period in particular. Indeed, the term as a way of referring to a particular way of utilizing the aesthetics of the past developed within Anglo-American and Francophone culture in the 1960s, when it was used to describe the Art Nouveau revival in the United Kingdom and the United States, as well as a group of films known as the *mode rétro* in France, which turned back to representing the Second World War.[28] Novotný's use of the word in the title of his review is thus telling for two reasons. First, it situates the way Viewegh appropriates and deals with the past outside of the postsocialist setting and within a wider trend in what could be termed Western culture. Second, if, as Elizabeth Guffey argues, retro's 'most enduring quality is its ironic stance',[29] then Viewegh's novel certainly falls into this category.

The appropriation of the past in *Bliss* shares certain characteristics with a retro mode 'that perhaps best describes versions of postmodern nostalgia: playful, ironic, and where the past is a storehouse of fashion'.[30] It is this shift from nostalgia to retro that forms a key component of the Czech cultural memory of socialism: retro is concerned with surface and style and exemplifies what Jean Baudrillard and Fredric Jameson have both differently expressed as postmodern culture's lack of engagement with history – as a 'void' of history and politics, or a lack of 'historicity' respectively.[31] Memory becomes style and the past is consumed as an aesthetic artefact, divorced from sentimental longing. Retro has been discussed in scholarly literature as a postmodern phenomenon, and consideration of postmodernism – understood less as a means of periodization than as a stylistic repertoire – is missing from both the Czech literature on dealing with the past and the scholarship on *Ostalgie*. Yet such considerations are relevant: Jameson identified a basic convergence between developed forms of capitalism, which are marked by constant crises, and postmodern stylistic repertoires that display historical depthlessness and self-referential citationism.[32] With the fast-tracked introduction of a capitalist market economy in Central and Eastern Europe after 1989/1991, a postmodern aesthetic also saw the interest of artists in the region, Michal Viewegh among them.

Viewegh's narrative techniques serve well to exemplify the link between nostalgia, retro and the postmodern. *Bliss* displays several significant characteristics of postmodern stylistic repertoires: a pastiche of various styles and forms (Kvido's diaries, scripted scenes) and multiple layers of self-reflexivity (Kvido's childhood narrative as told from the retrospective perspective of his adult self, the meta-narrative of the adult Kvido discussing his manuscript with his editor, the inclusion of the plot of one of Viewegh's own earlier novellas as Kvido's first literary attempt). This is no coincidence: in his next novel *Bringing up Girls in Bohemia* (*Výchova dívek v Čechách*), Viewegh openly stylizes himself as a postmodern writer.[33] His case shows that Czech retro is not an isolated phenomenon arising only from a specifically postsocialist situation; it resonates with wider practices across Western culture and it engages with them deliberately.

Jameson has bemoaned postmodern nostalgia's lack of historicity, arguing that cultural artefacts such as the 'nostalgia film' have given up on efforts to represent historical content, replacing it instead with a stylized 'pastness'.[34] Yet Jameson's framework does not take into account that in certain contexts, precisely this deliberate elision of grand historical narratives can be viewed as politically significant. In the early 1990s in the Czech Republic, literary critics perceived Viewegh's escape from the seriousness of vilifying the communist regime that was happening elsewhere in the public sphere as an important move towards coming to terms with the past. *Bliss Was It in Bohemia* was to an extent read as a *Vergangenheitsbewältigung* – as a text that brought about a more nuanced and rounded view of the period.[35] Contemporary reviews appreciated Viewegh's ability to reclaim the spaces of everyday experience, which were necessarily affected by political pressures on some level, but at the same time afforded a platform for those *wonderful years* of the title to take place.

Bliss was closely followed in 1993 and 1994 by a series of newly published as well as reissued short stories by Petr Šabach (1951–2017). Having started his writing career already before the fall of the Iron Curtain, Šabach's stories of childhood reminiscence could easily move between the pre- and post-1989 reading context through their illusion of being concerned wholly with the private. Reviewers remarked on certain affinities with Viewegh, highlighting his comedic approach to the past and ironizing stance.[36] Though less concerned with style and self-reflexivity, Šabach's episodic narratives play on the same juxtaposition of adult and childhood views of the period. Adopting an at times faux-naïve child's perspective, the retrospective narration once again generates humour in relation to (de)politicized everyday occurrences, creating a nostalgic mood through a longing for childhood innocence, which is at the same time comically tempered by the politically informed adult view.

Šabach achieved recognition when his short story 'Jackal Years' ('Šakalí léta') from his 1986 collection *How to Sink Australia* (*Jak potopit Austrálii*) was used as a basis by screenwriter Petr Jarchovský for Jan Hřebejk's 1993 musical comedy *Jackal Years* (*Šakalí léta*, dir. Jan Hřebejk, 1993). The film, set at the end of the 1950s in Prague's Dejvice neighbourhood, was initially met with mixed reviews and a moderate audience response.[37] As in the case of *Black Barons* and *The Tank Battalion*, reactions to the film focused mainly on questions of genre, in this case that of the musical. The choice of this particular genre enabled Hřebejk to employ a stylized aesthetic, evoking the 1950s through rich-coloured costumes juxtaposed with a homely neighbourhood feel. Reviewers passed little comment on how the film engaged with the period in which it was set; when they did, they felt that it failed on this account.[38] For example, journalist Jiří Peňás writing in the daily *Mladá fronta Dnes* criticized the use of historical detail as a mere aesthetic backdrop: 'the whole period of red neck scarves, sputniks and architecture in the style of socialist realism served as a splendid decoration for "a pretty good blast"'.[39]

Šabach's original story 'Jackal Years' was published in 1986. Turning to the late 1950s, the nostalgia of the narrative does not require the political break of the Velvet Revolution to be effective – it finds its locus purely in youthful reminiscence, the period of the 1950s being sufficiently distant in terms of atmosphere and its material universe to warrant such a return. Šabach emphasizes the period's *pastness*, its social rituals now obsolete: 'In those times, when people would spit at a kiss in public, Bejby and his sweetheart unashamedly kissed on every corner. And how they kissed!'[40] However, Hřebejk's film adds another dimension to Šabach's nostalgia for a time long gone. Termed a retro-musical by several critics, the film is primarily concerned with an aestheticization of the period, relishing such details as the main character Bejby's platform shoes or semi-acoustic guitar. In an essay published in the daily *Lidové noviny*, Zdenko Pavelka was the only critic to remark on the film's engagement with postmodern modes of representation. As evidence, he quotes the degree of stylization, the use of symbols, a disjointed narrative and, most significantly, the fact that 'the benchmark for the reconstruction of the period setting is not exact historical accuracy, but an approximate resemblance in combination with the conception of the authors and the viewers, who (mostly) do not remember the period, or experienced it as children'.[41] Pavelka has thus captured an important principle of the retro aesthetic so prevalent in Czech cinematic and televisual representations; it represents the past, but does not strive to re-create it with an eye to accurately capturing historical detail.

Retro is distinguished by choosing markers of the past that also appeal to contemporary aesthetic tastes. Visually, *retrochic*, as Raphael Samuel terms it, 'plays with the idea of the period look, while remaining determinedly of the here-and-now'.[42] It thus produces a pastiche of styles. In visual texts, this is often most apparent in costume design: in the case of *Jackal Years*, while the shapes and cuts of the 1950s are quoted and reproduced, materials will often employ a wider and fuller colour palette than would have been available at

Figure 2.1 *Šakalí léta* (*Jackal Years*), Jan Hřebejk (director, screenwriter) and Petr Jarchovský (screenwriter), 1993. © Image Space Films.

the time to create a more contemporary look. *Jackal Years* is a strong example of this kind of retro aesthetic; its genre lends itself particularly well to hyperbole and visual spectacle (Figure 2.1).

The over-the-top aesthetic of Hollywood musicals has often been associated with camp, understood as an aesthetic mode that self-consciously emphasizes its own artifice.[43] Indeed, the Hollywood musical is a reference point for *Jackal Years* and camp as a self-aware, tongue-in-cheek stylization, can also effectively be applied to the film's retro look.[44] What a film like *Jackal Years* shares with Viewegh's novel is a participation in postmodern modes, through a foregrounding of stylistic mechanisms, which are less interested in accurately portraying historical content as they are in paying attention to self-reflexive textual detail or visual aestheticization. The past, whether dealt with in a retro mode or not, can of course only be apprehended through the lens of the present. However, a retro way of seeing is characterized, in the words of Paul Grainge, by 'a more acute sensitivity ... to the fact that access to the past is never direct or natural but realized through a complex history of representations'.[45] Thus, *Jackal Years* references as much the golden era of Hollywood musicals as the time period it ostensibly portrays.

Sentiment and Kitsch

Not all representations in the 1990s turned to socialism through postmodern retro devices and camp visuals. In contrast to the ironic distance of retro, other representations employed kitsch to exploit the audience's emotional identification with those who stood 'on the right side' of history. A significant film of the period was the box-office success *Kolya* (*Kolja*, dir. Jan Svěrák, 1996),⁴⁶ which was awarded an Academy Award for Best Foreign Language Film. While *Kolya* was also hailed as a retro-film,⁴⁷ its participation in retro modes is less clear than in the case of the previously discussed texts. The lapse of time between the narrative presence of *Jackal Years* and the film's making enables a clear stylistic differentiation of the past, but in the case of *Kolya*, the time gap is much narrower and stylized retro markers are thus much less apparent. Set mostly in the final months of the socialist regime in 1989, the film returns to a period only a few years earlier, of which the majority of contemporary viewers would have had clear memories. In this case, the Velvet Revolution serves as a definite historical and structural break, which allows a narrative set so recently to indicate pastness. Reviewer Lucie Štaudová, for example, remarks on how the film highlights what has changed in the period since the Revolution.⁴⁸ 'Retro' was thus used by reviewers as a generic term to connote a narrative set in the past, without reference to its postmodern dimension.

However, critical attention to the portrayal of the period was largely drowned out in a response to the strong emotional charge of the film.⁴⁹ Detailing the development of a tender bond between an ageing bachelor and his unexpected adoptive child, the five-year-old Russian boy Kolja, the film employs the narrative techniques of classical Hollywood cinema to achieve its affective goals, which are furthered through its lovable child protagonist, a stylized colour palette that endows all images with a warm golden light and a soaring orchestral score. The mood of *Kolya* is thus sentimental rather than nostalgic. This sentiment turns not so much to the socialist past itself as to the moment of its overcoming: the emotional highpoint of the film is the Velvet Revolution. Yet the film does engage with nostalgic strategies. The picture is narrated with an unobtrusive, kind-hearted humour,⁵⁰ characteristic of the work of screenwriter Zdeněk Svěrák, which creates a predominantly benign portrayal of the period. Thus, as his son, director Jan Svěrák, noted in an interview, even the repressive aspects of the communist regime are depicted with humorous detachment, such as the character of the menacing secret police interrogator, whose threatening persona is comically deflated by pairing him up with a bumbling colleague.⁵¹

On a visual level, the camera filter envelopes the period setting, both physically and figuratively, in a golden glow (Figure 2.2). It is the socialist setting itself that allows the narrative to unfold: the main protagonist, disgraced cello player Louka only comes to take care of Kolja because his mother has emigrated to the other side of the Iron Curtain, but it is only its fall that enables the story's resolution. The boy is immediately reunited with his mother once

Figure 2.2 *Kolja* (*Kolya*), Jan Svěrák (director) and Zdeněk Svěrák (screenwriter), 1996. © Biograf Jan Svěrák.

the borders are reopened and the bachelor Louka is compensated for his loss by the pregnancy of his lover as he finally returns to the symphony orchestra he had to leave for political reasons. In one of the final scenes, shots of Louka are spliced into historic footage of Rafael Kubelík conducting Bedřich Smetana's cycle of symphonic poems *Má vlast* (*My Homeland*) on Prague's Old Town Square in 1990. The jubilant tones convey the hopes of the new era and consolidate the film's ultimate reconciliatory message: all will be well in the new order.

Even so, *Kolya* does not shy away from depicting the unpleasant aspects of the period – a political misdemeanour prevents Louka from playing with the Czech Philharmonic and he is forced to scrape a living by providing music at funerals; he is interrogated by the secret police and has a hostile encounter with social services. At the same time, the film shows how well Louka deals with all of this through acts of minor, personal resistance.

The depiction of ideas of heroism in representations of socialism and the political meanings they convey is closely tied to questions of genre. The comic aspects of *Kolya* touch upon what will become a significant trope in Czech representations of the period, which I term 'petty heroism'. This is a longing for a time when there was clearly something to fight against and when even a substandard joke could make an individual a temporary, local hero, because the joke itself, rather than necessarily its content, constituted an act of resistance. Humour can represent an attempt at heroism, which in turn evokes a nostalgia for this heroism in retrospective depictions. At the same time, an initially noncomic attempt at heroism inevitably results in comedy. An example is when Louka (heroically) tells his student/erotic interest Blanka that he will not be putting up flags in his windows for the upcoming Party anniversary. The impulse of nostalgia for heroism and its political resonance thus lies in a self-congratulatory mode in which the viewer, together with the characters who drive the narrative, revels in how well they managed to set themselves against communist authority. However, faced by the unexpected situation of having to take care of the child of an emigrée and thus potentially attracting the interest of the secret police, Louka's heroic gesture fails: he decides to conform and put up the flags after all with the words 'I'm a coward'.[52] His failure achieves its final deflation when Louka is in bed with Blanka and Kolja unexpectedly enters the room, unveiling the flags in the window with a loud bang of the blinds. The moral compromises of the period are thus treated with a humorous distancing.

The sentimental charge of the film as well as the kind of moral apologetics it offers in its portrayal of state socialism elicited a response from reviewers that introduced a new term into Czech discussions of depictions of the past: kitsch. The filmmakers anticipated that this accusation would be levelled at their picture; several articles quoted Zdeněk Svěrák's defence that 'the fact that this story touches us – and it really does touch us – does not necessarily mean it has anything to do with kitsch. It's only an expression of our emotions'.[53] However, critic Jiří Peňás was of a different opinion. His complaint with the film is based on the facile *Vergangenheitsbewältigung* it offers:

> Kitsch begins with an easy, uncritical self-identification. For example, in the moment when we recognize ourselves in the sympathetic protagonist of an all but flawless film and we are touched by this, for we have once again confirmed how infinitely humane and full of the most sympathetic qualities we are.[54]

Peňás refers here not so much to kitsch as an aesthetic property as he does to a particular emotional response famously defined by Milan Kundera in his novel *The Unbearable Lightness of Being*. Kundera's oft-quoted example of kitsch, which Peňás himself invokes, is that of two metaphorical tears that flow in quick succession when seeing children running on the grass. The observer is moved twice: first at the sight of the children and immediately after, he or she is moved at the thought of being moved, 'together with all mankind',[55] by the sight of children running on the grass. According to Kundera, 'it is the second tear that makes kitsch kitsch'.[56] Through a sentimentalized gaze, then, *Kolya* also evokes a private narrative like the representations discussed earlier.

However, the film further finds a cosy feeling of moral exculpation in this privacy: identifying with the protagonist Louka, the viewer can congratulate himself or herself that they too had lived through the period in commendable ways. Kitsch is a prevalent mode of dealing with the socialist past not only in the Czech Republic – and certainly much *Ostalgic* film production makes use of kitsch – because it offers a feeling of easy exculpation, obfuscating difficult questions of collaboration or tacit consent with the regime's repressive aspects.

The early 1990s thus saw a variety of cultural texts that set out different ways of retrospectively speaking about Czech socialism, adding further supportive but also dissonant layers to the strategies of dealing with the past in the political arena. A number of common tropes emerged. Although some attempts at dramatic representations of socialism were made, in particular by screenwriter Jiří Stránský and director Hynek Bočan, as discussed in the previous chapter, most frequently, comedic mechanisms were employed to create a gentle, nonthreatening image of the period. The structural device of childhood reminiscence allowed these texts to invest nostalgia in an ostensibly nonpolitical arena and to thus recover the sphere of everyday occurrences and rituals under socialism. Where the reader or viewer does not directly partake of the child's gaze, a child protagonist is looked *at*, as in the case of *Kolya*, thus also moving the narrative towards a perspective of political innocence. In the film, this innocence is exemplified by Louka and Kolja's deliberate escape from politics and into the privacy of holiday-making when they leave Prague after a particularly disagreeable encounter with social services.

Based on these representations from the 1990s, it is possible to begin to establish several trends in depictions of socialism, which can be applied not only to the Czech context. The return to the past was on the one hand connoted through a set of stylistic retro mechanisms; this postmodern mode contrasted, on the other hand, with the affective strategies of narratives like *Kolya* or, to an extent, the texts of Petr Šabach. Paul Grainge effectively captures this difference when he identifies a distinction between sentiment and style or what he terms 'mood' and 'mode'. It is worth quoting Grainge's distinction here at length:

> The nostalgia mood is principally defined in relation to a concept of loss …
> By contrast, the nostalgia mode has no necessary relation to loss or longing. As a commodified style, the nostalgia mode has developed, principally within postmodern theory, a theoretical association with amnesia.[57]

Mood thus refers to a sense of yearning for something long gone and lends itself to the portrayal of childhood or adolescence. *Mode*, on the contrary, ironizes this yearning. This framework can be expanded by introducing two aesthetic mechanisms with which this mood and mode operate: kitsch and camp. While kitsch is the result of sentimental portrayals, camp exemplifies the style of retro. Altogether, these stylistic repertoires can help us to analyse and identify the messages about the past conveyed by representations of the past that bring more nuance than the amorphous category of nostalgia. Representations produced in the 1990s operated with a plethora of techniques, yet the opposition set up between mood and mode is not a binary one. As we move towards the end of the 1990s and beyond in the next chapter, it will become clear that this opposition is not mutually exclusive, but can comfortably coexist within one text or practice, forming multilayered and complex responses to the socialist past.

Notes

1. An example among many is the musical *Smoke* (*Kouř*, dir. Tomáš Vorel, 1990), the genesis of which began already in the mid 1980s as one of Vorel's student films. However, it entered cinemas only after the changes of 1989 and incorporates a story of regime change on the local level.
2. See A. Pilátová, 'Filmová show po česku' ['Film Show the Czech Way'], *Právo lidu*, 6 June 1991, 4; M. Nezval, 'Tankový prapor' ['The Tank Battalion'], *Mladá fronta Dnes*, 13 May 1991, 4; J. Kopic, 'Černí baroni ze soukromých peněz' ['Black Barons from Private Money'], *Noviny*, 19 July 1992, x.
3. *The Tank Battalion* was the most successful domestic film of the 1990s. It was seen by over one million viewers in cinemas in the first two months following its opening. See 'Memento za vepřové' ['Memento for Pork'], *Mladá fronta Dnes*, 4 July 1991, 5. *Black Barons* was seen by an impressive number of 1.6 million viewers (although this figure is for Czechoslovakia as a whole). See *Filmová ročenka 1992* (Prague: Národní filmový archiv, 1993), 147.
4. J. Jaroš, untitled, *Zemědělské noviny*, 1 June 1992, no pagination.
5. See A. Prosnicová, 'Paradoxy Černých baronů' ['Paradoxes of the Black Barons'], *Noviny*, 25 June 1992, 9.
6. J. Krapfl, *Revolution with a Human Face: Politics, Culture and Community in Czechoslovakia, 1989–1992* (Ithaca: Cornell University Press, 2013), especially 19–31.
7. R. Hladík, 'Vážné, nevážné a zneváženě vzpomínání v postsocialistické kinematografii', in P. Kopal (ed.), *Film a dějiny 4: Normalizace* (Prague: Casablanca; ÚSTR, 2014), 461–75 (470–71).
8. Ibid., 474.
9. For more on how this tradition is present in Czech cinema, see P. Hames 'The Good Soldier Svejk and after: The Comic Tradition in Czech Film', in D. Holmes and A. Smith (eds), *100 Years of European Cinema: Entertainment or Ideology?* (Manchester: Manchester University Press, 2000), 64–76.
10. See, for example, L. Losev, *On the Beneficence of Censorship: Aesopian Language in Modern Russian Literature*, trans. J. Bobko (Munich: Otto Sagner in Kommission, 1984);

A. Terian, 'The Rhetoric of Subversion: Strategies of "Aesopian Language" in Romanian Literary Criticism Under Late Communism', *Slovo* 24(2) (2012), 75–95.
11. P. Bren, *The Greengrocer and His TV: The Culture of Communism after the 1968 Prague Spring* (Ithaca: Cornell University Press, 2010).
12. See P. Pająk, 'Czeska komedia dla początkujących (szkic z historii gatunku)', in M. Bogusławska and Z. Grębecka (eds), *Popkomunizm: Doświadczenie komunizmu a kultura popularna* (Cracow: Libron, 2010), 139–48.
13. Jan Čulík lists *Our Czech Song II* (*Ta naše písnička česká II*, dir. Vít Olmer, 1990) and *Was It Us?* (*Byli jsme to my?*, dir. Antonín Máša, 1990) as examples of such unsuccessful films. See J. Čulík, *Jací jsme: Česká společnost v hraném filmu devadesátých a nultých let* (Brno: Host, 2007), 50.
14. The first season of the TV series *A Land Gone Wild* (*Zdivočelá země*, dir. Hynek Bočan, 1997) ran to twelve episodes and was watched by a total of approximately 2,900,000 adult viewers. *The End of the Long Vacation* (*Konec velkých prázdnin*, dir. Miloslav Luther, 1996) had six episodes and was watched by a total of approximately 2,800,000 viewers. Ratings data source: Czech Television diary research (*Deníčkový výzkum ČT*), Czech Television Archive.
15. M. Mulkay, *On Humour: Its Nature and Place in Modern Society* (Cambridge: Polity Press, 1988), 17.
16. M. Viewegh, *Báječná léta pod psa* (Prague: Československý spisovatel, 1992).
17. The film was the sixth most-watched picture of the year in Czech cinemas, with 328,733 viewers. See *Filmová ročenka 1997* (Prague: Národní filmový archiv, 1998), 279.
18. *Bliss Was It in Bohemia* was republished in 1993, 1994, 1995, 1997, 2002, 2007, 2013 and 2018. See also L. Hloušková, 'Jsou na špičce, ale knihy je neuživí. Proč?' ['They're at the Top But Can't Make a Living out of Writing. Why?'], *Novinky.cz*, 23 December 2015. Retrieved 19 August 2019 from https://www.novinky.cz/zena/styl/388603-jsou-na-spicce-ale-knihy-je-neuzivi-proc.html.
19. Parts of the discussion of nostalgia in *Bliss Was It in Bohemia* and how it relates to the concept of 'petty heroism' have appeared in V. Pehe, 'Drobné hrdinství: Vzdor jakožto předmět nostalgie v díle Petra Šabacha a Michala Viewegha', *Česká literatura* 63(3) (2015), 419–34.
20. M. Viewegh, *Bliss Was It in Bohemia*, trans. D. Short (London: Jantar Publishing, 2015).
21. *The Hostage* was among the ten most-watched films in Slovak cinemas for three weeks. In the Czech Republic, it did not make it into the fifty most-watched films of the year.
22. 'Es war die schönste Zeit meines Lebens, denn ich war jung und verliebt'. *Sun Alley*, 1999.
23. P. Janáček, 'Groteska o velké lásce' ['A Grotesque about Great Love'], *Nové knihy*, 25 November 1992, 1.
24. Z. Sirový (director, screenwriter) and M. Švandrlík (screenwriter), *Černí baroni* (DVD booklet). Czechoslovakia, Space Films, 1992.
25. J. Tyl, 'Autorský subjekt jako osvoboditel (sebe sama)', *Iniciály* 4(36) (1993), 25–26 (26).
26. Sdk, 'Svěrákovské retro' ['Svěrákian Retro'], *Lidové noviny*, 23 February 1991, 8.
27. R. Starý, 'Ještě jedno nostalgické retro', *Prostor* 4(15) (1991), 137–39.
28. See E.E. Guffey, *Retro: The Culture of Revival* (London: Reaktion Books, 2006), in particular Chapter 1.
29. Ibid., 20.
30. P. Grainge, *Monochrome Memories: Nostalgia and Style in Retro America* (Westport: Praeger, 2002), 54.

31. See J. Baudrillard, 'History: A Retro Scenario', in *Simulacra and Simulations*, trans. S. Faria Glaser (Ann Arbor: University of Michigan Press, 1994), 43–48; and F. Jameson, *Postmodernism, or, the Cultural Logic of Late Capitalism* (New York: Verso, 1991), in particular 19.
32. See Jameson, *Postmodernism*.
33. M. Viewegh, *Výchova dívek v Čechách* (Prague: Český spisovatel, 1994).
34. Jameson, *Postmodernism*, 19.
35. V. Karfík, 'Báječná léta pod psa', *Literární noviny* 4(10) (1993), 7.
36. See, for example, P. Šrut, 'Nemusí hořet – stačí, když doutná' ['It Needn't Burn – Smouldering is Enough'], *Lidové noviny* (Sunday supplement), 4 February 1995, 10; and jú, 'Hovno prý hoří' ['Shit Allegedly Burns'], *Labyrint revue* (1) (1995), 4.
37. The film was seen by 144,166 people in cinemas, placing it thirty-fourth on the list of most-watched films in 1993. See *Filmová ročenka 1993* (Prague: Národní filmový archiv, 1994), 205.
38. See A. Halada, 'Proč a jak (ne)točit v Čechách muzikál' ['Why and How (Not) to Make a Musical in the Czech Republic'], *Mladý svět* (4)(51) (1993), 54; or, L. Korecká, 'Šakalí léta' ['Jackal Years'], *Magazín Dnes*, 9 December 1993, 26–27.
39. J. Peňás, 'V čem se dobře cítí humorista aneb ráj plandavosti' ['Where a Humourist Feels Good, or, the Paradise of Looseness'], *Mladá fronta Dnes*, 10 January 1995, 19.
40. 'V těhle časech, kdy si lidi uplivávali před veřejnou pusou, se Bejby se svým miláčkem bezostyšně líbali na každým rohu. A jak se líbali!' P. Šabach, *Jak potopit Austrálii* (Prague and Litomyšl: Paseka 1999), 46.
41. Z. Pavelka, 'Šakalí past' ['Jackal Trap'], *Lidové noviny* ('Echo' supplement), 19 March 1994, I.
42. R. Samuel, *Theatres of Memory: Volume 1: Past and Present in Contemporary Culture* (New York: Verso, 1994), 83
43. See, for example, J. Feuer, *The Hollywood Musical* (Bloomington: Indiana University Press, 1993), 140–41.
44. For more on camp, see S. Sontag, *Against Interpretation* (London: Vintage, 1994), espiecally the chapter entitled 'Notes on Camp'.
45. Grainge, *Monochrome Memories*, 55.
46. The film was seen by almost 900,000 people in Czech cinemas in 1996. More spectacularly, even though it had premiered in May 1996, it was also the most-watched film in Czech cinemas in 1997 with an additional 449,887 viewers. See *Filmová ročenka 1996* (Prague: Národní filmový archiv, 1997), 253; *Filmová ročenka 1997* (Prague: Národní filmový archiv, 1998), 279.
47. See, for example, (spa), 'Jan Svěrák našel hrdinu svého nového filmu v Moskvě' ['Jan Svěrák Found the Hero of His New Film in Moscow'], *Mladá fronta Dnes*, 18 August 1995, 16; or ham, 'Otcovství starého mládence' ['The Fatherhood of a Bachelor'], *Večerník Praha*, 16 May 1996, 13.
48. L. Štaudová, 'Dojemný film otce a syna Svěrákových míří do kin' ['Touching Film of Svěrák Father and Son Hits Cinemas'], *Denní telegraf*, 15 May 1996, 11.
49. See M. Spáčilová, 'Hezký český Kolja se netají tím, že se chce líbit' ['Nice Czech Kolya Does Not Hide, He Wants to Please'], *Mladá fronta Dnes*, 16 May 1996, 19; or J. Ovsíková, 'Rodinný tandem Svěráků ve filmové akci' ['Svěrák Family Tandem in Action'], *Práce*, 22 August 1995, 1.
50. Svěrák earned praise for this particular kind of humour from reviewer Oxana Tulajdanová in her review 'Nestyďte se za slzy, očistí vaši duši' ['Don't Be Ashamed of Your Tears, They Will Cleanse Your Soul'], *Lidové noviny*, 16 May 1996, 11.

51. J. Foll, 'Pozlacení, absurdita a rozšlapané autíčko' ['Gilding, Absurdity, and a Stepped-on Toy Car – Interview with Jan Svěrák'], *Lidové noviny* ('Národní 9' supplement), 11 May 1996, xiii.
52. 'Jsem srab'. *Kolya*, 1996.
53. S. Tesárová, 'Kolja i po několika týdnech v kinech neustále vyprodán' ['Kolya Still Sold Out Even after Weeks in Cinemas'], *Zemědělské noviny*, 5 June 1996, 14.
54. J. Peňás, 'Ekránové sny o sobě samých' ['Screen Dreams about Ourselves'], *Respekt*, 20 May 1996, 19.
55. M. Kundera, *The Unbearable Lightness of Being*, trans. Michael Henry Heim (London: Faber & Faber, 1995), 244.
56. Ibid.
57. Grainge, *Monochrome Memories*, 21.

Chapter 3

THE LATE 1990S

Contesting the Past through Popular Culture

Literary and cinematic representations were just one aspect of cultural returns to the past in the new postsocialist era. A significant presence in everyday life was the continuity of socialist-era entertainment – whether in the form of rescreenings of films and TV series on television or in the music industry. The 1990s were a time of infatuation with Western popular culture, which had for decades remained largely inaccessible, and 1989 thus represented a significant change in television programming, including the rise of new, commercial television stations. But as historian Martin Franc notes in relation to public broadcasting, 'already at the beginning of the 1990s it became clear that in the long term it is not viable for television to give up archival programming, for financial reasons among others'.[1] Socialist era-entertainment thus never truly left Czechoslovak, and later Czech, TV screens. A recurring format on both Czech and Slovak television are edited shows, which intersperse clips from Czechoslovak Television's archive with often humorous commentary by a host. In the Czech Republic, these included the programme *Proč bychom se nebavili, když nám Pánbůh archiv dal* (*Why Not Be Entertained When God Gave Us the Archive*, 1997, 2000–1) and the long-running programme *Retro* (2008–13), which combined an educational remit with an aesthetic captivation with the quirks of socialist material and cultural production. On Slovak public television, similar formats included the light-hearted *Noc v archíve* (*Night in the Archive*, 2009) and *Fetiše socializmu* (*Fetishes of Socialism*, 2014), which used archival footage to explore a different social or cultural phenomenon of life under state socialism in each episode.

This chapter, however, focuses on an earlier period. In the late 1990s, the continuity of socialist-era entertainment became the subject of controversy. I will trace the public contestation of the socialist past by looking at several events of the late 1990s that re-invigorated the cultural memory of the socialist period with both positive and negative valences. On the one hand, comedy films set during socialism enjoyed popularity, while the broadcast of a 1970s television series or the comebacks of socialist-era entertainers sparked vocal criticism in the media. Tracing the media debates of the time, this chapter shows how these controversies highlighted what appeared to be two competing memory regimes of rupture and continuity: while commentators in the mainstream media advocated the former, readers and particular audience groups called for the right to integrate the memory of socialist popular culture into the continuity of their own biographies. Yet a third position also emerged, which I suggest accommodated both an anticommunist rejection of the former regime's politics and a lenient memory of socialism's popular culture, through a number of rhetorical strategies that invoked categories such as 'professionalism', 'quality' and 'retro'.

The first indicator that socialist popular culture would start to attract media attention came in February 1998, when the by then almost forgotten king of Czechoslovak 1980s disco, Michal David, sang to a large crowd on Old Town Square in Prague, on the occasion of the return of the victorious Czech ice hockey team from the Olympic Games in Nagano. An analysis of press articles in the major Czech daily newspapers dealing with this event shows that David's comeback came as a surprise to many. It was also met with a wave of distaste, mainly because of his strong association with the previous regime, when he was known as the composer of songs for the *spartakiáda*, a heavily politicized mass gymnastics event held every five years.[2] Yet his performance was widely publicized.[3] His successful re-emergence inspired a number of other pop stars of the previous regime, who soon announced concert tours and new albums, such as the 1980s duo Petr Kotvald and Stanislav Hložek.[4]

Andrew Roberts interprets this revival of socialist-era entertainment at the end of the 1990s as a sign of nostalgia in Czech society.[5] This argument provides a convenient explanation, but does not adequately capture the complex cultural dynamics of these events. Already the example of David illustrates this well: the singer's comeback, paradoxically, did not come at a point when Czech society was turning back to the socialist period; although the late 1990s saw an economic dip that may have shaken the belief of some sections of society in market solutions, David's arrival was intimately linked to a forward-looking moment of national confidence, when the country had achieved international recognition through winning a gold medal at the year's largest international sporting event. If it is possible to speak about

David's re-establishment on the music scene as a manifestation of nostalgia, then such nostalgia came at a time that prevents it from being easily interpreted as a symptom of disappointment with the new era.

Furthermore, the genesis of David's comeback points to how a practice that is seemingly nostalgic for socialism is embedded in and generated through market mechanisms. When Olympic hockey team member Jiří Šlégr revealed to the daily *Právo* that he and his teammates listen to Michal David in their dressing room in Nagano,[6] the marketing potential of this ostensibly innocuous comment was seized upon by the Czech Ice Hockey Association, together with its sponsor Coca-Cola, which asked David to write an 'anthem' to welcome back the victorious team. One of the conditions of the commission was for the lyrics of the song to mention Coca-Cola.[7] Soon after, David's records experienced increased sales and the singer launched a new album and became a staple on the concert circuit.[8] One explanation is that records of artists such as David were not consumed only out of nostalgia, but also with a tongue-in-cheek irony – a significant form of reception of socialist artefacts. Socialist popular culture met with a number of at times contradictory reactions in the public sphere, pointing to the ongoing memory processes in relation to the socialist past. The disputes over the legacies of socialist entertainment can perhaps best be explored through the example of the icon of the Czech pop music scene, Karel Gott, and the crime series *The Thirty Cases of Major Zeman* (*Třicet případů majora Zemana*, dir. Jiří Sequens, Czechoslovak Television, 1974–79); these stand in stark contrast to the altogether unproblematic reception of the hit comedy film *Cosy Dens* (*Pelíšky*, dir. Jan Hřebejk, 1999), demonstrating the complex layers of memory at work in Czech society.

Karel Gott and the Controversies of Cultural Continuity

David's increased sales indicated the popularity that socialist-era cultural products enjoyed, as did the continued airing of a number of pre-1989 television programmes. Yet several commentators in the daily press, who had built their reputation on their anticommunist credentials, launched vociferous and at times aggressive debates on the merits of socialist popular culture, the underlying question being whether the entertaining memory popular culture carried did not dangerously obscure the regime's repressive side. For instance, a highly publicized case of the early 2000s was music critic Jan Rejžek's accusation that pop diva Helena Vondráčková's return was the work of what he ambiguously termed 'communist mafias', for which Vondráčková took him to court.[9]

But one star who did not require any comeback as he continued to hold an absolutely central position in the field of Czech popular music throughout the entire postsocialist period, until his death in 2019, was Karel Gott. Disputes around Gott at the end of the first postsocialist decade pointed to a discrepancy between elite and popular perceptions of the cultural legacy of socialism and became a site of competing memories. On the one hand, influential public figures called for a radical break with the socialist past represented by Normalization-era performers. On the other hand, if the popularity of singers like Gott can be interpreted as nostalgia, then it did so through a 'demand for continuity', as Irena Reifová argues, which she contrasts with the official mnemopolitics of discontinuity coming 'from above',[10] as represented by media columnists and representatives of the cultural elite in the case of the dispute around Gott.

Gott, a pop and soft rock singer, maintained constant popularity without any significant slump in his fifty-year career, not even in the early 1990s, when public taste longed for everything and anything imported from the West. Instead, he continued touring and recording under the guidance of influential music producer František Janeček, who quickly realized that in times of bewildering change, constancy too has its market potential. The fact that he won the popular vote contest *Zlatý slavík* (*Golden Songbird*), in the 1990s renamed the *Czech Songbird*, a staggering 41 times[11] attests to his unwavering popularity. In addition to the Czech Republic, Gott enjoyed star status in the genre of *schlagermusik* in neighbouring Germany and Austria, where he is known as the 'golden voice from Prague'. Having started his career in the 1960s, he is particularly strongly associated with the period of Normalization, during which his popularity abroad was a significant source of hard currency for the country. Openly supportive of the regime, he led the signing of the so-called 'Anti-Charter' in 1977, a proclamation of artists and cultural workers condemning the dissident manifesto Charter 77.[12] In 1985, he was awarded the country's highest artistic state title, *národní umělec* (national artist). His endorsement of the Normalization regime, as well as his political swing to the right in the 1990s, made him an object of criticism, but for his fanbase, he remained 'divine Karel' or 'The Master'. Two events in the late 1990s focusing on the singer showcased that not all were happy about his continued presence on the Czech music scene and what it represented.

The first of these was Gott's sixtieth birthday celebration in July 1999, which took the form of a three-hour televised show where virtually the whole Czech showbusiness establishment congratulated the singer. Even President Václav Havel sent a laudatory note in which he – probably not without irony – praised Gott for being a 'model of professional continuity'.[13] While the more left-leaning daily *Právo* asserted that the celebrations demonstrated why Gott is rightly considered the apex of Czech pop music,[14] others used the opportunity to open up debates about the role of entertainers in supporting and maintaining the socialist regime.

Columnist and writer Ondřej Štindl's opinion piece in *Lidové noviny* on the occasion argued that Normalization-era entertainers should take some responsibility for their collaboration with the regime. Štindl's focus on Gott stemmed from the singer being one of the regime's most lucrative export articles and also its most prominent faces with an explicit political investment: the story of Gott's aborted emigration to Germany in 1971 is now notorious thanks to Milan Kundera's novel *The Book of Laughter and Forgetting*, in which he details how President Husák offered Gott excellent conditions if he returned to Czechoslovakia after the singer had decided to stay in the West. As Štindl pointed out in a paraphrase of Kundera, Gott is a singer of forgetting: in the 1960s, his songs expressed the hopes of an era; in the 1970s, they encouraged Czechoslovaks to forget those hopes.[15]

Former dissident Bohumil Doležal continued the debate by asking whether the role of showbusiness personnel in supporting the regime is not exaggerated. A response from Adam Drda, a columnist and radio journalist, took issue with what he saw as Doležal's unnecessarily forgiving stance and called for open discussions of the 'amoral behaviour of Czech regime entertainers in the 1970s and 1980s'.[16] Here Gott was attacked from the typical anticommunist position pervasive in Czech public discourse at the time, which aimed to find specific culprits and perpetrators who could, in this view, atone for their past sins only by performing public penance. This position brought angry reactions in *Haló noviny*, the KSČM daily, and in the form of readers' letters in the mainstream press coming out in Gott's support, indicative of a popular counter-memory to that embodied by well-known columnists. Just as cultural producers in the previous chapter presented more conciliatory views of the past, public opinion mitigated the prevalent discourse of anticommunism that called for a wholesale condemnation of the previous regime, illustrating a clear cleavage between elite and popular perceptions of the cultural legacy of socialism.

The outrage over Gott was voiced by a handful of influential publicists pushing an anticommunist agenda, but the second affair surrounding the singer added much of the country's cultural elite to the mix. The scandal, which came to be known as 'Hannovergott', was sparked by a short article by architectural historian Zdeněk Lukeš. Reflecting upon Gott's planned performance at the World Fair EXPO 2000 in Hannover, Lukeš wrote: 'This zombie has been pursuing me since my childhood. Since the second half of the 1960s, he has been spoiling the taste of several generations.'[17] This assertion generated an extraordinary response. The singer let it be known that he was considering withdrawing his participation at the EXPO because of the offence caused to him.[18] This produced such a stir that the Minister of Culture himself implored Gott to reconsider his position in an open letter printed in *Lidové noviny*, the same daily that had published Lukeš's controversial text.[19] The Communist Party daily *Haló noviny* defended Gott's professional qualities[20] and further reactions in *Lidové noviny* also pointed to Gott's long-standing status as the Czech number one pop music performer.[21] After extensive discussions in both the serious and the tabloid press (*Lidové noviny* even published a special supplement dedicated to the singer), Gott was eventually persuaded to perform in Hannover.

What Gott represents became a version of the familiar dispute between high and low culture and a battle over what should be included or excluded from the cultural memory of socialism. In an interview, Lukeš, author of the inflammatory text that started the whole debate, cited Alfred Radok's multimedia theatre project *Laterna magika* at the 1958 EXPO as a successful example of the type of cultural endeavour that should represent the country abroad. Bohumil Doležal reacted to this with the words that even this 'surely tasteful and elegant show promoted a Russian colony ruled by a criminal and immoral regime. A dumpling variety show [*knedlíková estráda*] in honour of an after all much more democratic Czech Republic does not seem so bad to me in comparison'.[22] Doležal's comment exposes the logic of the anticommunist position: if any cultural artefact, even of dubious artistic merit, that has arisen in a democratic, free market system is by default more valuable than anything produced under socialism, then such a position places very little demand on the role of culture in the present, apart from legitimating the current political order. This was not a position to which public opinion subscribed; a poll conducted in this period brought the results that 84% of Czechs thought that Gott should represent the country at the EXPO.

The defenders of socialist popular culture felt that it formed a significant part of their lives and their cultural heritage and as such continues to function as part of their memory of the period.[23] Karel Gott, as Lukeš notes, indeed 'haunted', but also delighted, several generations since their childhood. For defenders of socialist popular culture, to deny this culture any validity is also to deny the validity of the lived experience of many. The controversy, then, has many parallels to the fundamental issue in discussions of *Ostalgie* in Germany, namely, as Paul Cooke summarizes, a 'sense of frustration prevalent amongst many Easterners that their experience of living in the GDR is being elided from the German historical record', accompanied by the feeling 'that the actual experience of everyday life in the East has been devalued and ignored'.[24] The voices of 'ordinary' fans of Gott in letters to the editor in both the serious and tabloid press revealed a sense of not being taken seriously by an intellectual elite who possessed the cultural and social capital to give their voice necessary weight in the media.[25]

However, it would be too simplistic to dismiss Gott as entertainment for 'the masses', disdained by intellectuals. Such an attitude was even the subject of critique formulated by the then President Václav Klaus in a preface to a book celebrating Gott's seventieth birthday.[26] While voices in the media demanded rupture with the socialist past, the reception of Gott actually points to continuity through recontextualization. Gott's success can be partially attributed to the absolute stability of his repertoire and genre. The title of a *Lidové noviny* article from 1999 says it all: 'Regimes Come and Go, the Golden Voice Remains.'[27] A rhetorical constant around Gott's persona is the category of 'professionalism', which is invoked even by his critics, as well as by his showbusiness colleagues as an accolade. It is Gott's professionalism that transcends the divide of 1989: an example can be drawn from Klaus's anniversary essay on Gott, in which he argued that 'in totalitarian Czechoslovakia, he became the first representative of show business'[28] and adds that although many structural limitations were in place, they could not thwart Gott's professional attributes. Klaus's analysis is emblematic of much postsocialist discourse in which a quality like professionalism is seen as 'universal' and 'extra-ideological', and thus in contrast to the inherently 'ideological' nature of the previous regime. Despite efforts to the contrary by his critics, the idea of professionalism allowed Gott to be extricated from the political implications of the past regime and to be co-opted into the vocabulary of present values. Such a position could accommodate a nostalgic indulgence of Gott's past performances, reminding audiences of the time of their youth, and a simultaneous condemnation of the political circumstances in which Gott's star persona was formed. A number of memory events that took place in 1999 reveal further layers of this multivalent reception strategy.

The 'Nostalgic Moment' of 1999

With the events surrounding first David and then Gott, 1999 became a truly 'nostalgic moment' for the Czech Republic. In April, Jan Hřebejk's highly popular and well-received retro comedy *Cosy Dens* was released.[29] Then in September, after months of intense discussions, the 1970s television series *The Thirty Cases of Major Zeman* was rescreened on Czech Television for the first time since the fall of the communist regime.[30] Contemporary media did not comment on the conjunction of these events at all, yet it seems significant that while the media raged in a vociferous debate largely condemning *Major Zeman*, Jan Hřebejk's nostalgic comedy was greeted with critical acclaim. Audiences were thus involved in active reminiscing about the past, but this did not mean that they longed for the return of the past regime. The conjunction of *Major Zeman* and *Cosy Dens* brought about a number of responses, both sentimental and condemning of the past, which at times cohabited comfortably.

Why was *Major Zeman* so controversial when other staples of socialist television entertainment, such as the series *The Engineer's Odyssey* (*Inženýrská odysea*, dir. Evžen Sokolovský, 1979) or *The Hesitations of Chef Svatopluk* (*Rozpaky kuchaře Svatopluka*, dir. František Filip, 1984), had been rescreened without comment earlier in the 1990s?[31] Similarly, films from the socialist era, in particular comedies from the 1960s and the period of Normalization, were rerun throughout the 1990s on both public and private television channels, without any raised eyebrows. *Major Zeman* also elicited responses from sections of the audience that perceived the series as simply an unproblematic part of Czech(oslovak) culture, but it was the politicized plot that brought about vocal opposition in 1999, making the series an excellent case study of the competing memory regimes present in the Czech public sphere at the time.

Made explicitly to showcase the good work of the communist police – with direct guidance from the Ministry of the Interior, as Paulina Bren details[32] – *Major Zeman* was perceived by critics as the most heavily ideologized product of socialist television, mapping the years 1945–75 through the story of the policeman Major Jan Zeman and the cases he solves. The proposal of Czech Television to rescreen the series in the 1990s garnered extraordinary attention from the time it was first publicly mentioned. Already in 1996, the director of the commercial TV station *Nova*, Vladimír Železný, condemned Czech Television's intention, stating that 'it is an opening of graves'.[33] Some warned of the morally corrupting potential of the series[34] and the Confederation of Political Prisoners (KPV) protested loudly against its allegedly insulting nature towards victims of communist oppression.[35] The discussion became so explosive that it eventually contributed to the dismissal of Czech Television director Jakub Puchalský, less than two years after the start of his tenure.[36]

While Czech Television officials were loath to admit it directly, motivations for the rescreening of the series were most likely commercial, after private Slovak channel Markíza's successful rerun of the series in 1998. The Slovak television channel had been regularly showing a number of Czechoslovak socialist-era programmes in an afternoon slot. *Major Zeman* was, however, shown at an unattractive time around midnight, suggesting that rather than commercial gain, the primary motivation may have been simply to fill late-night programming with a familiar show. The rerun proved an unexpected success, with high ratings throughout and even higher audience figures during the morning repeat of each episode – about 70% of total television audiences at the time.[37] Although the commercial channel did not need to puzzle over whether the series complied with a public broadcasting remit, an employee of Markíza's marketing section confirmed to the Czech press that the channel was aware of the controversial nature of the series and they were unsure what to expect. The audience response nevertheless positively surprised them.[38]

The Slovak reprise of the series led to VHS cassettes with individual episodes circulating not only in Slovakia, but also the Czech Republic and demand for the series clearly increased, for instance, through the creation of a dedicated internet fanpage.[39]

Czech Television did eventually begin rescreening the series in September 1999, accompanying each episode with a thirty-minute documentary, which aimed to reconstruct how historical events, distorted in the series, had really unfolded. In addition, after the documentaries, Czech Television also irregularly broadcast a series of studio debates with historians and other relevant experts, who discussed key aspects of the socialist past depicted in the series. However, by claiming that it wanted to 'set things right' (*uvést na pravou míru*) through the documentaries, Czech Television ended up in the precarious position of 'normalizing' history by offering a corrective interpretation of the past.[40]

Cosy Dens, on the other hand, received largely positive reviews and soon became a cult film of the period. The comedy was praised for its accurate re-creation of the 1960s setting in terms of props, set design and costumes, its acting, and for the period music on its soundtrack.[41] A term that often recurs in contemporary reviews is 'quality', be it of the acting, the screenplay and in particular the period music used, putting forward the idea that socialist pop culture was in many ways of a higher standard than the Westernized, imported culture that became prevalent after 1989.[42] Indeed, like in the case of Gott, quality was a significant strategy in this case of accommodating socialist-era culture into contemporary vocabularies.

The film, created by the same team as the retro musical *Jackal Years* of director Hřebejk and screenwriter Jarchovský, once again adapting a story by Petr Šabach, is set in the months directly preceding the 1968 Warsaw Pact invasion of Czechoslovakia and details the cohabitation of two neighbouring families with widely differing political opinions in one Prague house. *Cosy Dens* operates with well-established tropes already familiar from earlier representations from the 1990s: it is a family picture, reconstructing the private spaces of life, the 'cosy dens' of the title, where the characters are safe from outside pressures. The narrative is once again structured by the view of a teenage protagonist, fifteen-year-old Michal, who observes the personal and political bickering of his father with his neighbour, Kraus, with a sense of bemused disgust.

What then do *Cosy Dens* and the rescreening of *Major Zeman* have in common? These two events represent two very different types of text and practice: the past revisited (in the case of the television series from the 1970s) and the past re-created in representation (the film). Engaging directly with material reminders of socialism appeals to experience; the re-creation of the past in retrospective representation creates ground for comparison with lived experience and thus gives rise to new imaginings in the space between the creators' and viewers' conceptions of the past. The mediation of the past through this imaginative space may account for the widely differing reception that the series and the film received. For critics of the past regime, engaging with an image *of* the past is seen as much less threatening than engaging with an image *from* the past. Yet at the same time, there are a number of common mechanisms at play that connect *Cosy Dens* and *Major Zeman*. Although both texts, and *Major Zeman* in particular, also invited a number of other readings, the link between these two events can be traced in a retro mode of reception, which constituted one of the significant responses to both of these cultural products.

The opinions put forward in the debates surrounding *The Thirty Cases of Major Zeman* can be divided into several camps.[43] The 'repressive approach' was propagated by the anticommunist section of the press and public, and included many of the same commentators who simultaneously voiced their concerns over Karel Gott. Generally, adherents of this view felt that it was wrong for a public broadcaster to show a programme so blatantly defending an ideology they considered criminal. As in the Gott debates, the issue of the perceived immorality of socialist entertainment came to the fore. Concern was expressed about the effect the rescreening might have on young viewers;[44] others compared the obvious propagandistic intentions of *Major Zeman* to the films of Leni Riefenstahl.[45] Adam Drda once again questioned the moral 'cadre profile' of socialist-era entertainers. Commenting on the second accompanying studio debate broadcast on 23 September 1999, in an article tellingly entitled 'An Intellectual Catastrophe on the First Channel', Drda was disgusted by what he saw as *Major Zeman* actor Radoslav Brzobohatý's attempt to jovially ingratiate himself with former political prisoner Jiří Stránský, thus morally acquitting his role in the series.[46]

While columnists like Drda called for an (undefined) coming to terms with the past, the television debate itself demonstrated very clearly the unwillingness of representatives of various strands within society to broach this topic. Stránský's evasive comments that 'the table needs to be cleared' did not offer any constructive steps; columnist Tomáš Vystrčil was equally vague in stating that things should have been named clearly long ago. The other participants also failed to articulate what exactly would constitute such a coming to terms with the past, apart from optimistic historian Vilém Prečan, who believed that they were already setting the process in motion by simply attending the debate.[47] The discourse of the KPV was the clearest in offering concrete solutions: in the first television debate, KPV chairman Stanislav Drobný suggested that 'dealing with the past' should consist of 'punishing communist criminals'.[48] Although, as Kamil Činátl points out, the attitude of the KPV received considerable traction in the media, it failed to turn this rhetoric into specific gains. The broadcast of the series did go ahead and the lawsuit the organization filed against Czech Television was unsuccessful.[49]

Czech Television's promise to deliver a nationwide discussion of the past through *Major Zeman* thus had mixed results. Jiří Peňás's call for the series to become the equivalent of the German *Historikerstreit* did not materialize.[50] Instead, the competing 'quality narrative' pointed to the perceived continuity of socialist popular culture in certain sections of society. The 'quality' approach is perhaps nearest in character to Svetlana Boym's restorative nostalgia, which, she argues, turns to notions of 'tradition'.[51] The adherents of this view wish to reclaim this site of socialist popular culture, which they see as traditional and good-quality entertainment. This particular narrative, then, is interested in the continuity of popular culture and of the original viewing experience, sharing the initial impulse of validating socialist culture with the defenders of Karel Gott. The argument made is that *Major Zeman*, in spite of its ideological content, is in fact a solid piece of filmmaking and an entertaining detective series, superior to excessively violent and sexualized Western productions.[52] A similar dynamic can be seen in other postsocialist countries as well. Boym argues that:

> 1990s nostalgia for the Brezhnev era was partially based on the old Soviet movies that reappeared on Russian TV at the time. Many Russian viewers, tired of upheavals and lost illusions of the post-Soviet decade, tuned in and suddenly began to believe that Soviet life resembled those movies, forgetting their own experiences as well as their ways of watching those films twenty years earlier – with much more scepticism and double entendre.[53]

She thus points to the significant fact that a changing reception context can lead to new interpretations; despite an ostensible investment in recovering the original viewing experience, retrospective reviewing necessarily generates new ways of reading.

A complex reading landscape thus begins to emerge, where a number of strategies compete with one another. As mentioned in the previous chapter, a well-documented phenomenon in socialist culture was that readers and viewers searched for signs of political subversion between the lines, also known as 'Aesopian language', in cultural production (and cultural producers intentionally used this mechanism to avoid censorship).[54] This is the kind of 'double entendre' Boym refers to – or a code of political metaphors and allegories, which could be interpreted as critical of the regime or somehow subversive. While a rejection of Aesopian reading strategies leads to simply attending to the genre of the series and producing the 'quality' narrative, as Boym describes in her post-Soviet example, in other readings, attempts at decoding persist. 'Seeing through' the obvious ideological content of *Major*

Zeman became a significant part of its viewing pleasure for certain sections of the audience. This could perhaps best be termed the 'educational approach' – a number of contributors to the debate argued that the obvious ideological intentions of the series made it an excellent didactic tool for learning about the functioning of communist propaganda.[55] This was also the view propagated by academic writing on the subject.[56]

However, the decoding of Aesopian features generated another kind of response. This could best be described as 'ironic', though the word that appeared in the Czech media more frequently was *recese*. This term without a direct English equivalent denotes a certain type of practical humour and has a long tradition in Czech culture, encompassing the most beloved Czech prankster Švejk, but also, for instance, the theatre of Jára Cimrman, which only stages plays attributed to an entirely fictional genius and jack of all trades. An ironic reading does very little to reflect on politics. It is interested in the aesthetic level of practices and representations and thus takes a postmodern view – it uses socialist aesthetics for the purposes of its own playful pastiche of the past. Činátl's research corroborates that this reading mainly arose at a point when a generational exchange had taken place: ironic approaches to the series largely occurred when the viewer did not have a strong experiential investment in the period in which the series was made and was thus able to approach it with the kind of detachment that facilitates irony.[57] It was exemplified, for instance, by Michal Zavadil, chairman of an unofficial *Major Zeman* fanclub and member of the generation of viewers who first watched the series as young children. In the first TV debate accompanying the series, he called *Major Zeman* 'wonderful postmodern entertainment'.[58]

The ironic approach turns *Major Zeman* into a retro artefact, where similar features to those already determined in some of the representations from the early 1990s can be discerned. The shift that has taken place here is that while retro mechanisms are inscribed in texts like *Bliss Was It in Bohemia* or *Jackal Years*, in the case of *Major Zeman* a particular type of response attributes retro characteristics to an artefact that was not made with any such discernible strategy. This retro reading arises from viewing the series with a camp sensibility that could be summarized with the slogan 'it's so bad that it's good'. Over-the-top performances and overcoding of certain phenomena, such as the exaggerated portrayal of drug use in the episode 'Mimikry' ('Mimicry') create a hyperbolic mode inviting ironic interpretations. This episode allows the viewer to engage in several levels of decoding and thus to partake of an 'in-joke' situation – the pleasure is derived from a kind of intellectual flattery of the viewer who can congratulate himself or herself on recognizing the reference. Depicting alternative rock music, a real-life hijacking of a plane in 1972, and heroin addiction in wildly unrealistic terms, watching the episode becomes an entertaining game of spotting ideological fabrications.

Such an ironic enjoyment in consuming the past is not unique. Amongst many other examples, a similar effect occurred when Karel Gott headlined the country's largest contemporary rock music festival, Rock for People, in 2013. Initially, the reaction to the announcement of Gott's performance – hardly rock and no longer that contemporary – was perceived as a joke by the music press, but the performance proved to be a massive success. The audience, which largely consisted of people of a generation whose parents were fans of Gott, clearly perceived the singer with a combination of genuine and ironic enjoyment. Young audiences could simultaneously indulge memories of their own childhood that was accompanied by Gott's rendition of the theme song to the Japanese/German 1970s cartoon *Maya the Bee*, as well as approach the singer with a camp sensibility. The latter turned his performance into retro in a strategy reminiscent of what Alexei Yurchak has identified 'the new sincerity' in Russian art,[59] a peculiar mixture of acutely self-aware postmodern irony and sincere appreciation of artefacts of the past.

Political Contracts

Examples such as *Major Zeman* and *Cosy Dens* frustrate attempts to divide practices of consuming the past into neat categories and show how nostalgic sentiments for specific aspects of the past can coexist with a host of other feelings and attitudes, including a political condemnation of the communist regime. If then we understand nostalgia as an emotion that sentimentalizes particular aspects of the past, restorative and reflective nostalgia need not be as mutually exclusive as Svetlana Boym suggests. Both types amalgamate in situations like the rewatching of *Major Zeman*, where wistful responses can mingle with more ironic enjoyments, or in *Cosy Dens*, where nostalgic mood and mode coexist and a sentimental investment in the period coincides with a detached appreciation of retro aesthetics. Ironic retro readings deliberately elide political questions and aestheticize the past, yet, as we will see, they necessarily operate with specific political assumptions.

Stylistically and narratively, *Cosy Dens* is structured around a number of material objects from the 1960s. The private setting of the film, with interiors dominating over exteriors, allows it to become a showcase for a number of retro markers, such as interior decorations, furniture, fabrics, hairstyles and fashions, both in the film's mise-en-scène and its narrative structure. The aesthetics of the film revels in the deficiency of these objects, laughing at the inadequacy of the products portrayed, and elevates these defects to a retrospectively 'hip' status. This is a viewing strategy akin to the joking or ironic approach to *Major Zeman*. In the series, it is precisely those aspects that appear substandard, such as the stilted dialogues, the lack of action or long

Figure 3.1 *Pelíšky* (*Cosy Dens*), Jan Hřebejk (director) and Petr Jarchovský (screenwriter), 1999. © Image Total HelpArt THA.

scenes of narratively redundant political meetings, which are highlighted as that which becomes retrospectively amusing. In a similar way, deficient fashions and objects of the 1960s, 1970s or 1980s in retrospective representations possess a certain retro-attractiveness precisely because of their perceived unsightliness, just as Gott appears as a relic of the past to younger audiences.

The design of *Cosy Dens* creates a dense pastiche of at times ahistorical nostalgic markers, generating a recognizable semblance of pastness for the viewer, while retaining a contemporary aesthetic appeal. But the film also produces nostalgic affect to a greater extent than, for instance, *Jackal Years*. The film, in its evocation of cosy and comfortable family spaces, very much plays on the concept of the everyday. Like *Kolya*, which employed glowing golden visuals to create an inviting, sentimentalized gaze, *Cosy Dens* uses a yellowish camera filter to endow all interior shots with a radiant warmth. Socialism is largely depicted in warm shades of brown (Figure 3.1). Like the representations of the early 1990s, *Cosy Dens* relies on a retrospective narrative strategy to generate a sense of nostalgic longing for youth gone by. Events are recounted through voiceover by an older version of teenager Michal, who, despite living through formative moments of his life at the time of the political upheaval of the Prague Spring, is solely concerned with his own private problems, in particular his unrequited love for his neighbour Jindřiška. The story, revolving around family events and rituals, remains in the personal realm, focusing on a limited group of characters and their relationships with one another. *Cosy Dens* thus makes use of the same structure as Michal Viewegh's and Petr Šabach's texts, setting aside an explicit thematization of the politics of the past and, like in *Kolya*, adopting a sheltered, forgiving view of the period.

The film thus mines sentiment through a twofold investment: the nostalgic mood by definition turns to a lost time, and *Cosy Dens* strengthens this through focusing narratively on unfulfilled moments or moments of loss. This is the case with the main protagonist's unsuccessful attempts to woo his neighbour and, on a larger level, the Warsaw Pact invasion, marking the end of an era and lamented in the film by a plaintive rendition of the national anthem on the piano by one of the characters. To use Paul Grainge's typology, mood and mode cohabit in the film: the comic mode of portraying the everyday, with its world of amusing styles and objects, shifts to the sentimental mood of the exceptional, a technique that grants the scene of the invasion all the more potency by disrupting the cosy domesticity that preceded it. Both ironic and sentimental readings can sit side by side in the interpretation of this representation of the past.

The fiction of *Cosy Dens* operates on an implicit political contract between the filmmakers and the viewer: the politics of the period do not need to be explicitly addressed, because it is understood that the audience does not sympathize with the socialist system. The structure of the narrative itself prevents viewers from doing so – the narrative arc is carried by teenage protagonists who set themselves up against the regime, while characters who make use of the system to further their own goals are portrayed in a negative light (such as the careerist teacher and later headmaster Saša Mašlaň). Like *Kolya*, Hřebejk's film allows the viewer to engage in a kind of nostalgia for resistance. Films such as *Cosy Dens* ask us to identify with characters who resist communist authority; the viewer sympathizes with, but is simultaneously amused by, their acts of petty heroism. For example, in an iconic scene, the otherwise despotic head of the family, Kraus, steps out onto his balcony and with boyish relish shouts a rather innocent antiregime obscenity – 'Proletarians of the world, go fuck yourselves' (*Proletáři všech zemí, vylížte si prdel*). The moment of laughter comes at the gesture's futility, when Kraus gleefully returns inside to his wife with the words 'What a relief' (*To se mi ulevilo*).

Such moments of petty heroism generate humour in the film, allowing the viewer to indulge in the kind of 'liberating laughter' that critics praised Viewegh for. But while the film would appear to offer the possibility to laugh away the repressive aspects of the period, like in *Kolya*, this leads to a rather facile apologetics. As film critic Kamil Fila has observed, the narrative structure of the film guides the viewer towards an anticommunist stance, which allows the audience to dismiss all communists as the caricatured 'Other'.[60]

Representations that make use of nostalgic tropes turn to a morally more clear-cut time: a black-and-white portrayal of 'us' and 'them', good and evil, where the viewer is always by default positioned in the camp of those who at least in small, petty ways disagreed with the regime. Nostalgia for resistance thus allows the viewer, together with the characters who drive the narrative, to revel in how well they managed to set themselves up against the 'Other' communists. The genre of retro-comedy further adds to this contract established through the narrative structure: by assuming that viewers share a condemnation of the past regime, the film can set an explicit depiction of politics aside and indulge instead in the pleasing and amusing retro aesthetics of the past, which are thus rendered nonthreatening.

Similarly to *Cosy Dens*, while many readings of *Major Zeman* may not be explicitly political, they once again operate with certain assumptions. The aforementioned practice of 'seeing through' and laughing at the overly ideologized elements of a series like *Major Zeman* enables the viewer to also engage in a kind of retrospective oppositional attitude. Thus, both representations and revisitings of the past afford the viewer the possibility of setting himself or herself 'above' the period ideology and reaffirming the superiority of the ideology of the present. In the case of retrospective representations, this is achieved through a narrative strategy in which the viewer is asked to identify with antiregime characters. In period representations, the narrative is driven by characters who support the regime – thus the 'petty heroism' is transferred to the viewer who, with retrospective knowledge, creates a resistant reading of the ideology displayed in the television piece or film in question.

The multiple reading strategies discussed in this chapter point to a many-layered cultural dynamic that cannot easily be subsumed under a local version of the *Ostalgie* framework. When discussing postsocialist nostalgia, it is less useful to speak of categories into which representations and practices can be grouped, rather than a set of particular mechanisms that representations and practices utilize. While the elegiac tone of German *Ostalgie* laments the loss of the East German state, Czech practices and representations of socialism accommodate this past into a continuum with the present.

Czech cultural reflections of socialism in the late 1990s thus displayed a twofold drive: they turned, necessarily, to a sense of rupture with the socialist period; at the same time, they spoke to a particular politics of the present. But by inscribing a dismissal of the politics of socialism into their very structure, the aesthetics of the past are used to establish a narrative of linear progress from socialism into market capitalism. Relics of the past are co-opted into this continuity by means of rhetorical strategies that separate them from socialism's politics, invoking seemingly neutral categories such as quality or professionalism. Mining comedic potential and thus debunking the ideology and material culture of socialism, viewing practices set the consumers of both socialist popular culture and retrospective representations in a historically comfortably superior position, thus ultimately forming not so much a narrative focused on lamenting the loss of the past as one focused on an implicit justification of the present.

Notes

1. M. Franc, 'Ostalgie v Čechách', in M. Kopeček and A. Gjuričová (eds), *Kapitoly z dějin české demokracie po roce 1989* (Prague and Litomyšl: Paseka, 2008), 193–216 (195).
2. V. Dušánek and J. Hymp, 'Stotisícový dav fanoušků přivítal v metropoli své hrdiny z Nagana' ['Hundred-Thousand-Strong Crowd Welcomes its Heroes from Nagano in the Capital'], *Mladá fronta Dnes* ('Praha' supplement), 24 February 1998, 1; dub, zup, 'Někdo děkoval, jiní agitovali' ['Some Gave Thanks, Others Campaigned'], *Lidové noviny*, 25 February 1998, 3.
3. See, for example, M. Králová, 'Překvapení ze Staroměstského náměstí' ['Surprise from Old Town Square'], *Liberecký den*, 24 February 1998, 7; O. Štindl, 'Michal David – principál národních veselic' ['Michal David – Bandleader of National Celebrations'], *Lidové noviny*, 25 February 1998, 3.
4. See O. Bezr, 'V začarovaném kruhu' ['In a Vicious Circle'], *Týden*, 6 July 1998, 42.
5. A. Roberts, 'The Politics and Anti-politics of Nostalgia', *East European Politics and Societies* 16(3) (2002), 764–809 (765).
6. Čtk, 'V šatně poslouchají Davida' ['They Listen to David in the Dressing Room'], *Právo*, 20 February 1998, no pagination.
7. Anon., 'Michal David zpívá o coca-cole, protože její výrobce patří mezi sponzory hokeje' ['Michal David Sings about Coca-Cola Because its Manufacturer Sponsors Ice-Hockey'], *Mladá fronta Dnes*, 25 February 1998, 4.
8. V. Vlasák, 'Které nahrávky se nejlépe prodávají' ['Which Records Sell Best'], *Mladá fronta Dnes*, 28 February 1998, no pagination; M. Kučerová-Turková, 'Fosílie, nebo hit?' ['Fossil or Hit?'], *Týden*, 6 July 1998, 40–45.
9. See Renata Kalenská's interview with Rejžek: R. Kalenská, 'Dívčí válka' ['The Maidens' War'], *Pátek: Magazín Lidových novin*, 16 October 2000, 11; and J. Marek, 'Helena Vondráčková prohrála soudní při s hudebním kritikem Janem Rejžkem' ['Helena Vondráčková Loses Legal Battle with Music Critic Jan Rejžek'], *Radio Praha*, 15 January 2002. Retrieved 19 August 2019 from http://www.radio.cz/cz/rubrika/udalosti/helena-vondrackova-prohrala-soudni-pri-s-hudebnim-kritikem-janem-rejzkem.
10. I. Reifová, 'The Pleasure of Continuity: Re-reading Postsocialist Nostalgia', *International Journal of Cultural Studies* 21(6) (2018), 587–602 (598).
11. See čtk, lidovky.cz, 'Nic nového. 41. Slavíka získal Karel Gott, cenu převzala jeho dcera' ['Nothing New. Karel Gott Received His Forty-First Nightingale, His Daughter Collected the Award'], 26 November 2016. Retrieved 19 August 2019 from http://

www.lidovky.cz/na-slavikach-nic-noveho-zpevacku-roku-vyhrala-bila-nejlepsi-kapelou-je-kabat-1vc-/kultura.aspx?c=A161126_214443_ln_kultura_ele.
12. See Roberts, 'The Politics and Anti-politics of Nostalgia', 778.
13. A. Drda, 'Gott a disent: srovnatelná selhání?' ['Gott and Dissent: Comparable Failures?'], *Lidové noviny*, 30 July 1999, 11.
14. J. Tluchoř, 'Karel Gott je právem králem' ['Karel Gott Is Rightly King'], *Právo*, 15 July 1999, 12.
15. O. Štindl, 'Gott mit uns a my s ním' ['Gott with Us and We with Him'], *Lidové noviny*, 14 July 1999, 1, 20 (20).
16. Drda, 'Gott a disent: srovnatelná selhání?'.
17. Z. Lukeš, 'Hannovergott', *Lidové noviny*, 6 January 2000, 17.
18. J. Tluchoř, 'Gott odmítl vystoupit na EXPO, Dostál jej chce přemluvit zpět' ['Gott Refused to Perform at EXPO, Dostál Wants to Convince Him Back'], *Právo*, 11 January 2000, 3.
19. P. Dostál, 'Nedejte se otrávit' ['Do Not Let Yourself Be Annoyed'], *Lidové noviny*, 11 January 2000, 10.
20. D. Strož, 'A budou bez Gotta' ['And They'll Be without Gott'], *Haló noviny*, 11 January 2000, 5.
21. M. Zapletal, 'Lidovým novinám nepoděkuji' ['I Will Not Thank Lidové noviny'], *Lidové noviny*, 12 January 2000, 11.
22. B. Doležal, 'Knedlíková estráda není hlavní problém' ['Dumpling Variety Show not the Main Problem'], *Lidové noviny*, 19 January 2000, 11.
23. Columnists were mainly critical of Gott and any endorsement of the singer remained cautious, while acknowledging his immense popularity. His defenders came from the ranks of readers who expressed their opinions in letters to the editor, in the major dailies, as well as tabloid papers such as *Blesk*. See, for example, Anon., 'Na jaké místo v naší kultuře řadíte Karla Gotta?' ['Where in Our culture Do You Place Karel Gott?'], *Slovo*, 13 July 1999, 7; or V. Chourová's letter to the editor in 'Dopisy Blesku' ['Letters to Blesk'], *Blesk*, 22 July 1999, 10.
24. P. Cooke, 'Performing "Ostalgie": Leander Haussmann's *Sonnenallee*', *German Life and Letters* 56(2) (2003): 156–67 (160).
25. See (tr), 'I hudba se dnes dá ideologicky zneužít…' ['Music Too Can Be Ideologically Misused Nowadays…'], *Haló noviny*, 2 October 1998, 4; red, 'Dopisy nedělnímu Blesku' ['Letters to Blesk on Sunday'], 23 January 2000, 20; M. Musil and O. Neuman, 'Je nebezpečné dotýkat se hvězd' ['It Is Dangerous to Touch the Stars'], *Lidové noviny*, 19 January 2000, 17.
26. M. Remešová and D. Mácha, *Karel Gott: Zlatý hlas z Prahy* (Prague: Eminent, 2009).
27. čtk, 'Režimy přicházejí a odcházejí, zlatý hlas zůstává' ['Regimes Come and Go, the Golden Voice Remains'], *Lidové noviny*, 15 July 1999, 12.
28. V. Klaus, 'Místo prologu', in M. Remešová and D. Mácha (eds), *Karel Gott: Zlatý hlas z Prahy* (Prague: Eminent, 2009), 7–9 (8).
29. The film was seen in cinemas by an audience of over one million, a staggering number in a country of ten million inhabitants. Taking into account its wide availability on DVD and frequent repeats on both private and public television, its impact is truly remarkable.
30. The following discussion of *The Thirty Cases of Major Zeman* draws on V. Pehe, 'Retro Reappropriations: Responses to *The Thirty Cases of Major Zeman* in the Czech Republic', *VIEW Journal of European Television History and Culture* 3(5) (2014), 100–7. Retrieved 19 August 2019 from http://ojs.viewjournal.eu/index.php/view/article/view/JETHC060/129http://ojs.viewjournal.eu/index.php/view/article/view/JETHC060/129.

31. See J. Peňáš, 'Nesmrtelní hurvínci' ['Immortal Hurvíneks (children's cartoon character – my note) '], *Respekt*, 6 May 1996, 3; P. Bren, *The Greengrocer and His TV: The Culture of Communism after the 1968 Prague Spring* (Ithaca: Cornell University Press, 2010), 237; Roberts, 'The Politics and Anti-politics of Nostalgia', 771.
32. Bren, *The Greengrocer and His TV*, 81.
33. Anon., 'Železný váhá směnit kanál s Premiérou kvůle mjr. Zemanovi' ['Železný Hesitant to Exchange Channel with Premiéra Because of Major Zeman'], *Právo*, 27 May 1996, 2.
34. See, for example, P. Šafr, 'Do našich domovů se vrací Rudý Honza' ['Red Honza is Returning to Our Homes'], *Lidové noviny*, 16 September 1999, 1; T. Vystrčil, 'V debatě o Zemanovi nikdo vážně diskutovat nechce' ['Nobody Wants to Talk Seriously in Zeman Debate'], *Lidové noviny*, 29 September 1999, 9; M. Pavlata, 'Vysílání majora Zemana není ve veřejném zájmu' ['Broadcast of Major Zeman Not in Public Interest'], *Lidové noviny*, 15 October 1999, 1.
35. See, for example, Anon., 'Major Zeman se vrací na obrazovky' ['Major Zeman Returns to the Screens'], *Mladá fronta Dnes*, 1 October 1998, 6; M. Spáčilová, 'Česká televize hledá argumenty pro uvedení Majora Zemana' ['Czech Television Searching for Arguments for Screening Major Zeman'], *Mladá fronta Dnes*, 16 September 1999, 6; J. Chochola, 'Protestují vězni, poslanci i odboráři' ['Prisoners, MPs and Trade Unionists Are All Protesting'], *Mladá fronta Dnes*, 16 September 1999, 6.
36. J. Perglerová and K. Miketa, 'Puchalský položil funkci' ['Puchalský Resigned'], *Právo*, 16 December 1999, 1.
37. brp, jkl, 'Major Zeman usiluje o návrat' ['Major Zeman Strives for Return'], *Mladá fronta Dnes*, 1 August 1998, 1.
38. brp, jkl, 'Risk Markízy diváci ocenili' ['Viewers Appreciated Markíza's Risk'], *Mladá fronta Dnes*, 1 August 1998, 4.
39. B. Paklík and J. Kábele, 'Lidé mají o seriál zájem, Česká televize váhá' ['People are Interested in the Series, Czech Television Is Hesitating'], *Mladá fronta Dnes*, 1 August 1998, 1.
40. The formulation that the documentaries would 'set things right' (*uvést na pravou míru*), appeared repeatedly in the press; see e.g. M. Spáčilová, 'Česká televize hledá argumenty pro uvedení Majora Zemana' ['Czech Television Searching for Arguments for Screening Major Zeman'], *Mladá fronta Dnes*, 16 September 1999, 6; fik, ces, 'Představiteli majora Zemana se uvedení seriálu s komentářem nelíbí' ['Major Zeman Actor Not Happy with Broadcast of Series with Commentary'], *Lidové noviny*, 2 October 1998, 4; E. Harantová, 'Je návrat Zemana na obrazovky chybou, nebo záslužným počinem?' ['Is the Return of Zeman to the Screen a Mistake or a Commendable Act?'], *Lidové noviny*, 10 September 1999, 23.
41. See, for example, Anon., 'Hřebejkův nový film Pelíšky se vydává do českých kin' ['Hřebejk's New Film Pelíšky Hits Cinemas'], *Hradecké noviny*, 6 April 1999, 8; A. Matušková, 'Pelíšky mi umožňují cestovat volně v čase' ['*Cosy Dens* Enable Me to Travel Freely in Time – interview with Petr Jarchovský'], *Lidové noviny*, 10 April 1999, 13.
42. See, for example, V. Míšková, 'Humor filmových Pelíšků zalézá až pod kůži' ['The Humour of *Cosy Dens* Gets under the Skin'], *Právo*, 9 April 1999, 12.
43. I am indebted to both Kamil Činátl's typology in the chapter 'Návraty majora Zemana' from his book *Naše české minulosti* (Prague: Nakladatelství Lidové noviny, 2014), 177–202, and Jan Kohoutek's categorization of responses to *Major Zeman*, as detailed in his MA dissertation, 'Veřejná polemika o uvedení seriálu Třicet případů majora Zemana v České televizi po roce 1989 (diskurzivní analýza českého celostátního tisku)', MA dissertation, Masaryk University Brno, 2011.

44. Many press articles make reference to the 'morally corrupting' potential of the series for young viewers, but then go on to refute it. *Lidové noviny*, for example, published an article entitled 'Young People are Not Interested in Zeman at All' (M. Keries, 'Mládež se o Zemana vůbec nezajímá', *Lidové noviny*, 17 September 1999, 4).
45. J. Rejžek, 'Major Zeman na hrad?', *Literární noviny* 10(39) (1999), 4.
46. A. Drda, 'Intelektuální katastrofa na ČT 1' ['An Intellectual Catastrophe on the First Channel'], *Lidové noviny*, 25 September 1999, 10.
47. Debate accompanying the series *The Thirty Cases of Major Zeman* entitled 'Tlustá čára za minulostí?' ['A Thick Line Behind the Past?'], Czech Television, broadcast on 23 September 1999, dir. Marek Straka, Czech Television Archive, IDEC: 299 322 22469/0002.
48. Untitled debate accompanying the series *The Thirty Cases of Major Zeman* ['Beseda k seriálu Třicet případů Majora Zemana'], Czech Television, broadcast on 16 September 1999, dir. Marek Straka, Czech Television Archive, IDEC: 299 322 22469/0001.
49. Činátl, *Naše české minulosti*, 187.
50. J. Peňás, 'Asimilovaná lež' ['Assimilitated Lie'], *Respekt*, 12 October 1998, 19.
51. S. Boym, *The Future of Nostalgia* (New York: Basic Books, 2001), 45.
52. See M. Komárek, 'Jedni tajtrlíci se vracejí, druzí už tu jsou' ['Some Clowns Return, Others are Already Here'], *Mladá Fronta Dnes*, 13 November 1998, 15. This attitude was also particularly marked in responses from newspaper readers – for example, 'Hlasy čtenářů: Návrat majora Zemana – je to vtip, či nebezpečí?' ['Readers' Voices: Return of Major Zeman – Joke or Danger?'], *Mladá Fronta Dnes*, 7 August 1998, 11.
53. Boym, *The Future of Nostalgia*, 61.
54. The phenomenon has been studied particularly in the Soviet context. For an exploration of its use in Soviet cinema, see K. Moss, 'A Russian Munchhausen: Aesopian Translation', in A. Horton (ed.), *Inside Soviet Film Satire: Laughter with a Lash* (Cambridge: Cambridge University Press, 1993), 20–35. For its literary applications, see L. Losev, *On the Beneficence of Censorship: Aesopian Language in Modern Russian Literature*, trans. Jane Bobko (Munich: Otto Sagner in Kommission, 1984).
55. (spa), 'Je to skvělá studijní látka...' ['It's Great Study Material…'], *Mladá fronta Dnes*, 16 September 1999, 6. The educational value of the series was also one of Czech Television's official arguments for rescreening *Major Zeman*. See e.g. Anon., 'Major Zeman bude od září na obrazovkách ČT' ['Major Zeman Will Return to the Screens from September'], *Právo*, 26 August 1999, 1; or J. Šídlo, 'Třicet případů majora Puchalského' ['The Thirty Cases of Major Puchalský'], *Respekt*, 30 November 1998, 5.
56. P.A. Bílek, 'Předmluva', in P.A. Bílek (ed.), *James Bond a major Zeman: Ideologizující vzorce vyprávění* (Příbram: Pistorius and Olšanská, 2007), 7–9 (9).
57. Činátl, *Naše české minulosti*, 194.
58. Untitled debate accompanying the series *The Thirty Cases of Major Zeman* ['Beseda k seriálu Třicet případů Majora Zemana'], Czech Television, broadcast on 16 September 1999, dir. Marek Straka, Czech Television Archive, IDEC: 299 322 22469/0001.
59. A. Yurchak, 'Post-post-communist Sincerity: Pioneers, Cosmonauts, and Other Soviet Heroes Born Today', in T. Lahusen and P.H. Solomon, Jr. (eds), *What Is Soviet Now? Identities, Legacies, Memories* (Berlin: Lit Verlag, 2008), 257–76.
60. K. Fila, 'Muž na rozcestí' ['Man at the Crossroads'], *Respekt*, 26 November 2012, 52–58 (58).

Chapter 4

PETTY HEROISM

Nostalgia for Resistance

This chapter moves into the first decade of the twenty-first century, analysing the ways in which the socialist past was represented in literature and film. In this period, comedy still continued to dominate the cultural memory of the state socialist past in the Czech Republic. Within this generic setting, nostalgia often appeared as a mood and motif, but, as we will see, in a somewhat counter-intuitive turn, it looked back upon the oppressive aspects of the regime. A feature shared by practically all Czech comedic representations of socialism that is strikingly absent from discussions of postsocialist nostalgia in other national contexts is a longing for resistance against authority, for bringing it down with small, private gestures. To an extent, this chapter thus explores mechanisms already encountered in previous chapters: the use of humour and child narrators, and the failure of heroic attempts. What it adds is a closer look at the precise implications of cultural producers assuming that readers and viewers share a condemnation of the past regime with the protagonists of fictional narratives and defines the 'ordinary heroism' projected by cultural mediations of the socialist past.

Throughout the postsocialist era, humorous portrayals of the previous regime – whether written or cinematic – overwhelmingly turned to the period of so-called Normalization. The widely used term refers to the last twenty years of state socialism, from the definitive end of the movement towards liberalization known as the Prague Spring in 1969 to the fall of communist rule in 1989. This period saw a return to a more hardline regime under the rule of Gustáv Husák following the Warsaw Pact invasion of August 1968.

Unlike the hopes and disappointments associated with the building of socialism in the 1950s, the political crimes and persecutions of the same decade, or the cultural and political rebirth of the 1960s, late socialism is typically seen in both representation and historiography as lacking large historical events. How can we speak about a time of such perceived 'eventlessness'? Writers and filmmakers have resolved this problem by focusing on the personal sphere, recounted through self-enclosed episodes, often with a comic punchline. What gives these episodes structure are very often gestures of resistance. In such a scenario, we may ask what the purpose of setting such personal narratives in the past is if the stories they tell do not hinge on a broader historical context. In other words, to what end is Normalization narrated as a time when nothing happened?

Recounting Normalization in this way leads to a specific political interpretation: at a time when there are few large events with accompanying heroes to focus on, heroism becomes the domain of 'ordinary' characters. The preoccupation with the personal and with individual resistance rather than collective stories in these comedies sits conveniently with a dominant post-1989 narrative of keeping any probing of collusion or consensus with the regime at a safe distance within popular memory. Michal Viewegh's novel *Bliss Was It in Bohemia* (*Báječná léta pod psa*, 1992), a number of Petr Šabach's short stories, as well as the films *Kolya* (*Kolja*, dir. Jan Svěrák 1996), Jan Hřebejk's *Pupendo* (2003), Irena Pavlásková's *An Earthly Paradise for the Eyes* (*Zemský ráj to napohled*, 2009), Ondřej Trojan's *The Identity Card* (*Občanský průkaz*, 2010), Richard Řeřicha's *Don't Stop* (2012), the television series *Tell Me a Story* (*Vyprávěj*, 2009–13) – all of these are predominantly set in the 1970s or the 1980s. Through a close reading of several of these representations from the 2000s, this chapter argues that the two key factors of genre and understandings of heroism play into the political interpretation of the socialist period as a time that was rejected and resisted.

Irena Dousková's Jolly Anticommunism

In previous chapters I pointed out that cultural representations practically never evince a longing for the period of state socialism as a whole. A nostalgic appraisal of certain aspects of the previous regime is thus not at odds with its political rejection – especially if the object of this nostalgia is an antiregime stance displayed by characters. Literary authors often found humorous potential in this seeming paradox, especially if employing a child's perspective. Throughout the 1990s, popular authors such as Michal Viewegh, Petr Šabach and Irena Dousková consolidated a postsocialist canon of comic literature about the previous regime recounted from the perspective of a child or teenager. While Viewegh's *Bliss Was It in Bohemia* was discussed in Chapter 2, Dousková and Šabach will be the subject of the present chapter. The latter's work in particular illustrates that anticommunism can coexist with nostalgia; Dousková's indulgent and humorous view of the period also sits alongside an interpretation of the socialist past condemning everything associated with the communist establishment.

Before entering the 2000s, a slight detour back into the 1990s is necessary. In 1998, Dousková (born 1964) published the novel *Hrdý Budžes* (translated as *B. Proudew*).[1] The title of this novel is a play on the words *hrdý buď, žes* ('be proud that you') from Stanislav Kostka Neumann's 1949 poem, which the young protagonist of the novel, eight-year-old Helenka, constantly mishears when learning it at school. Told from Helenka's faux-naïve child's perspective, the book humorously details the period of the early 1970s in a provincial town near Prague. The reviews of the novel upon its publication, which were not numerous, remarked that the 'confrontation of the language of children with the language of adults is a building block of humouristic literature'[2] and likened Dousková's style to the canonical prose of Karel Poláček (1892–1945). In particular, they referred to the popular children's novel *There Were Five of Us* (*Bylo nás pět*, first published in 1946), which Dousková's use of colloquial language can be seen as referencing.

The meagre number of reviews indicates that the publication of the novel did not have a large impact. Dousková only became much more widely known when she adapted *B. Proudew* for the stage in 2002 and the novel was republished. Premiered in Příbram, the town where Dousková grew up, and where *B. Proudew*, under the fictive guise of the name Ničín is set, the play soon became a cult production. In 2004, the daily *Mladá fronta Dnes* reported that *B. Proudew* has 'become a phenomenon on the Czech theatre scene',[3] quoting the large number of repeat showings and the fact that the show was sold out for months in advance. That a major daily chose to cover a provincial show attests to the play's significance. A recording of the production was broadcast on Czech Television on 8 November 2003. The leading actress Barbora Hrzánová, who portrayed eight-year-old Helenka, won the prestigious *Thalia* award in the same year,[4] and the production moved from the provincial theatre in Příbram to Prague's Theatre without Balustrades in 2003, a popular commercial theatre, where it has been continuously showing ever since. In 2006, Dousková published *Onegin Was a Rusky* (*Oněgin byl Rusák*), a sequel to *B. Proudew*, which now saw Helenka in the final year of her high school studies in 1980s Prague.[5] The novel was once again successfully adapted for the stage by the Theatre in Dlouhá in Prague.[6]

The tragicomic treatment of socialism in Dousková's texts was likened to Michal Viewegh's *Bliss Was It in Bohemia* several times by reviewers, as well as to the stories of Petr Šabach or the films of Jan Hřebejk.[7] The setting of

Douskova's popular texts amongst these authors attests to the consolidation of a benign, humorous representational discourse on the socialist past, even to the point of oversaturation. Already in 2002, in an article entitled 'It's Not Possible to Mine Jokes out of the Absurdities of Socialism Forever', theatre critic Jana Machalická complained that the topic had already been dealt with 'earlier, more aptly, and more humorously'[8] by authors including Viewegh and Šabach. However, the continued repeats of both *B. Proudew* and *Onegin was a Rusky*, as well as the production of a number of other representations that operate with humour to portray socialism in this period, demonstrate that audiences were indeed still willing to 'mine jokes' from the past.

Dousková uses the discrepancy between a child's or teenager's view and that of their parents to generate humour and simultaneously offer political commentary on the past regime, though unlike Viewegh's Kvido in *Bliss*, Helenka doesn't narrate events from a position of ironic hindsight, but with disarming in-the-now sincerity. She naïvely demands to be allowed to partake in communist rituals, as she does not understand their political dimension, while automatically reproducing the anticommunist discourse her parents teach her at home and that the text asks the audience to sympathize with. For example, Helenka complains that her mother 'doesn't want to let me go to the Sparkies [the younger version of the Pioneers], cos the Sparkies and the Pioneers are supposed to be little Communists. So I don't know, out of our class the whole class goes and I'd like to go, too'.[9] Dousková generates a nostalgia for the period that lies in a fascination with its outward, formal characteristics – its form and symbolism, here the institution of the Sparkies – but not its content.

This tendency was captured in a minor controversy that erupted after Barbora Hrzánová, the actress playing Helenka in the stage adaptation, paraphrased the script of the play in her televised acceptance speech at the *Thalia* award ceremony: 'I'm really happy that I'm doing this show, because saying in public that the Ruskies and communists are bastards, only you're not allowed to say it … it feels so good after all those years that I wish all of you could try it.'[10] Dousková's comedies thus perpetuate a situation in which audiences indulge a benevolent laughter at something they at the same time denounce. It is precisely this humorous indulgence that is key to identifying the nostalgic elements in these texts – the joy provided by recognizing the period's outward attributes in combination with a judgement of their ideological defectiveness. In *Onegin*, this becomes even more marked, as Helenka is no longer a naïve child who wants to join the Sparkies without realizing the political implications, but an opinionated teenager whose anticommunism is a matter of course, though her courage in expressing this conviction is limited to gestures of teenage rebellion, such as displaying a sign saying 'EAT PLENTY – YOU'RE NOT GOING TO BE SORRY'[11] at a May Day parade. The case of Dousková and her popularity shows not only how widespread this particular representational strategy of socialism had become, but in its (public and paratextual) condemnation of communism, it also brought home the pedagogical character of this seemingly nostalgic discourse, which aims to educate its recipients towards a 'correct' interpretation of history.

Normalization as Timelessness

Kamil Činátl has argued that 'the times of Normalization resist grand narratives, and so lend themselves to a hypertrophy of plots that are connected with small stories, with the banal time of the everyday, with personal memory'.[12] Indeed, the memory of late socialism throughout the former Eastern Bloc is dominated by notions of a suspended temporality, frozen in a state of stasis, when, as Anikó Imre writes, 'everyday life was permeated by a sense of being stuck between a past of (longing for) heroic communism, forever out of reach, and a future without hope since no one expected socialism to fall'.[13] In the Czech context, the period is often referred to by means of the metaphor of 'timelessness'. This is not a new term. It already existed in contemporary, particularly dissident discourse – symptomatic perhaps as a way of thinking about a period by people who had been denied access to any decision-making processes by state power and thus were not able to partake in actions that would allow them to turn Normalization into an 'eventful' time. In a 1987 essay, Václav Havel wrote that he remembers the early 1970s as a time when 'history stopped' and argued that the 'totalitarian system is fundamentally (that is, in its basic principle) "anti-narratively" oriented'.[14] And since time is only experienced through narrative and history, Havel argues, the very experience of time began to disappear.

The year 1977, in which the until then fragmented dissident movement coalesced around the manifesto Charter 77, could be seen as one significant marker that punctures this period. Yet producers of popular culture after 1989 have rather tended to avoid this subject. Sune Bechmann Pedersen speaks of a 'disenchantment with dissidence'[15] when it comes to portraying the milieu around the Charter in cinema and remarks that only few post-1989 films have taken up dissent as a topic, including *An Earthly Paradise for the Eyes, Kawasaki's Rose* (*Kawasakiho růže*, dir. Jan Hřebejk, 2009) and *Walking Too Fast* (*Pouta*, dir. Radim Špaček, 2009). This lack of attention is linked not only to the ambivalent legacy of dissent in the Czech public sphere, but also to a general wariness towards portraying heroes in comedies, a feature of Czech representational culture that I will return to.

Of the above representations, only *An Earthly Paradise for the Eyes* devotes itself fully to the dissident 'scene'. Scripted by Tereza Boučková, the film records some of her first-hand experiences of being the daughter of prominent dissident playwright Pavel Kohout. The fragmentary story meanders somewhat aimlessly through the smoky apartments of only thinly fictionalized figures such as Kohout or Havel, where heroism stems more from the desire for attention on the part of self-involved men rather than a genuine concern with the problems of society: dissent is portrayed as one big party. In a similar vein, the Czech Television production *Wisdom Teeth* (*Osmy*, dir. Jiří Strach, 2014) shows dissidence as an accident, not a wilful political act – the main protagonist becomes a hero against his own will when he signs the Charter in a drunken haze. The exception of dissent sits uncomfortably with popular memory, as it requires some form of reckoning with the fact that a few people attempted to actively (and publicly) resist injustice, implying that the vast majority compromised with the ruling power. Such a view is a hard sell for mainstream popular culture aimed at a wide audience, which rather tends to revel in a reconciliatory and benign view of the past that does not antagonize its viewers.

With the absence of grand narratives such as that of dissent, representations of late socialism turn to portraying private stories. Historians generally tend to agree that Normalization was marked by a strong distinction between the public and the private, both on the level of everyday life and state-sponsored policy.[16] According to this conception, the Normalization regime concluded a 'social contract' with the people, placating them with consumer goods and an officially sanctioned retreat into privacy, in exchange for a display of outward loyalty towards the socialist system.[17] However, closer examination reveals a more complex dynamic, which, a new generation of historians suggests, displays not only contractual but also consensual aspects.[18] As Paulina Bren has argued, the return to the private sphere and domesticity was simultaneously encouraged by the state and functioned as an expression of resistance and disregard for the political demands of public life.[19] Television, in Bren's argument, was at the forefront of state efforts to market the ideals of the 'quiet life' to its citizens. It is thus not surprising that retrospective representations took up the private as a setting for resistance, a trope that will have resonated with viewers with an empirical memory of the period.

The eventless atmosphere of late socialism is usually represented through grey, that least expressive of colours. Journalist Jiří Peňás's comment in an interview confirms the widespread popular prejudice about the colour scheme of Normalization: 'one of the distinctive signs of communist civilization in the Soviet Bloc was that its industry was not able to produce nice bold colours'.[20] Exemplified in a 2013 production of Prague's Theatre on the Balustrades entitled *Grey Seventies, or, Husák's Quiet* (*Šedá sedmdesátá, aneb Husákovo ticho*),[21] this colour attribution refers to the material universe of the period, while the metaphor of quietness also points to a perceived lack of eventfulness. The Theatre on the Balustrades thus contrasts late socialism with its previous production, *Golden Sixties* (*Zlatá šedesátá*),[22] portraying a decade of dynamic reform, and through this colour metaphor pointing to the different set of valences the 1960s bear in the Czech popular imagination.

This is by no means an argument to say that everyday life during Normalization did actually lack eventfulness for those who lived through it; rather, I am pointing to a prevalent popular mythology already perpetuated to an extent by the popular culture of the period. The narrative poverty of Normalization – or rather the possibilities of what could be said under censorship requirements and the relative stability of 'real existing socialism' – was evident in contemporary representations of everyday life. Havel complained about this in the late 1980s, establishing a connection between popular culture and the emptiness of public time in the already-mentioned essay. Referring to a number of unspecified popular comedies, he objected to the lack of historical grounding in these films, which are reduced to purely personal narratives.[23] A prime example of this aesthetic is the cinematic adaptation of Bohumil Hrabal's *The Snowdrop Festival* (*Slavnosti sněženek*) by Jiří Menzel in 1983, which saw an absolute lack of plot development, focusing instead on the most mundane of everyday occurrences.

Stories lacking an overarching narrative and concentrating on the banality of the everyday did not, of course, emerge only during Normalization. They have an established tradition in Czechoslovak cinema at least since the New Wave of the 1960s, with the early films of Miloš Forman perhaps being the best-known examples. But neither in historiography nor popular discourse are the 1960s associated with timelessness – if anything, it is seen as a rather happening decade, epitomized in the everyday usage of the phrase 'golden sixties'. Retrospective works of popular culture have also captured this sense of social and historical momentum. Apart from cinematic appraisals of 1968, which will be discussed in more detail in the next two chapters, an example of constructing the 1960s as a time when the small stories of the personal became intimately intertwined with the large stories of dynamic political developments comes from neighbouring Slovakia in Anton Baláž's novel *Just One Spring* (*Len jedna jar*).[24] The author sets out to remind readers that the Prague Spring did not happen just in the capital, but that the 'Bratislava Spring' was equally eventful and indeed 'happening', in a story focusing on several creative young people experimenting with new forms of artistic expression and their sexuality just as Czechoslovak society experiences a political awakening.

The representational culture of late socialism also did not jettison grand narratives and social questions; nevertheless, this aspect of cultural production has not made it into the cultural canon of how Czechs remember this period. For instance, the theme of work and work problems emerged as a productive site of drama and even tragedy. Films such as *The Young Man and the White Whale* (*Mladý muž a bílá velryba*, dir. Jaromil Jireš, 1978) or *Scalpel, Please* (*Skalpel, prosím*, dir. Jiří Svoboda, 1985) explore serious topics relating to the work worlds and moral dilemmas of their protagonists, whether in the sphere of chemical engineering or medicine. And as historian Pavel Kolář points out, late socialist cinema explored a range of other socially critical themes, including feminism, ecology, violence or, later in the 1980s, new phenomena such as drugs.[25] But it is rather works that show the paucity of events under Normalization that are frequently rescreened on television to this day, often in a pastoral setting with nationalist overtones in particular in Menzel's rendition, the most typical example here being *My Sweet Little Village* (*Vesničko má, středisková*, dir. Jiří Menzel, 1985).

Yet another genre of popular representation tried to convince viewers that this lack of societal narratives was a result not of the utopian impulse behind the socialist project being depleted, but because there was nothing left to desire. A typical example is the TV series *The Woman Behind the Counter* (*Žena za pultem*, dir. Jaroslav Dudek, 1977), which was first screened in the same year as the publication of Charter 77. The brimming supermarket in which the story is set presents a society where time stands still: the grand narratives that marked the period after the communist takeover of Czechoslovakia are a thing of the past. Now in real existing socialism, as the saleswoman Anna tells her bosses, 'we have stores which we wouldn't even have dreamt about'. Public time is suspended; only the personal and the intimate structures the everyday. Where no sustained narrative can be drawn, the narrative mode of Normalization timelessness becomes supremely episodic, a strategy that is also employed by retrospective representations.

Failing Heroic Gestures

The chief representative of the episode as a genre is undoubtedly Petr Šabach, one of the most prominent Czech raconteurs of socialism, whose works were adapted for the screen several times by screenwriter Petr Jarchovský after 1989.[26] The comic prose writer is the author of numerous novellas and short stories set mainly during the pre-1989 years. Recounting stories over a glass of beer is how Šabach's characters most often communicate and how his narrators impart the narrative to the reader. His works comprise a series of loosely linked reminiscences on the pleasures of youth; they embody the small stories and personal memory that Činátl has identified as emblematic of the narrative possibilities of Normalization.[27] To generate narrative, Šabach uses gestures of resistance against the regime to structure the eventlessness of the period. To illustrate this point, I will focus primarily on Šabach's novella *The*

Identity Card (*Občanský průkaz*, 2006)[28] and its subsequent film adaptation (dir. Ondřej Trojan, 2010), though these observations are equally applicable to other Šabach-Jarchovský films, and indeed comedies about the socialist past in general.[29]

Gestures of resistance in Šabach's narratives function to create clear hierarchies for his characters – the more protagonists define themselves against the ruling authorities, the more the reader is asked to sympathize with them. Yet fictional narratives hardly ever take up large heroic gestures as an object of portrayal. Already Viewegh's 1992 novel *Bliss Was It in Bohemia* generated comic effects through petty heroic gestures and their failure, with the moral dilemmas of the characters treated with deprecating humour. For instance, the character of the father of the protagonist Kvido experiences his greatest moment of heroism when he and Kvido's mother accidentally run into hounded playwright and dissident Pavel Kohout, who has been banished to the provincial town where they live and accept his invitation to visit him. Kvido's parents display a certain ambiguity about their feelings in relation to this act: 'Later, following a reprise, they failed to agree who had seen the persecuted playwright first and so should have given the signal to retreat in time.'[30] The narrator further comments on the conflicting emotions involved: '"If I wanted to cosy up to enemies of the regime, I could have stayed in Prague", Kvido's father lamented for appearance's sake, but somewhat in thrall to his own civic pluck.'[31] The father's heroism is then humorously deflated in the scene of the actual visit in Kohout's garden, when he tries to disguise his growing anxiety at the situation by loudly appreciating the food, only to nervously vomit into the hedge moments later. Here, heroism ultimately fails. Petty heroism thus contributes to an ironic mode by creating self-deprecating humorous situations.

Such petty heroism once again finds its precursor in interpretations of the overly eager compliance with authority as a display of subversion in Jaroslav Hašek's character of the good soldier Švejk. Švejk's apparently imbecilic servility and over-identification with the orders he is given by his superiors or any figures of authority is reminiscent of what Alexei Yurchak terms *stiob* in the late Soviet context, which he defines in the following way:

> a peculiar form of irony that differed from sarcasm, cynicism, derision, or any of the more familiar genres of absurd humour. It required such a degree of overidentification with the object, person, or idea at which the *stiob* was directed that it was often impossible to tell whether it was a form of sincere support, subtle ridicule, or a peculiar mixture of the two.[32]

Švejk is so compelling as a character precisely because of this peculiar mixture, though considering the place that Švejk has gained in the Czech canon as a representative of national character, interpreting him as a cunning trickster certainly has more flattering implications than viewing him as simply the imbecile he claims to be.[33]

While *Švejk* is set during the First World War, gestures of attempted or intended, though not necessarily successful, heroism have also been employed in canonical narratives of the Second World War. Novelist Josef Škvorecký, who emigrated to Canada in 1969, famously builds on the Švejkian tradition with his character of Danny Smiřický, protagonist of his debut novel *The Cowards* (*Zbabělci*, written in 1948–49 and published in 1958), the title of which already betrays the attitude towards heroism this text takes. The novel fell into disfavour with the authorities immediately after publication for its unheroic and 'ideologically unsound' portrayal of the end of the Second World War. The small town where Danny lives is preparing for an uprising, but all he can think about is his love, Irena, and that acting heroically would impress her: 'I didn't have anything against an uprising. But that was the only good reason I could see for fighting for any patriotic or strategic reasons. The Germans had already lost the war anyway, so it didn't make any sense. It was only because of Irena that I wanted to get into it. To show off.'[34] In comedic representations, the general resistance to heroism translates into a certain refusal to acknowledge exceptionalism, which may account for the discomfort in portraying the exception of dissidence within the framework of Normalization. It also, as we will see, relates to an 'equal distribution' of resistance via everyday actions.

In Šabach's work, heroism remains petty, on the level of slightly subversive jokes. This is best illustrated in *The Identity Card*, where a group of male friends, whom the text follows from their teenage years in the late 1960s into adulthood, enact their own daily 'tiny revolutions',[35] to use George Orwell's phrase, in ways that temporarily upset the established order, but never pose a sustained challenge. The subversive gestures these characters engage in could be referred to by the Czech term *švejkovina*, denoting a Švejk-like prank. The novella opens with a scene in which the unnamed narrator and his friends receive their identity cards from a policeman in an official ceremony. In a gambit with echoes of *stiob*, the characters perform a prank in which they over-identify with the form of the ceremony, squeezing the policeman's hand so tightly when shaking it that they crack his knuckles. The difference here between the subtle parody of *stiob*, or indeed Švejk, is that there is no dilemma about where the characters position themselves and how their acts should be interpreted. In a review of the film adaptation, Petr Lukeš notes: 'the antipathy of the heroes towards the regime is a matter of course, we do not witness any hesitation or doubt'.[36] The resistant gestures of Šabach's characters always reaffirm their a priori anticommunist stance, which the text assumes the reader shares with them.

The novella is a nostalgic celebration of the pleasures of youth and the narrator repeatedly reminds the reader that no matter what the circumstances, being young was always fun: 'Those were good times. Hangovers were usually laughable, one just threw up a bit in the morning and then simply went on. What more can one wish for?'[37] To an extent, Šabach thus uses the most obvious mechanism for generating nostalgia, namely reminiscing about youth gone by. Adolescent rebellion and intergenerational conflict remain timeless themes not tied to any particular political system and much nostalgia looks back at precisely this life stage. However, in Czech representations of socialism, it is not only young people who feel the need to define themselves against authority; this is a feature that serves to elicit sympathy for protagonists of all age groups. An essential ingredient of this nostalgia are thus also the unpleasant, directly oppressive aspects of the regime: the episodic narrative of the book version of *The Identity Card* is structured around the encounters of the narrator and his friends with the police well into adulthood and details the ways in which they, through more or less petty heroic gestures, managed to outwit the authorities. The text thus nostalgically captures the excitement that carrying out semi-legal activities afforded in an authoritarian regime.

To an extent, these activities seem devoid of any conscious political meaning in particular in the early stages of the narrative – the characters' actions are motivated simply through an apparently innate teenage desire to rebel. Resistance is portrayed as peer pressure, as a means of achieving appreciation in one's friendship group. For example, the narrator's friend Venca suggests to the group that, just like his older brother, they should all tear out page thirteen from their identity card booklets, because 'the thirteenth congress of the KSČ is coming up, and if you have page thirteen torn out, it means: I disagree with the regime!'[38] When the rest of the group are somewhat taken aback by this, it transpires that Venca was boasting too much: 'All of my brother's mates tore *the edge* of page number thirteen'.[39] Reminiscent of Danny Smiřický's petty motives for wanting to become a hero, the attempted act of heroism is humorously deflated by Venca's admission that he is essentially only trying to imitate his brother (whose heroism is also put into question by not going as far as to tear out the whole page) rather than extending a genuine political gesture. Nevertheless, it is precisely the regime, with its multitude of rules and limitations, which is nostalgically looked back upon as a facilitator of teenage rebellion, as it always provided clear boundaries of what was permissible and what already bore the irresistible tinge of resistance. Thus, the narrator can be satisfied with his circumstances, commenting on the group's attendance at the youth festival Majáles, known for its liberal atmosphere in the 1960s: 'We were fourteen years old and we thought: "Yeah, this is exactly it! We're in the right place to be alive!"'[40]

According to this logic, the more strictures the regime imposes, the easier it is to display resistance. Thus, as the story moves beyond the pivotal year of 1968, the repression of Normalization only reinforces the narrative structure, as now, in the new hardline regime, the police represent even more obviously something against which the characters can define themselves. As one reviewer noted, the narrative drive arises from 'the need to boast about dangers overcome, about how difficult the situations we have managed to live through were, and with how many absurdities we met in their course'.[41] Even once the story moves into the characters' adulthood, the narrator still brags that he holds the neighbourhood record in the number of times he was brought to the police station. It is thus no surprise that screenwriter Petr Jarchovský and director Ondřej Trojan chose to set the 2010 film adaptation in the 1970s only, the more hardline time of Normalization, which also provides the very readily visually recognizable framework for portraying resistance in the form of the underground music movement, with which the protagonists sympathize, marked by long hair and a distinctive dress style.[42]

If resistant gestures aim at ultimately overthrowing the regime, then the stories they tell about the present should be different from the ones told about socialism. Yet the picture is somewhat more complicated: examples of petty heroism express a nostalgia for a perpetually resistant way of life, which ostensibly aims at ending socialism, but paradoxically thrives on its own sense of oppositional purpose. When songwriter Jiří Dědeček, in a well-known song from the early 1990s, ironically demands 'Give me back my enemy',[43] he taps into the phenomenon of a longing for a time when boundaries were clearly defined and 'good' and 'evil' stood in stark opposition, granting actors a sense of purpose and identity.

In *The Identity Card*, Šabach captures how characters deal with this paradox in post-1989 realities: the police – the bane of the characters throughout their teenage years and twenties – still represent power which the ordinary person must resist; they are still the butt of jokes. An illustrative example is an episode set in 2005, where the group of friends discuss the police over beer in the pub, which reveals that Venca, whom we encountered earlier in the heroic gesture of tearing his identity card, now describes himself as neurotic because every time he sees a policeman, he reflexively reaches for his identification papers. Likewise, other characters complain that policemen are corrupt and ask for bribes. The narrator nostalgically reminisces about 'Good old, Rusňák',[44] referring to the overzealous officer who terrorized his group of friends in the 1960s. The characters need the police to function in the same way as under the previous regime for the construction of their identities. If anything, such self-construction was easier under socialism, and the characters use it to retrospectively validate their resistant credentials. The grammar of the narrator's utterances now changes to the past conditional – had I been this, I would have done that. The nostalgia of petty heroism thus lies in a set of values that were lost with the changes of the new liberal democratic regime and that the characters struggle to reconstruct.

Šabach's ability to generate nostalgia rests on the total identification he expects with his protagonists from the reader. We laugh with the protagonists when they make a good joke, but their behaviour is never exposed as ridiculous in the same way as that of the police, whom we laugh at. The petty heroism of the characters reconfirms a binary vision of the past where, as reviewer Aleš Smutný has effectively captured it, 'the communists and their sympathizers are either unconditionally stupid, insidious, or ugly, or a combination of all of the above. On the other hand, those who resist the regime are noble, vulnerable, humane and in their core kind and understanding … One then has to ask where these communists came from, if they were all so stupid and primitive'.[45] The kind of anticommunism that Dousková promoted under the veneer of nostalgia for the rituals and symbols of socialism is here inscribed into the very narrative structure of Šabach's text: in order to sympathize with the protagonists, the reader is automatically placed on the 'right' side of those who resisted the regime. Each exploit of the characters against authority constitutes a self-enclosed episode, and it is these episodes of resistance that enable the timespan of Normalization to be structured and narrated. Ondřej Trojan's film adaptation only underscores this episodic structure by transposing Šabach's narrative into the 1970s, thus avoiding representing the grand historical narrative of 1968.

Nostalgia for resistance is certainly not unique to the Czech Republic and, indeed, as nostalgia finds a grateful locus in the period of youth and its accompanying rebellion against authority, it is somewhat thematically inevitable as a longing for a time that will never return. Yet this phenomenon has received little attention, despite numerous examples. Russian retrospective representations of the Soviet Union have employed this mechanism: the rebellion of the *stilyagi*, fashionable urban youths in 1950s Moscow in Valery Todorovsky's eponymous film (2008), against the uniformity and conformism of the Komsomol structures much of the narrative; in *The House of the Sun* (*Dom Solntsa*, dir. Garik Sukachev, 2010), Sasha, a girl from a well-placed Moscow family, is seduced by the countercultural appeal of the hippy Solntsa and his gang; the Polish film *All That I Love* (*Wszystko, co kocham*, dir. Jacek Borcuch, 2009) also sees some of the happiest moments of the main protagonist Janek's adolescence take place as he achieves recognition and self-realization in a politically subversive punk band.

Even more similarly to *The Identity Card*, Leander Haußmann's *Sun Alley* (*Sonnenallee*, 1999), perhaps the inaugural film of the German *Ostalgie* wave, is predicated on main character Micha and his friends' opposition to the local border guard in their East Berlin street, who intentionally makes life difficult for them. Yet the *Ostalgie* literature does not identify this nostalgia for opposition against the regime as a significant feature in the debate, and the kind of underlying anticommunist dynamic observed in Czech representations of socialism lacks attention in the German context. Interpretations of nostalgia in Germany focus on salvaging the positive aspects of the GDR, such as its social values of a promise of a more just society and the antihegemonic resuscitation of socialist-era consumer products; they fail to recognize that the negative aspects of state socialism can generate a nostalgia of their own kind.

Postsocialist nostalgia is thus able to find an unlikely object, in that it turns to the repressive aspects of the regime. It idealizes a fictional community of anticommunists, to whom this mechanism ascribes moral value through representation. Two dimensions are key for such an interpretation of the past: first, the choice of genre, namely comedy, which by way of humour offers a conciliatory view of the past through attempts at resistance most often in the form of a joke or prank. Second, these representations work with an understanding of resistance that rejects the notion of heroism as exception: resistant gestures are available to most characters, including at times those who are implicated in the state's structures of power, though we may doubt their sincerity or laugh at their inefficacy.

Politically, nostalgic representations participate in a wider discursive strategy that seeks to find perpetrators of 'the system'. They cast out communists, while generating a nonparticipatory image of socialism for 'ordinary' people. The motif of petty heroism is used as an expiating gesture, while the simultaneous failure of resistance also acts as an implicit excuse for the longevity of the regime, which is perpetuated by 'someone else', but not 'us', a category into which representations invite readers and viewers. By presenting characters who themselves did not contribute to sustaining the regime's power, these comic portrayals of socialism contribute to generating a cultural memory that bolsters the trope of widespread 'inner resistance' – a discrepancy between public acquiescence and private disagreement. Through petty heroism, protagonists find themselves quietly resisting, with small and sometimes bigger gestures, though generally with a whimper rather than a bang.

Notes

1. I. Dousková, *Hrdý Budžes* (Prague: Hynek, 1998). English translation: I. Dousková, *B. Proudew*, trans. M. Clarke (Brno: Pálava Publishing, 2016).
2. A. Dušková, 'A Hrdý Budžes vytrval' ['And B. Proudew Persisted'], *Literární noviny* 10(4) (1999), 7. See also M. Jungmann, 'NEON stále bez záře' ['NEON Still without Glow'], *Týden* 6(8) (1999), 59; A. Hama, 'Poláčkovské téma z jiné perspektivy' ['A Poláčkian

Topic from a Different Perspective'], *Nové knihy* 39(1) (1999), 4; J. Brabec, 'Druhá původní novinka...' ['Second Original New Book'], *Literární noviny* 10(7) (1999), 16.
3. Fk, 'Hrdý Budžes se stal fenoménem' ['Hrdý Budžes Has Become a Phenomenon'], *Mladá fronta Dnes*, 19 May 2004, 8.
4. For a list of *Thalia* award holders, see http://www.ceny-thalie.cz/historie.php. Retrieved 26 August 2019.
5. I. Dousková, *Oněgin byl Rusák* (Brno: Druhé město, 2006).
6. As of the end of 2019, *B. Proudew* still regularly featured in the programme of the Theatre without Ballustrades in Prague. *Onegin was a Rusky* finished its almost ten-year run at Prague's Theatre in Dlouhá in June 2017.
7. J.P. Kříž, 'Budžes nebyl indián ani partyzán' ['Budžes Was Neither an Indian nor a Partisan'], *Právo*, 18 December 2002, 15; Ondřej Horák, 'Další nemilé věci Helenky Součkové' ['Helenka Součková's Further Displeasing Things'], *Lidové noviny*, 11 April 2006, 18; P. Mandys, 'Mladá intelektuálka, úchylové, komouši' ['A Young Intellectual, Perves and Commies'], *Týden*, 10 April 2006, 84.
8. J. Machalická, 'Nelze donekonečna dolovat humor z absurdit socialismu' ['It's Not Possible to Mine Jokes out of the Absurdities of Socialism Forever'], *Lidové noviny*, 14 November 2002, 25.
9. '... mi nechce dovolit chodit do jiskřiček, protože jiskřičky a pionýři jsou prý malý komunisti. Tak já nevím, z naší třídy tam chodí celá třída a já bych tam taky chtěla chodit.' I. Dousková, *Hrdý Budžes* (Brno: Petrov, 2002), 9. English tanslation by Melvyn Clarke. I Dousková, *B. Proudew* (Brno: Pálava Publishing, 2106), 15–16.
10. F. Žák, 'Příbramská Helenka pobouřila komunisty' ['Příbram's Helenka Has Angered Communists'], *Příbramský deník*, 22 April 2004, 15.
11. 'JEZTE HODNĚ – NEBUDE.' I. Dousková, *Oněgin byl Rusák* (Brno: Druhé město, 2006), 211. English translation by Melvyn Clarke: I Dousková, *Onegin Was a Rusky* (Brno: Pálava Publishing, 2018), 236.
12. K. Činátl, 'Časy normalizace', in P.A. Bílek and B. Činátlová (eds), *Tesilová kavalérie: popkulturní obrazy normalizace* (Příbram: Pistorius and Olšanská, 2010), 166–87 (167).
13. A. Imre, 'Why Should We Study Socialist Commercials?', *VIEW Journal of European Television History and Culture* 3(2) (2012), 65–76 (75).
14. V. Havel, 'Příběh a totalita' in V. Havel, *Eseje a jiné texty z let 1970–1989: Dálkový výslech* (Prague: Torst, 1999), 931–59 (937).
15. S. Bechmann Pedersen, *Reel Socialism: Making Sense of History in Czech and German Cinema since 1989* (Lund: Lund University/Media-Tryck, 2015), 242.
16. Paulina Bren argues that after 1968, the mutually interdependent desire of state and people for normality led to the widespread ethos of a 'quiet life', which meant 'not merely acceptance of what was most certainly another descriptive cliché of the time – people's political apathy – but the state's active endorsement of it. The call for calm and order, and the way in which it became synonymous with normalization, was not merely programmatic; it was also ideological'. See P. Bren, *The Greengrocer and His TV: The Culture of Communism after the 1968 Prague Spring* (Ithaca: Cornell University Press, 2010), 89.
17. A. Liehm, 'The New Social Contract and the Parallel Polity', in J. Leftwich Curry (ed.), *Dissent in Eastern Europe* (New York: Praeger, 1983), 172–81. See also L. Kopeček, *Éra nevinnosti: Česká politika 1989–1997* (Brno: Barrister and Principal, 2010), 11; M. Otáhal, *Opozice, moc, společnost 1969–1989: příspěvek k dějinám 'normalizace'* (Prague: Ústav pro soudobé dějiny AV ČR, 1994), 33.

18. The argument that the Normalization regime drew its legitimacy from a particular form of social consensus is put forward succinctly by Michal Pullmann in his book *Konec Experimentu: přestavba a pád komunismu v Československu* (Prague: Scriptorum, 2011).
19. Bren, *The Greengrocer and His TV*, 174.
20. J. Machalická et al., 'Vyprávěj: policejní režim s lidskou tváří' ['Vyprávěj: A Police Regime with a Human Face'], *Lidové noviny*, 30 October 2010, 28.
21. J. Mikulášek and D. Viceníková, *Šedá sedmdesátá aneb Husákovo ticho*. Theatre on the Balustrades, dir. Jan Mikulášek, 2013.
22. P. Juráček, *Zlatá šedesátá aneb Deník Pavla J*. Theatre on the Balustrades, dir. Jan Mikulášek, 2013.
23. Havel, 'Příběh a totalita', 953–56.
24. Anton Baláž, *Len jedna jar* (Bratislava: Marenčin PT, 2013).
25. P. Kolář, 'Čtyři "základní rozpory" východoevropského komunismu', in P. Kolář and M. Pullmann (eds), *Co byla normalizace? Studie o pozdním socialismu* (Prague: Nakladatelství Lidové noviny and Ústav pro studium totalitních režimů, 2017), 132–34.
26. These adaptations include *Jackal Years* (*Šakalí léta*, dir. Jan Hřebejk, 1993); *Cosy Dens* (*Pelíšky*, dir. Jan Hřebejk, 1999); *Pupendo* (dir. Jan Hřebejk, 2003); *The Identity Card* (*Občanský průkaz*, dir. Ondřej Trojan, 2010).
27. Činátl, 'Časy normalizace', 167.
28. Petr Šabach, *Občanský průkaz* (Prague and Litomyšl: Paseka, 2006).
29. For further discussion of *The Identity Card*, see V. Pehe, 'Drobné hrdinství: Vzdor jakožto předmět nostalgie v díle Petra Šabacha a Michala Viewegha', *Česká literatura* 63(3) (2015), 419–34.
30. 'Později, když si střetnutí znovu rekapitulovali, se nedokázali shodnout, kdo z nich pronásledovaného dramatika uviděl jako první a měl tedy včas vyhlásit signál k ústupu.' M. Viewegh, *Báječná léta pod psa* (Prague: Český spisovatel, 1995), 126–27. Trans. D. Short, *Bliss Was It in Bohemia* (London: Jantar Publishing, 2015), 153.
31. '"Kdybych se chtěl přátelit s oponenty režimu, mohl jsem zůstat v Praze", hořekoval naoko Kvidův otec, trochu okouzlený vlastní občanskou odvahou.' Ibid., 130; translation *Bliss Was It in Bohemia*, 157.
32. A. Yurchak, *Everything Was Forever, Until It Was No More: The Last Soviet Generation* (Princeton: Princeton University Press, 2006), 250–51.
33. For instance, Radko Pytlík, who has written extensively on Hašek and Švejk, offers an extremely positive interpretation of the character when he claims that Švejk is 'an expression of a generous, deep humanity, which is connected with the transfer from an old world into a new one'. R. Pytlík, *Jaroslav Hašek a Dobrý voják Švejk* (Prague: Panorama, 1983), 60.
34. J. Škvorecký, *The Cowards*, trans. Jeanne Němcová (Harmondsworth: Penguin, 1972), 27.
35. A phrase coined by George Orwell to describe a joke which 'in some way that is not actually offensive or frightening … upsets the established order'. G. Orwell, 'Funny, But Not Vulgar', in S. Orwell and I. Angus (eds), *The Collected Essays, Journalism and Letters of George Orwell: Vol. 3, As I Please, 1943–1945* (London: Secker and Warburg, 1968), 283–88 (284).
36. P. Lukeš, 'Bylo nebylo' ['Once Upon a Time'], *Host* 1 (2011), 96.
37. 'To byly dobrý časy. Kocoviny bejvávaly v tý době většinou k smíchu, člověk si ráno prostě ublink a pak zas pokračoval dál. Co víc si člověk může přát?' P. Šabach, *Občanský průkaz* (Prague and Litomyšl: Paseka, 2006), 43.

38. '… teď bude třináctej sjezd ká es čé, a když máš vytrženou stránku třináct, tak to znamená: Nesouhlasím s režimem!' Ibid., 8.
39. 'Všichni kámoši mýho bráchy si natrhli stránku číslo třináct.' Ibid., 9 (emphasis added).
40. 'Bylo nám čtrnáct a říkali sme si: "Jo, přesně tohle je vono. Sme na správným místě k žití!"' Ibid., 34.
41. E.F. Juříková, 'O esenbácích, estébácích a dalších fízlech', *Host* 12(9) (2006), 37.
42. The film was a moderate success, ranking eleventh in audience figures for the year.
43. 'Give me back my enemy.' J. Dědeček and J. Burian, *Vraťte nám nepřítele* (Panton – SP, 1990), compact disc.
44. Šabach, *Občanský průkaz*, 174.
45. A. Smutný, 'Občanský průkaz', *Cinema* 20(11) (2010), 24.

Chapter 5

THE POLITICS AND AESTHETICS OF RETRO

Throughout the previous chapters, retro has repeatedly made an appearance as a stylistic repertoire and reception mechanism in the cultural memory of socialism. This chapter gathers together these strands that have been running throughout the book so far to conceptualize retro in both its aesthetic and political dimensions. I have already suggested that retro captures more adequately the relationship to the past witnessed in Czech cultural artefacts than the vocabularies associated with the nostalgia paradigm, if understood as a postmodern, ironic, tongue-in-cheek and unsentimental form of appropriating the past. While cursory attempts have been made to understand various appropriations of the socialist past as retro in other national contexts, the concept lacks a more systematic theorization. This is surprising, as retro also proves relevant as a designation for a particular relationship towards the past outside the postsocialist space and applies not just to representations, but also to material artefacts.

Generally seen as a postmodern phenomenon by scholars, retro shares postmodernism's scepticism towards grand narratives.[1] But retro is not just a postmodern version of nostalgia; it is a memory regime in its own right. The term's usefulness lies in its temporal dynamic: unlike the sense of historical rupture and loss posited by nostalgia, what unites retro in both material culture and artistic representations is an effort to integrate the past into a continuum with the present. Much like the culture of Normalization discussed in the previous chapter, retro refuses to read socialism as grand narrative; the stories it is able to tell are necessarily small and episodic. For this reason, retro is most suited to recounting uneventful periods such as the perceived 'timelessness' of Normalization rather than the era of building socialism of the 1950s with its grand narrative of creating a better society. This chapter examines retro's pervasiveness, but also the limits of its representational potential: emotionally wrought moments and grand historical narratives, such as the crushing of the Prague Spring in 1968, do not lend themselves to being rendered through retro's ironic detachment.

As a mode of appropriating the past, retro has received some attention in the post-Soviet context. Kevin Platt, writing about the 'New Wave' song competition – the post-Soviet answer to Eurovision – observes that what distinguishes retro from nostalgia is its projection of a sense of continuity between the past it returns to and the present moment from which this past is narrated. In Platt's words, 'whereas nostalgia is out of sync with time's flow, retro is at home in time – able to reach back into the past in order to reproduce in unproblematic fashion what was'.[2] As we saw in Chapter 3, the Czech cultural memory of socialism is also able to integrate socialist popular culture into the fabric of present-day values through rhetorical strategies of accommodation. In contrast to the break of nostalgia, retro does not necessarily play on a sense of absence, but on the availability of the past for reappropriation and pastiche. This is made possible by the firm retrospective view with which retro operates, where the present order is posited as the *telos* towards which earlier histories always strove.

Selling the Past

Unlike nostalgia, retro captures a relationship to the past devoid of affect. It is precisely this unemotional approach that allows for irreverent appropriations that can exploit symbols associated with the repressive aspects of communist regimes, as seen in the souvenir industry with its plethora of Soviet-themed memorabilia, or indeed in a TV series like *Major Zeman*. This lack of emotion ostensibly leads, to an extent, to a levelling of hierarchies of value; in her exploration of the culture of fashion and style revivals, Elizabeth Guffey has argued that retro pillages the past at random, applying a pick-and-mix attitude.[3] While such an interpretation can lead to the unexciting conclusion that retro is the ultimate symptom of a postmodern malaise of meaninglessness, other scholars have attempted to reclaim retro's critical potential. Looking at material culture, Sarah Elsie Baker argues that rather than decontextualization, the valuation of certain objects as retro involves recontextualization and the production of new meanings.[4] In other words, retro does have an implicit framework of values. In the context of furnishings that Baker examines, these values are tied to class taste; only members of particular social classes with sufficient cultural capital are able to recontextualize old pieces of furniture that would appear simply outdated among other groups and use them, in Bourdieu's sense, as a marker of distinction.

Indeed, it was material culture that led to initial theorizations of retro in relation to the art nouveau revival in Great Britain in the 1960s. Much of the debates on postsocialist nostalgia have also focused on material objects and consumer products, yet their discussion as retro is largely absent from the literature on *Ostalgie* and other national contexts. This is a striking absence, as some of the phenomena subsumed under *Ostalgie* would benefit from being clearly identified as retro. Westerners appropriating Eastern products as 'hip', various tongue-in-cheek kitsch artefacts mocking the symbols of communist repression, cafés that nod to the design of the previous era – all of these share the assumption that the position from which they narrate the past is 'knowing'. They do not return to this past to nostalgically wallow in better times gone by, but to assert that consumers have arrived in a position of confidence from which the past is exploited at will.

Of course, many critics have also read the enduring popularity of East German consumer products as a sign of a genuine sentimental attachment to the previous regime. While the validity of such explanations must not be underestimated, we should also not forget that the consumption of socialist-era or socialist-themed products is embedded in market practices, and even the utopian dimension of socialism has been co-opted into capitalist marketing as a selling point. Maya Nadkarni and Olga Shevchenko effectively demonstrate this point when they argue that during state socialism, the West was imagined as a consumer paradise. 'The characteristics of this utopia, however, were markedly socialist in that this abundance was fantasized as available to everyone',[5] Nadkarni and Shevchenko write. That this fantasy of equality was purely utopian became apparent in the post-1989 era, which brought stark inequalities in wealth distribution: 'As a result, once-disparaged items of socialist mass production have acquired the authenticity that Western products are now perceived to lack. They are now embraced as vehicles of the once-utopian dreams and desires for the idealized West.'[6] In the Czech case, this perceived authenticity builds on the notion of tradition, which similarly to the continuity narrative prevalent in appropriations of socialist popular culture integrates socialist-era products into a larger story of Czechoslovak manufacturing history.

Illustrative of this point are the shoe brand Botas and the soft drink Kofola. Manufactured by the eponymous shoe company from Skuteč in Eastern Bohemia, together with the Prestige trainer from Zlín, Botas effectively held a monopoly on sports footwear in Czechoslovakia.[7] In fact, the Czech term *botasky* has come to stand in for any type of sports shoe, much like 'hoover' is used to designate a vacuum cleaner in Britain. While Botas seemed to be one of those socialist brands that would find it difficult to survive in the face of competition after 1989, the company received an unexpected boost when two students from Prague's Academy of Arts, Architecture and Design chose to rework the classic 1966 model of Botas trainers as part of an assignment in 2008.[8] The designers kept the original shape of the shoe practically intact, but updated the model in terms of colours and materials. The shoes were widely hailed as an example of retro in the press,[9] which commented on the unexpected appeal of the new collection to the young generation, while also retaining some charm for those who remembered and wore the original model. As one commentator put it, 'the shoes may be intended for the young, but their parents or grandparents are happy to give them money for them, for instance out of nostalgia'.[10]

This kind of generational exchange, in which the past is consumed mainly as a style, lends itself to a retro reception, which can be understood as a sensibility in relation to the past akin to Raymond Williams's structure of feeling. Williams posits that a structure of feeling is a set of dominant perceptions and values in a particular generation that manifest chiefly in the cultural production of a period.[11] In this sense, retro as a structure of feeling can be viewed both as a particular response to the socialist past shared across members of a generation that came of age at the very end of socialism or only after its demise and as an aesthetic inscribed in representations of the past produced by this generation. The concept of structure of feeling provides a loose enough framework to be able to speak about a recognizable general sensibility – one not imbued with any particularly strong sentiment towards the past in this case – available to members of a generation as well as those observing the generation from the outside, without suggesting that such an attitude must necessarily be universal across that generation.[12] Retro thus appeals not only to those for whom objects, fashions and music of the past act as memory triggers; its lack of experiential investment in the period allows for precisely the kind of distance that facilitates irony and thus enables an appreciation of the playful and at times irreverent appropriation of the past.

Botas presents its trainers as a traditional Czech product. The brand's website explicitly places the shoes in a larger family of quality products of the socialist era: 'BOTAS shoes together with the Kofola drink as well as Supraphon recordings belong to the high-quality products made in our country in the period of normalization.'[13] The focus shifts away from the shoes as mementoes of socialism to the brand as a representative of tradition, where it no longer matters when exactly the product in question was inaugurated. This marketing strategy focused on 'time-tested quality' may seem counter-intuitive at first: if anything, socialist products were perceived as deficient compared to those manufactured to the west of the Iron Curtain.

Historian Martin Franc explains this by the fact that after 1948, two parallel cycles of manufacture developed: one for the domestic and the other for the export market. Inevitably, some export products made their way back on to the domestic market (and could be purchased for hard currency in the specialist *Tuzex* chain of shops), and this possibility of comparison made domestic products come out unfavourably.[14] Films like *Cosy Dens* (*Pelíšky*, dir. Jan Hřebejk, 1999), discussed in Chapter 3, draw much of their comedy precisely from the laughable inadequacy of socialist products. However, *Ostalgie* literature speaks to a valuation of GDR objects if not as quality, then as durable and time-proven.[15]

Botas presents itself as part of local production (the designers insisted that all materials should be manufactured in the Czech Republic),[16] and through its surrounding discourse of tradition paints socialism and its culture as embedded in a larger narrative of Czech history (Figure 5.1). While a temporal-historical distancing is required for objects to be identified as retro (and in the Czech case the events of 1989 conveniently provide such a distancing), at the same time, retro sutures this break by projecting a continuity; it returns to a moment from the past that has not been lost, but, on the contrary, to which a direct link can be traced – hence the emphasis in the press on the fact that Botas had never, in fact, stopped manufacturing shoes before receiving its redesign boost. Given the emphasis on national tradition, it is perhaps not surprising that some of the bestselling models of the new Botas 66 range were ones decorated with national symbols such as the Czech Lion or presented in national colours.[17]

Figure 5.1 Botas store, Prague. The sign in the window reads 'Traditional Czech Product'. Photo by the author.

A similar discourse can be witnessed around the soft drink Kofola, which the Botas website quotes as another traditional brand of the socialist era. Czechoslovakia's alternative to Coca Cola, Kofola was first manufactured in the early 1960s. While Western cola-style drinks gained a large share of the market after 1989, Kofola made a successful comeback in the early 2000s.[18] The press once again remarked how popular this product was with the younger generation who had hardly experienced socialism.[19] Kofola was marketed predominantly as a product bringing back the era of the 1960s. The 1960s theme was also used in the drink's fiftieth anniversary campaign, which introduced a short advertising spot that re-enacted a fictional story of the invention of the drink in period costume. As Franc points out, 'the 1960s – the thaw, echoes of the hippie movement descending from beyond the borders, the success of domestic cinema – that is the ideal exploited by both *Kofola* and *Botas*'.[20]

But retro does not focus only on resurrecting quality and tradition and does not shy away from the repressive aspects of the previous regime, which it renders harmless through ironic distancing and ridicule. The work of acclaimed Czech designer Maxim Velčovský (born 1976), characterized by playful pastiche of socialist-era objects and styles, is a pertinent example of the ways in which a retro aesthetic is consciously exploited in a process that takes inspiration from lowbrow forms to create an institutionally validated 'high culture' product. An example of this type of work is his porcelain bust of Lenin entitled 'Ornament and Crime', the face of the leader covered with a traditional 'blue onion' pattern, which Velčovský perceives as 'the ornamental symbol of Bohemia'.[21] At the same time, he has also appropriated objects of everyday use and design icons from the socialist era and set them in porcelain, creating, for instance, a candleholder in the shape of a Trabant car, entitled 'Spirit of the East'.

Velčovský takes a generational view, claiming in an interview that while the older generation fought for higher goals in 1989, his generation demanded coke in a can.[22] It is this consumerist dimension that also contributes to retro as a structure of feeling for the generation that Velčovský describes. If Velčovský's work can be seen to have an affective aspect at all, then it presents nostalgia for a more authentic consumerism as described by Nadkarni and Shevchenko, while itself dispensing with the egalitarian dimension of consumption under socialism it references (Velčovský's works sell for hundreds of pounds). But the appeal of Velčovský's design lies in 'kitschfying' the symbols of the past. Although kitsch is conventionally understood as a mark of bad taste, in its conscious employment in the design of these artefacts, it becomes an aspect of irony: 'Spirit of the East' or 'Ornament and Crime' only work if viewers are sufficiently 'in the know', recognizing kitsch as kitsch. The past is once again appropriated from a position of superior knowledge. Retro thus does not suggest a return to the past in order to resurrect aspects of 'better' times; instead, through taking the old and combining it with the new, it posits a linear narrative of progress. I suggest that retro representations work in a similar fashion, granting readers and viewers a position of historical privilege.

Where Memory Becomes Style

Amongst Czech representations of socialism, the film *The Rebels* (*Rebelové*, dir. Filip Renč, 2001) and the series *Tell Me a Story* (*Vyprávěj*, dir. Biser Arichtev, 2009–13), produced in five seasons by Dramedy Productions for Czech Television, are perhaps the most emblematic of retro as both an aesthetic and a relationship towards the past. The film and TV series are both successful examples of their respective forms – *The Rebels* was the fourth most-watched film in cinemas in 2001, seen by almost 400,000 people, while the Czech Television series had consistently high ratings, especially in its first season.[23] Though different in form, these artefacts lend themselves to comparison as they share a number of themes in terms of their content, as well as a host of stylistic devices. Both turn to the 1960s and the period of the Warsaw Pact invasion, which they present in a heavily visually stylized manner, exploding with the colours of socialism. *The Rebels* is a musical comedy that constructs its narrative around a pre-existing canon of 1960s songs, detailing the love stories that develop between three teenage girls and three young men who have deserted from military service. *Tell Me a Story*, on the other hand, is a soap opera that follows the stories of three generations of an 'average' family from 1964 onwards. By this, the series' makers meant, as producer Filip Bobiński summarized for the daily newspaper *Hospodářské noviny*, characters who were neither committed communists nor fought against the regime.[24]

Both the film and TV series are also united in making more than just a nod to the country's shared past with Slovakia. *The Rebels* does so by featuring a Slovak as one of the fleeing soldiers. However, the character of the shy and sensitive Eman does little more than acknowledge that Czechoslovakia was indeed a country shared by both Czechs and Slovaks, and mines a few jokes out of the differences between the Czech and Slovak languages. *Tell Me a Story*, on the other hand, is one of the few post-1989 Czech representations that engages more fully with the common Czechoslovak past. The central family of the Dvořáks comprises a Czech husband and a Slovak wife, other Slovak-speaking characters regularly feature on the show, and the heroine Eva switches freely between spoken Czech and Slovak depending on the situation. Yet the apparent shared memory is narrated from a deeply Czech perspective. Like many Czech representations of socialism, it focuses on

Prague. To an extent, this preponderance for setting narratives about the past in the capital arose from their literary origins: several of the representations discussed in this book are based on Petr Šabach's autobiographical works of prose, in which he reminisces about his childhood and adolescence in the capital. While *Tell Me a Story* is not connected to Šabach in any way, setting the story of this long-format TV series, which structures many of its plots around particular socialist practices and consumer products, in the capital city enabled the creators to display a wide array of features of everyday life under socialism. In contrast, the story's Slovak aspect is depicted in a strikingly exoticizing manner. Episodes featuring visits to Eva's family in a remote Slovak village often focus on the comedy of the culture shock her Czech husband Karel experiences, especially when he cannot keep up with the pace at which the locals down juniper brandy. Slovakia as exotic Other is compounded by the musical accompaniment in these episodes, which feature a recurring motif from a traditional Slovak folk song, positing rural Slovakia and its inhabitants as folksy, salt-of-the earth, but also somewhat backward characters. The supposed Czechoslovakism of *Tell Me a Story* thus speaks mainly to a Czech imaginary where Slovakia figures as periphery. In this, *Tell Me Story* is not in any way exceptional to how the shared memory of Czechoslovakia has featured in Czech culture.

Renč's 'song-filled retro-film' (*písničkový retrofilm*), on the other hand, is exceptional at least in its choice of genre, with musicals appearing relatively rarely in post-1989 Czech film production. The story of summer love is constructed in such a way as to justify and accommodate the inclusion of a number of well-known 1960s pop songs. Referencing not only the music itself, *The Rebels* also refers to the 1960s Czechoslovak musical as a genre, and the songs' original transmission in the form of television songs (*televizní písničky*), the Czechoslovak precursor to the music video, with their angular decorations in a studio setting. The film is thus oversaturated with references to the popular culture of the 1960s. But not all of the numbers in the film feature period recordings: certain tracks were rerecorded by the film's actors, while the rest were used in their original versions as performed by artists such as Josef Zíma, Waldemar Matuška and Olympic. This mixing of original product and reconstruction is also typical of the visual strategy of both the film and the TV series. The camp visuals of the film make use of the aesthetic of retrochic, which, as Raphael Samuel argues, references historical styles, but remains contemporary.[25] Like *Jackal Years* (*Šakalí léta*, dir. Jan Hřebejk, 1993), in which we could first observe this feature in Chapter 2, *The Rebels* updates the colour palette of the 1960s to give costumes a present-day appeal (Figure 5.2).

The visualization of the past in *Tell Me a Story* is also less concerned with historical accuracy than it is with packaging the series in a visually attractive

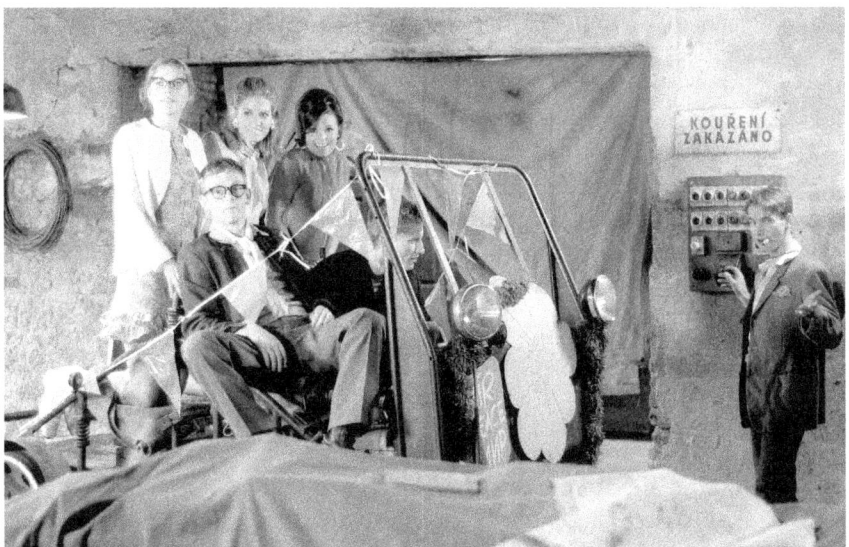

Figure 5.2 *Rebelové* (*The Rebels*), Filip Renč (director, screenwriter) and Zdeněk Zelenka (screenwriter), 2001. © Image S Pro Alfa Film.

retro-look. The full-hued costumes, chic hairstyles and bright make-up the characters wear are primarily designed to appeal to a contemporary audience. Hence the costumes often employ not only period polyester and other synthetic fibres, but also present-day, evidently higher-quality materials. Costume shapes and cuts also introduce a twenty-first-century aspect. In an interview, the costume designer of the series, Libuše Pražáková, emphasized that this was a deliberate strategy in the visual packaging of *Tell Me a Story*: 'In spite of my memories, I went in for more colours. The producers also asked me to try to achieve a close successive relation between the clothing and today's fashions, so that young spectators would recognize themselves in it, just as in the music.'[26] The visual style of the series thus deliberately modernizes past looks for contemporary appeal.

The serial form of *Tell Me a Story*, with its long-run format of twenty-seven fifty-minute episodes in the first season, necessarily incorporates a wider range of techniques for evoking the past than *The Rebels*. The series is structured around the interplay of large historical and small personal events, represented by four generations of the Dvořák family. In order to give their stories historical grounding, each episode is framed by two segments of archival footage. This footage anchors each episode in contemporary political events, but often also reminds viewers of period music, theatre or film. Kamil Činátl observes the importance of media within the fictional world of the series: passing shots of television screens in the characters' apartments frequently offer a glimpse of popular stars of the day, and scenes are often accompanied by period hits playing intradiegetically on the radio.[27] The incorporation of historical pop-culture examples into the daily lives of the fictional protagonists serves to raise the credibility of the narrative of their everyday experiences. Visually stylized to a lesser degree than *The Rebels*, *Tell Me a Story* nevertheless features a plethora of period markers. The retro aesthetic of the series manifests itself in an eclectic evocation of the past, where material and popular culture, and informal practices, are displayed with a kind of frenzy: a single episode may draw attention to obtaining under-the-counter goods or dwell with narratively redundant shots on design details such as the shape of beer bottles or display posters of Western pop stars. The level of stylization is already evident from the opening credits of the series, which (literally) frame the past with whimsical period objects. Socialism is figured through an overabundance of period markers, which represent the past, but do not aim to re-create it accurately.

The visual style of *Tell Me a Story* thus works analogously to the musical aspects of *The Rebels*, which employ both old and new recordings and sit between periodization and contemporaneity. On both the production design and the musical level, these texts function as pastiche, which selects recognizable elements from precursors and models. As Richard Dyer remarks, a characteristic of pastiche is that 'for it to work, it needs to be "got" as a pastiche. In this sense, it is an aspect of irony. This implies particular competencies on the part of the audiences'.[28] Recognizing references is a powerful tool for creating a multilayered viewing community. That the period music used captured the attention of viewers was also shown on the discussion page of the series' website.[29] At the time of the series' airing, the website featured a lively discussion board, where one of the most frequent type of posts saw users asking for details of songs that were played in various episodes. The key here is the kind of eclecticism with which the past is appropriated. In this sense, it is no surprise that representations such as *The Rebels* and *Tell Me a Story* occasionally reach to pop culture references that are anachronistic. Markers of the past are exploited without regard for periodization.

Nevertheless, the aesthetic project of *The Rebels* and *Tell Me a Story* differs from more demonstrably postmodern attempts at dealing with the past, such as the 2008 Russian film *Hipsters* (*Stilyagi*, dir. Valery Todorovsky, 2008). Visually reminiscent of *The Rebels* with its loud colours, Todorovsky's film is also a musical comedy, which returns to 1950s Moscow. Songs are used indiscriminately, with the 1950s musically figured in 'anything goes' style 'through a collage of musical numbers in which cult underground rock numbers from the eighties are put to original lyrics pertaining to the plot'.[30] *The Rebels* and *Tell Me a Story*, despite not always respecting chronology, are much stricter in their use of music that can be identified as roughly from the period the film and series represent. Especially the first few episodes of *Tell Me a Story*, which feature a subplot revolving around the main protagonist Karel's band, rehearse the same catalogue of 1960s songs that also featured in *The Rebels*, including the well-known and beloved numbers *Oliver Twist* and *Hvězda na vrbě* (The Star on the Willow Tree). The inclusion of these particular songs suggests that they are not only part of a shared canon, but that they also assume the role of 'quality' products here. The fact that the soundtrack to *The Rebels* became the bestselling album in the Czech Republic in 2001 indicates that the reintroduction and recontextualization of 1960s pop captured the imagination of a wide cross-generational audience.[31] A cursory survey of responses to the film online on such platforms as the Czechoslovak Film Database also indicates that the songs themselves and their restaging were privileged by users of these websites over the actual narrative of the film.

What I identified as the 'quality narrative' in responses to the rescreening of the *Thirty Cases of Major Zeman* emerges in the present examples as well as a significant response to the popular culture of the socialist era. Film scholar Jan Čulík offers a variation on this view, rating the music used in *The Rebels* highly: 'The popular songs that the film brings back to the viewers were often remarkable works of art whose genuinely poetic texts were profoundly metaphorical.'[32] The press reception of *The Rebels* also focused on the quality of the music.[33] Both of these responses – just like the marketing of retro products like Botas and Kofola – suggest that the culture of the 1960s, associated as it is with a period of increased artistic freedom of political and cultural liberalization leading up to the Prague Spring, holds a special place in this kind of 'quality narrative' in the Czech context. In its pastiche approach, retro is not necessarily consistent; the culture of the 1960s is clearly positively valued and used as a means of historical authentication by the film and TV series, but this label of quality simultaneously allows the filmmakers to extricate it from the politics of the previous regime, which, as we will see, are treated with an anticommunist levelling of the entire socialist period into a single undifferentiated era of dictatorship.

The political agenda of *The Rebels* and *Tell Me a Story* recedes into the background, as both representations construct narratives that are primarily personal (love stories, family stories). Indeed, communists remain entirely peripheral characters in *The Rebels*; even the schoolteachers as representatives of authority are not explicitly depicted as proponents of the regime. Given that the central premise of the plot rests on three soldiers escaping from military service, the ostensible function of the communist state hovering in the background is to provide a general framework for the fleeing soldiers to rebel against (despite the film's title, this seems to be the only real instance of rebellion) and to introduce the emotionally charged moment of the Warsaw Pact invasion. The interactions of the teenage characters in the summer of

1968 – a moment in Czechoslovak history that tends to be remembered as a time when everyday life was arguably intensely politicized – are not in the least marked by political concerns. The purpose of this observation is not simply to point out an apparent historical inaccuracy in the portrayal of the period (and indeed it is entirely plausible that teenagers in a provincial town were simply not interested in the reform processes of the Prague Spring going on at the state level). *The Rebels* is full of small details that do not fit the historical picture of the 1960s – indeed, the story of three soldiers escaping to an imagined and dreamt-of West while a smear campaign is being conducted against them in the media appears slightly incongruous set in the summer of 1968, when the country had undergone extensive liberalization and legal travel to the West was no longer as highly restricted as it had been in previous years. But it is less important to evaluate a film – especially one that through its genre makes little pretence at realism – against its historical backdrop than to examine what purposes such ahistoricity may serve. As Sune Bechmann Pedersen argues, through ignoring such political contexts, the film performs a 'collapse of 1968 with the Normalization period'.[34] Much like the indiscriminate periodization of the music used, the different stages of Communist Party rule in Czechoslovakia are effectively levelled and nondifferentiated through the film's ahistorical setting. By their very elision of political narratives, representations such as *The Rebels* shape an interpretation of the past that blurs the distinctions between reform socialism and its subsequent suppression (or indeed its previous Stalinist iterations).

Tell Me a Story illustrates this even more clearly. The Dvořák family, in particular the main hero Karel, his father and staunchly anticommunist grandmother, who all prefer to stay out of active politics, present models for living through socialism in a comfortable, yet uncompromising manner. Karel's friend Tonda, on the other hand, who engages in oppositional activities, is not portrayed as favourably; in Season 3, Episode 20, the two friends fall out when Karel accuses Tonda of being an *androš*, a derogatory term for a member of the underground. *Tell Me a Story*'s pedagogy is thus focused on the notion of the 'ordinary person'. There is no doubt as to what the correct ways of living through socialism were, demonstrated for us through the family of the Dvořáks. Karel consistently refuses to give petty bribes, a widespread practice, while his father Josef successfully manoeuvres out of being pressured to join the Communist Party by his boss. Often the subplot of an episode will dramatize precisely such a moral problem and its model resolution: for instance, Season 1, Episode 9 tackles a widely perceived stereotype of state socialism, namely that pilfering from the workplace was socially acceptable behaviour. However, Josef obviously disapproves of his colleague and friend Mirek as he takes home an extra pair of work overalls from the railway depot where they work.

Karel, Josef and his mother Běta are portrayed as sharing an innate democratic sentiment, which structures their principles. Symbolically, this sentiment is embodied in the bust of Tomáš Garrigue Masaryk, Czechoslovakia's first democratic President, in Běta's apartment. Karel is a particularly pertinent example of this: he is above politics, as in his view the communists are not to be trusted, never were and never will be. While the idealist activist and later dissident Tonda ends up in prison for his political activity, Karel's obstinate ignorance of politics even at the height of the Prague Spring, similar to that of the protagonists of *The Rebels*, is portrayed as the most efficient strategy for survival in socialism. When Tonda asks him in the summer of 1968 on a canoeing holiday what he thinks about the political situation, Karel happily replies: 'We're completely cut off from the world here, we don't know anything.'[35] He waits patiently until the fourth season of the series, when the changes of 1989 retrospectively validate his view and he finally sets up his own company in a newfound enterprising zeal. A seemingly apolitical entrepreneur-in-waiting, Karel embodies the Czech national myth that harks back to the democratic and market tradition of the First Republic, suppressed by communist oppression, now making its triumphant comeback. The series' selection and reuse of certain elements of socialist popular culture becomes a mechanism of incorporating the socialist period into this larger narrative of continuity, which enables the narrativization of everyday life under socialism, suggesting that Czechs never endorsed communist ideology while existing within it.

With their protagonists who stay out of socialist politics, representations of socialism build on a wider national narrative of continuity with the First Republic, perpetuating the myth of the Czechs as an inherently democratic nation.[36] In contrast to German *Ostalgie*, the nationalist agenda of Czech representations of socialism manifests in their implication of a foundational myth of Czech democracy in which socialism is viewed as an externally imposed aberration on a democratic Czech identity, endangered during this period and only fully regained with the Velvet Revolution. Such a position is made possible by the retrospective teleology that these representations inscribe into their narratives; the reader and spectator view the past from a privileged position of knowing how history unfolded. In keeping with the peripheral treatment of Slovaks in the series, this continuity of Czech history is presented only through the Czech side of the family, presided over by the symbol of Masaryk.

Characters such as Karel or the gracious father-entrepreneur of the main heroine in *The Rebels*, who runs the first privately owned pub in the region – the filmmakers' apparent nod to their idea of 'liberalization' in the 1960s – are possible because the market values of capitalism are already retrospectively inscribed onto the moral compass of the characters during socialism. Such a move is described by Mieke Bal as 'paronthocentrism', which 'assumes that one's own position is normal, the standard, beyond questioning, hence universal and transparent'.[37] The values that the characters endorse fall under a broad notion of 'freedom' for which they oppose communist rule, and that is most clearly articulated in the idea of the freedom of the market. Such representations of socialism reaffirm an anticommunist politics where liberal, free-market democracy is seen as the culmination of the trajectory of Czech history.

However, this kind of implicit political framework does not contradict the aesthetic fetishization of the period on which retro representations build their popularity. As Činátl convincingly argues in his analysis of responses to *Tell Me a Story*, despite the obvious inscription of value judgements into the narrative structure, the reception practices of actual viewers often tend to disregard these and focus instead on the authenticity of the material objects on display.[38] The relationship towards the material culture of socialism, while fetishizing the quirky and the outdated, also participates in a generally superior attitude towards the past. In the canon of Czech depictions of socialism, this mechanism is most memorably captured in *Cosy Dens*, which generates humour from the laughable inadequacy of socialist-era products in two key scenes. The efforts of Šebek, an army man and convinced communist, to demonstrate the quality of socialist manufacturing fall flat: in the first instance, he embarrasses himself in front of his close family at Christmas when 'unbreakable' glasses from Poland reveal themselves to be easily broken by his teenage son. In the second episode, Šebek's humiliation is even more complete when he gives plastic spoons as a wedding gift to his neighbour Kraus, a staunchly anticommunist veteran of Second World War resistance. 'These are spoons developed by researchers in the GDR',[39] Šebek says emphatically to Kraus, who admires anything of Western provenance. The scene's humorous resolution arrives when the plastic spoons melt in the hot coffee that the wedding guests are served. The comedy of this episode hinges on the one hand on the material inferiority of socialist-era products; on the other hand, the spectator is able to laugh at this precisely because in the present, they are better off – not only do they have access to quality material goods, but they also do not have to stand in long queues to procure them. In this example, these products are portrayed as inferior; unlike Botas or Kofola, they have not been rhetorically marked as 'quality' or 'traditional', which would enable their disassociation with socialist politics. On the contrary, their socialist origins in Poland and the GDR are emphasized for comic effect.

The mechanisms described above are not limited just to the postsocialist space. A moral hierarchy from which the present emerges as a moment of self-congratulation on the progress made since the times represented can be witnessed in a range of retro representations. A prominent example of retro is the successful American television series *Mad Men* (Weiner Bros., 2007–15). Although the relationship to the material culture of the 1960s United States, where the series is set, is one of abundance and luxury rather than the scarcity and inadequacy in portrayals of socialism, the political message of the show arguably shares some similarity with retro as discussed in the Czech context. Set in a 1960s advertising agency in New York, the world of the series is one of extravagance, and the spectator too is treated to a vicarious enjoyment of fruits that are often considered forbidden in the present. These include not only heavy drinking and smoking, but also a time when political correctness was not a concern and sexist, homophobic and racist remarks did not raise any eyebrows. The reason why a contemporary American television series is able to depict such a world is because it operates with the assumption that the viewer will be able to distinguish the characters' behaviour precisely as racist, sexist, homophobic or, for instance, environmentally insensitive. Mark Greif has termed this mechanism 'Now We Know Better':[40] aimed at a liberal viewer, the series continuously reaffirms the superiority of the progressive politics of the present. Jerome de Groot suggests that this is typical of American popular culture: 'America is of course the pre-eminent country in the world for representations of various particular pasts that work towards the focal point of now, a rejecting of the "old ways" for the compelling modernity of the self-in-nowness.'[41] However, there is no reason to assume that this is a mode of representation specific to the United States; the Czech representations I have been discussing work analogously.

Similarly to *Mad Men*, the nostalgia of Czech retro texts lies not in the politics of the period, but in a narrative of their eventual surpassing. Precisely because it builds a linear narrative of progress, retro can also choose to cast certain aspects of socialist culture as outdated, while others, such as fashions, are updated for contemporary consumption. For the same reason, *Mad Men* does not require a historical discontinuity to look back at the past with an attitude of simultaneous fascination and smugness. The pastiche of the retrospective view selects what on the one hand can be included into the narrative of continuity and what on the other hand is cast out. The knowledge of the present's superiority gives retro a wide discursive scope that can survive its own ridicule: socialism can be figured through both deficiency and quality, as a time of suffering and a time to joke about, as an 'Other' to be rejected from national memory, or raided for its more redeemable, 'traditional' features. The implicit framework of anticommunism, with its narrative of condemning the past, compounds this sense of historical progress in the Czech context. And while Czech retro draws on culturally specific traditions, in particular the high cultural legitimacy of comedy, the wider processes of retro are not geographically specific, but rather speak to a more general cultural dynamic beyond the postsocialist space.

Beyond Retro: 1968 as Grand Narrative

The one common point where affectless retro gives way to a different emotional repertoire in both *The Rebels* and *Tell Me a Story* is the portrayal of the 1968 Warsaw Pact invasion of Czechoslovakia. Echoing the shift in tone already witnessed in capturing the invasion in *Cosy Dens*, these representations discard a retro 'mode' and adopt a nostalgic 'mood' by indulging sentiments of solidarity, self-pity and victimhood. In *The Rebels*, which concludes with the heroine's emigration in the wake of the invasion, the bright colours, slapstick comedy and postmodern pastiche of 1960s songs surrender to a much more sombre narrative. In an emotionally charged scene, the heroine Tereza passes through the main square of her hometown in a car with her father and his partner, watching her fellow citizens trying to deliberate with Warsaw Pact soldiers sitting on tanks, accompanied by the plaintive tones of Judita Čeřovská's Czech-language cover of 'Where Have All the Flowers Gone?'. Passing her classmate Olda, who has been desperately in love with her throughout the film, she calls out to him as the car drives by; Olda's face registers resignation and regret as Tereza's car recedes into the distance. In a gesture of farewell and loss, he throws a stack of leaflets he has been handing out into the air; the camera captures their fluttering down to the ground in slow motion. The music and the sloweddown pace in this scene create an elegiac tone, compounding several layers of loss through mourning the loss of a loved one, the departure from one's country and the end of the hopes associated with the Prague Spring. In classical tragedy, the heroes die; here the tragic tone is compounded by the passing of an era.

Tell Me a Story uses a similarly melodramatic storyline to capture the affective charge of the invasion. The heroine Eva and her young son Honzík are on their way to Slovakia by train. However, the train gets held up – in an act of somewhat heavy-handed symbolism on the part of the script – near a village called Bezpráví (Lawlessness) by a convoy of Russian tanks. One of the passengers experiences a heart attack. Eva, in a courageous gesture, attempts to implore the sympathy of a Russian soldier by explaining that the man needs to be taken to hospital. The soldier deliberates, but ultimately points his gun at the group of passengers who have gathered outside the train around the ill man, shouting at them in Russian to move back. The camera then pans slowly across the faces of the passengers, their expressions registering fear, but also disappointment and a sense of collective solidarity and silent resistance. The scene thus attempts to create an affective community between the characters of the Czech and Slovak train passengers and the viewer, all united against the invading soldiers.

The ability of these scenes to generate affect is built on the moment of 1968 as a grand narrative: unlike the perceived timelessness of Normalization, here there is a story to tell. Writing about the revolutions of 1989, Tim Beasley-Murray proposes 'a distinction between the low-key anecdote that illustrates the normal and the grand narrative or story of exceptional events and deeds'.[42] Such a distinction can apply to the events of 1968 as well: by narrating a moment of exception, these representations can break out of the small and the personal and overcome the narrative impossibility of the socialist everyday. In other words, to tell a big story, these representations make use of big emotions: Eva's appeal to the conscience of the Russian soldier or a scene of Tereza's teacher in *The Rebels* throwing a Czechoslovak flag over a tank are no longer gestures of petty, but of genuine heroism. The marshalling of emotion in these scenes is a technique that serves to validate the historical understanding of the invasion as a moment of exception and national tragedy as opposed to the light-hearted portrayal of everyday life.

Such moments evoke history as trauma, rejecting the postmodern playfulness of retro, and instead employ more linear narrative techniques to create a story of national memory as a memory of suffering and tragedy. In these instances, the difference to the retro mode with which these representations otherwise work is one of genre. As we have seen, the dominant genre of representing socialism in the Czech Republic had been comedy, structured around self-enclosed humorous episodes rather than a sustained narrative arc. Even *Tell Me a Story*, although a soap opera, has its fair share of comic moments. Humour functions as a distancing mechanism; it is a convenient tool for generating a self-deprecating look at the past. It enables an apologetic attitude towards the moral compromises the period demanded. For instance, in *Tell Me a Story*, the fact that Karel's father Josef is coerced into attending a May Day parade despite his ideological opposition is turned into a humorous gag. Josef's mother, to whom he lied about his attendance – saying instead that he was going to visit his father's grave – spots him in television footage of the parade and then indignantly insists that she will immediately move out of their shared flat. The result is an apologetic look at partaking in the performative aspects of socialist daily life. Josef elicits sympathy twice: by having to endure the parade and by incurring the anger of his mother (when she should be pitying him for having to attend an obligatory rally in which he obviously takes no enjoyment, but feels he must participate in for the sake of appearances). In the case of petty heroic gestures, which emerge every so often in representations of socialism, humour arrives precisely at the point when these gestures fail or are downplayed: laughter is a reaction to the absence of a moral resolution.

But humour is no longer necessary when there are no moral dilemmas involved – *The Rebels* and *Tell Me a Story*, but also *Cosy Dens*, where the

Warsaw Pact invasion disrupts a family wedding, employ August 1968 as an unequivocal moment of trauma where the whole nation was united in collective resistance against the invading forces. Of course, the Warsaw Pact invasion is a traumatic moment not only in Czech but also Slovak history, and while Slovak cinema has not taken up this historical event as a theme, a number of Slovak novels are dedicated to capturing the tragic qualities of 1968.[43] Casting particular historical moments as trauma and depicting them as tragedy rather than humorously marks a generic shift that connotes different political meanings. Whereas the retro mode saw heroism being carried out by ordinary characters in small and petty ways, in depictions of 1968, resistance is transferred from the individual to the collective. Moreover, it takes on a much clearer object than the vague representatives of the regime towards whom gestures of petty resistance turned. Here the nation is seen as united against Soviet imperialism.

Popular representations portray the Warsaw Pact invasion as primarily a Russian undertaking and it is anti-Russian sentiment that they mobilize. In *Cosy Dens* in the wake of the invasion, Kraus asks his daughter how to say 'bastards' in Russian and goes on to shout the word from his balcony. A peculiar twist on this narrative is presented in *English Strawberries* (*Anglické jahody*, dir. Vladimír Drha, 2008), a hybrid genre film set entirely during the first days of the invasion in a small town outside of Prague, which sits somewhat uncomfortably between attempts at comedy, love story and psychological drama. Like its comic predecessors, *English Strawberries* features gestures of petty heroism and an apolitical stance of its young protagonists, as opposed to the quashed political hopes of the committed communism of the older generation. Here, the generational revolt of the youngsters manifests in being indulgent, or indeed sympathetic, towards the invading soldiers as an act of resistance against the despair of their parents – a move that confused one reviewer, who complained that 'what emerges most strongly from the film is a conciliatory tone which excuses all those poor occupiers ... The relatives of the victims of the former gentle occupiers probably won't be impressed'.[44] The film's insipid depiction of the invasion also did not meet with an audience response – it was seen by fewer than 12,000 people throughout 2008.

Another film that defied the convention of narrating the invasion as trauma, and perhaps the only picture to engage with other national representatives of the Warsaw Pact, is the whimsical Czech-Polish coproduction *Operation Danube* (*Operace Dunaj*, dir. Jacek Głomb, 2009). The film casts both the Czech patrons of a provincial pub and a bumbling crew of invading Polish soldiers as victims of the Soviets. *Operation Danube* was a box-office flop in the Czech Republic and not a big hit in Poland either;[45] it appears that audiences did not endorse the move to completely subvert the widely perceived traumatic qualities of August 1968. The negative reception of the film was encapsulated by reviewer Mirka Spáčilová, who warned that the farcical rendering of the invasion 'may deeply offend witnesses of August 1968',[46] echoing the reviews of *English Strawberries*. The concern for the memory of eyewitnesses of this particular historical event points to the idea that a tragic depiction can more 'authentically' capture the trauma of the past – a notion that historical dramas of the late 2000s and 2010s, explored in the next chapter, also exploit.

The moment of 1968 thus defies two significant features of portraying state socialism in the second postsocialist decade in the Czech Republic, which it underscores and validates by way of contrast: the trope of petty heroism and the retro mode. These portrayals of 1968 foreshadow the directions Czech cultural memory will take moving on further into the new millennium. Petty heroism enables a forgiving approach to the failure and futility of resistance. This arises from the very nature of comedy, which generally seeks reconciliation and as such lends itself to placing its characters in situations of moral compromise that the audience can laugh at. Retro adds a certain comfort to this laughter, because it provides readers and viewers with a vantage point that allows for appropriating as well as ridiculing aspects of the past. The politics of the former regime are pushed safely into the background, and its pleasant or laughable aesthetic aspects come to the fore – a move reiterated by retro also outside the postsocialist space. Such a position does not necessarily hinge on the idea of 1989 as a radical break that would generate a need to recover something lost – hence the shift from more sentimentally laden nostalgia to retro. The films and TV series discussed in this chapter, with their anticommunist patterns of identification, turn to an imagining of the past where state socialism functions as a colourful aesthetic veneer that allows characters to perform minor acts of moral exemplarism in a world where the object of their defiance has been relegated to the margins of both narrative and history.

Notes

1. 'The collapse of grand narratives' was identified as a feature of postmodernism by Jean-François Lyotard in *The Postmodern Condition: A Report on Knowledge* (Minneapolis: University of Minnesota Press, 1984), first published in French in 1979.
2. K.M.F. Platt, 'Russian Empire of Pop: Postsocialist Nostalgia and Soviet Retro at the "New Wave" Competition', *The Russian Review* 72(3) (2013), 447–69 (464).
3. E.E. Guffey, *Retro: The Culture of Revival* (London: Reaktion Books, 2006), 163.
4. S.E. Baker, *Retro Style: Class, Gender and Design in the Home* (London: Bloomsbury, 2013), 21.

5. M. Nadkarni and O. Shevchenko, 'The Politics of Nostalgia: A Case for Comparative Analysis of Postsocialist Practices', *Ab Imperio* 2 (2004), 487–519 (495).
6. Ibid.
7. B. Sedláčková, 'Retro kecky z VŠUP mají úspěch' ['Retro Sneakers from Academy of Arts Are Successful'], *Lidové noviny*, 7 August 2009, 17.
8. M. Komrsková, 'Botasky: reinkarnace české klasiky' ['Botas: Reincarnation of a Czech Classic'], *Hospodářské noviny*, 18 August 2008, 24.
9. See, for instance, J. Hubený, 'Baťa a Botas podnikají spolu' ['Baťa and Botas Do Business Together'], *Mladá fronta Dnes*, 10 June 2009, 2; E. Tichá, 'Botasky jsou zpět' ['Botas Is Back'], ONA Dnes, 15 June 2009, 6; (rd), 'České retro táhne' ['Czech Retro Is Attractive'], *Ekonom*, 18 June 2009, 25; Ond, 'Retro botasky nadchly Čechy' ['Retro Sneakers Have Enthused Czechs'], *Lidové noviny*, 18 June 2009, 15.
10. Hubený, 'Baťa a Botas podnikají spolu', 2.
11. See R. Williams, *The Long Revolution* (London: Penguin, 1965), 63–65.
12. The concept of structure of feeling has been employed in a similar fashion by Ekaterina Kalinina in her discussion of post-Soviet nostalgia. I find the concept more applicable to the narrower designation of 'retro'. See E. Kalinina, *Mediated Post-Soviet Nostalgia* (Huddinge: Södertörn University, 2014).
13. Retrieved 20 August 2019 from http://www.botas.cz/Text/Detail/PROCBOTAS.
14. K. Čopjaková, 'Historik: Výrobky z dob komunismu se vrací: Nestýská se nám po režimu, ale po dětství' ['Historian: Products from the Times of Communism Are Coming Back: We Don't Miss the Regime, But Our Childhood'], *ihned.cz*, 2 June 2012. Retrieved 20 August 2019 from http://byznys.ihned.cz/c1-56001770-historik-vyrobky-z-dob-komunismu-se-vraci-nestyska-se-nam-po-rezimu-ale-po-detstvi.
15. Martin Blum rightly points out that even within a planned economy, not all products displayed the same level of mediocrity. He illustrates this using the example of 'high-quality' Florena cream produced in the GDR, while noting that time-tested cleaning products like Spee did not change or develop for decades. See M. Blum, 'Remaking the East German Past: Ostalgie, Identity, and Material Culture', *Journal of Popular Culture* 24(3) (2000), 229–53, in particular 235–41.
16. Komrsková, 'Botasky', 24.
17. Ond, 'Retro botasky nadchly Čechy', 15.
18. In 2002, the server *idnes.cz* noted that since 1996, the sales of the drink had tripled. See L. Kratochvíl, 'Bublinky Kofoly znovu stoupají vzhůru' ['Kofola's Bubbles Once Again Rise to the Top'], *idnes.cz*, 11 October 2002. Retrieved 20 August 2019 from http://ekonomika.idnes.cz/bublinky-kofoly-znovu-stoupaji-vzhuru-fck-/ekonomika.aspx?c=A021011_155529_ekonomika_klu.
19. M. Penconek and F. Čekal, 'Značky, které právě letí' ['Brands That Are In], *Marketing a media*, 11 October 2004, 18.
20. Čopjaková, 'Historik'.
21. P. Svoboda, 'Pankáč v porcelánu', *Týden* 15(49) (2008), 42–43.
22. M. Frajtová, 'Chtěli jsme kolu v plechovce', *Instinkt* 4 (50) (2005), 70.
23. The first season was watched on average by 1.3 million viewers per episode, a significant audience. Ratings quoted in I. Carpentier Reifová, K. Gillarová and R. Hladík, 'The Way We Applauded: How Popular Culture Stimulates Collective Memory of the Socialist Past in Czechoslovakia: The Case of the Television Serial *Vyprávěj* and its Viewers', in A. Imre, T. Havens and K. Lustyik (eds), *Popular Television in Eastern Europe during and since Socialism* (New York: Routledge, 2013), 199–221 (206).

24. I. Hejdová, 'Vyprávěj: Chystaný rodinný seriál České televize cílí na pamětníky' ['Vyprávěj: Family Series in the Making by Czech TV Aims at Eyewitnesses'], *Hospodářské noviny*, 2 July 2009, 10.
25. R. Samuel, *Theatres of Memory: Volume 1: Past and Present in Contemporary Culture* (New York: Verso, 1994), 83.
26. S. Absolonová et al., 'Zpátky do studentských let' ['Back to Student Years'], *Top Seriál Vyprávěj* 1 (2009), 61.
27. K. Činátl, *Naše české minulosti, aneb, jak vzpomínáme* (Prague: Nakladatelství Lidové noviny, 2014), 157.
28. R. Dyer, *Pastiche* (New York: Routledge, 2007), 3.
29. Retrieved 20 August 2019 from http://www.ceskatelevize.cz/porady/10266819072-vypravej/diskuse.
30. Y. Meerzon, 'Dancing on the X-rays: On the Theatre of Memory, Counter-memory, and Postmemory in the Post-1989 East-European Context', *Modern Drama* 54(4) (2011), 479–510 (499).
31. V. Vlasák, 'Rebelové si přišli na své' ['The Rebels Have Come into Their Own'], *iDnes.cz*, 27 February 2002. Retrieved 20 August 2019 from http://kultura.zpravy.idnes.cz/rebelove-si-prisli-na-sve-0hm-/hudba.aspx?c=A020226_193822_hudba_ef.
32. J. Čulík, *A Society in Distress: The Image of the Czech Republic in Contemporary Czech Feature Film* (Eastbourne: Sussex Academic Press, 2013), 95.
33. See, for example, D. Křivánková, 'Renč vystavěl pomník šedesátým létům' ['Renč Has Built a Monument to the Sixties'], *Lidové noviny*, 9 February 2001, no pagination; J. Sedláček, 'Rebelové', *Cinema* 3 (2001), 50–53; V. Míšková, 'S Rebely přichází smích, hudba i pláč,' ['With the Rebels Comes Laughter, Music and Tears'], *Mladá fronta Dnes*, 8 February 2001, 13.
34. S. Bechmann Pedersen, *Reel Socialism: Making Sense of History in Czech and German Cinema since 1989* (Lund: Lund University/Media-Tryck, 2015), 185.
35. 'Jsme tady úplně odříznutý od světa, nic nevíme'. *Vyprávěj*, 2009–13, Season 1, Episode 6.
36. This is also one of the myths in Kieran Williams' analysis of Czech national mythopoeia. Others include the myth of Slav reciprocity or the peculiar 'myth of mythlessness', which sees Czechs as too rational to sustain an extensive national mythology. See K. Williams, 'National Myths in the New Czech Liberalism', in G. Hosking and G. Schöpflin (eds), *Myths and Nationhood* (London: Hurst, 1997), 132–40 (135).
37. M. Bal, *Quoting Caravaggio: Contemporary Art, Preposterous History* (Chicago: University of Chicago Press, 1999), 19.
38. Činátl, *Naše české minulosti*, 154–76.
39. 'To jsou lžičky, které vyvinuli výzkumníci z NDR'. *Pelíšky*, 1999.
40. M. Greif, 'You'll Love the Way It Makes You Feel', *London Review of Books* 30(20) (2008), 15–16 (15).
41. J. de Groot, '"Perpetually Dividing and Suturing the Past and Present": Mad Men and the Illusions of History', *Rethinking History* 15(2) (2011), 269–85 (276).
42. T. Beasley-Murray, 'Ruins and Representations of 1989: Exception, Normality, Revolution', in D. Gafijczuk and D. Sayer (eds), *The Inhabited Ruins of Central Europe: Re-imagining Space, History, and Memory* (London: Palgrave Macmillan, 2013), 16–39 (32).
43. These include P. Rankov, *Stalo sa prvého septembra (alebo inokedy)* (Bratislava: Kalligram, 2008); V. Klimáček *Horúce leto 68* (Bratislava: Marenčin PT, 2011); P. Krištúfek, *Dom hluchého* (Bratislava: Marenčin PT, 2012); A. Baláž, *Len jedna jar* (Bratislava: Marenčin

PT, 2013). For an analysis of the various literary strategies taken up by these authors to depict the events of August 1968, see D. Pucherová, 'Trauma a pamäť augusta 1968 v súčasnom slovenskom románe', *World Literature Studies* 6(2) (2014), 64–77.

44. I. Hejdová, 'Anglické jahody: sovětská konzerva s něžnými okupanty' ['English Strawberries: A Soviet Tin Can with Gentle Occupiers'], *Lidovky.cz*, 12 November 2008. Retrived 20 August 2019 from http://magazin.aktualne.cz/kultura/film/anglicke-jahody-sovetska-konzerva-s-neznymi-okupanty/r~i:article:621822.

45. The film was seen by fewer than 27,000 viewers in cinemas in the Czech Republic, a meagre number considering the all-star cast of the film. In Poland, it ranked seventeenth among Polish films in cinemas that year. Data retrieved 14 November 2018 from http://www.pisf.pl/rynek-filmowy/box-office/filmy-polskie?cat=651.

46. M. Spáčilová, 'Recenze: Polský tank nabořený v české hospodě zabil šanci Operace Dunaj' ['Review: Polish Tank Rammed into Czech Pub Killed Opportunity for Operation Danube'], *iDnes.cz*, 23 July 2009. Retrieved 20 August 2019 from http://kultura.zpravy.idnes.cz/recenze-operace-dunaj-0tu-/filmvideo.aspx?c=A090722_173728_filmvideo_ob.

Chapter 6

CHANGING MEMORY LANDSCAPES IN THE 2000S

The year 2007 saw a major intervention in efforts of the Czech state to shape the memory of both the Nazi occupation and communist rule with the opening of the Institute for the Study of Totalitarian Regimes (Ústav pro studium totalitních režimů (ÚSTR)). This chapter explores the attendant changing memory paradigms witnessed both in official memory politics and cultural representations.[1] From around the middle of the first decade of the new millennium onwards, Czech literature and film saw a departure from the retro-comedy so prevalent in the memory of state socialism up to this point. Looking at both political developments and a host of representations, I argue that just as anticommunism as the dominant post-1989 memory narrative was increasingly coming under fire from various quarters, its adherents both on the level of institutional actors and cultural producers attempted to fortify a memory of anticommunist resistance.

The opening of ÚSTR brought to the fore an official memory politics that instituted an understanding of state socialism as a period of totalitarianism – as already apparent from the Institute's name – and actively sought to promote a national memory founded on the notion of heroic resistance. However, ÚSTR was not unique. These developments were part of a wider European trend of state-sponsored 'memory institutes', following the establishment of the Polish Institute of National Remembrance (2000) and Slovakia's Nation's Memory Institute (2002), among others.[2] Like its counterparts in neighbouring countries, ÚSTR investigates the crimes of both Nazism and communism, effectively equating the two. This position was officially sealed on an international level by a number of European intellectuals and politicians in the Prague Declaration on European Conscience and Communism of 2008. This document called for European-wide education about, and condemnation of, the crimes of communism, comparing them to the crimes of Nazism.[3] Yet this implication was not met with consensus in the Czech public sphere; the vociferous controversies accompanying the Institute from its inception are the most visible marker in a changing memory landscape from the mid 2000s onwards.

In parallel to these developments, the state as a caretaker of memory increasingly became a direct object of representation for writers and filmmakers. For instance, in the 2006 novella *The Identity Card*, Petr Šabach has his main protagonist consult his secret police file in the Security Services Archive reading room in Pardubice after the liberalization of the law allowing access to StB documents in 2004. For Šabach's protagonist, the visit is just another chance to retrospectively reconfirm his (petty) heroism; as his wife tells him after he finds out that the secret police had indeed kept a file on him: 'Even now one can see how chuffed you are that somebody was informing on you. You think it makes you a bit more interesting to others.'[4] This chapter explores this new trend in thematizing archives, remembrance, personal explorations of the past and the changing notions of heroism accompanying it.

It would nevertheless be an overstatement to trace a direct link between the new official memory politics and representational strategies. Rather, most representations reacted to broader memory developments only implicitly, providing evidence of a changing memory discourse that could be witnessed in parallel in the public sphere. After 2005, many Czech novels and films evinced a new 'search for heroes'. This search consisted of attempts to present positive role models for living in a repressive regime, whether through active resistance or strong moral positions, resonating with wider attempts of institutions such as ÚSTR to forge a resistance-based national memory. Where the comic retro mode condemned the regime while also looking back fondly at small, everyday occurrences, this new narrative trend de-emphasized the everyday and positively valued public acts. In what can be termed a 'dramatic turn', literature, film and television production increasingly tackled large historical moments and issues, such as the self-immolation of Jan Palach, the collectivization of the 1950s, the practices of the secret police, or the Velvet Revolution. While film comedies about socialism continued to be made, after the large-scale production *The Identity Card* (*Občanký průkaz*, dir. Ondřej Trojan, 2010), comedy as the genre of choice for portraying socialism receded into the background. A few humorous depictions of Normalization did emerge even after this date, but have garnered less attention from both critics and audiences.[5] The result has been an increasingly plural memory landscape, where different interpretations of the socialist past compete in both public discourse and cultural production.

Battles for the Past: From ÚSTR to Third Resistance

Efforts at inscribing a state-sponsored memory of the past did not meet with unanimous approval; on the contrary, the controversies surrounding the opening of ÚSTR suggested that the anticommunist consensus that had dominated Czech postsocialist public discourse was slowly losing ground. ÚSTR polarized the debate about the previous regime, pitting against each other those who wished to continue the anticommunist line by preserving primarily a memory of repression and those who called for understanding repression as just one of the aspects of a wider memory of state socialism, bringing to the fore a conflict that would continue to dominate the Czech memory landscape for years to come.

An initiative of the right-of-centre coalition in power at the time, ÚSTR, which studies the period 1938–89, has arguably been associated primarily with two tendencies: identifying victims and oppressors of the communist secret police, and the glorification of the heroes of both the Second World War and anticommunist resistance. The research, educational and commemorational institution is directly linked to the Security Services Archives (Archiv bezpečnostních složek (ABS)), formally an independent body, whose collections ÚSTR is dedicated to studying. For the purposes of this chapter, rather than recounting in detail the political conflicts around the Institute, it will suffice to summarize the main implications of the Institute's mission for official state-sponsored mnemopolitics and its most controversial actions. Though the situation around ÚSTR arguably stabilized after the last leadership change in 2014, the first few years of its existence generated a veritable 'battle for the past', to borrow a phrase from the title of a book by the Institute's first director, Pavel Žáček.[6]

The state institution's very remit was cast into doubt from the outset by a coalition of forces, including a number of academic historians, public intellectuals and left-wing politicians. They feared that the Institute, whose board is directly appointed by the upper chamber of parliament, would produce research unduly susceptible to political pressures. Academic historians have been among ÚSTR's most sustained critics, not necessarily, as one commentator suggested early in the debate, because they feared having to directly compete with another institution,[7] but because ÚSTR's form and mission raised serious questions about the kind of historical knowledge it could produce. Indeed, a number of historians actively entered the debate and frequently wrote in to various media outlets or were interviewed by them. Michal

Kopeček summarized the concerns of this group when he pointed out that the Institute has four main aims, some of which are, in his view, inherently contradictory. First, it is home to the ABS; second, it promotes a memory of anticommunism, e.g. by helping to administer applications for official status as anticommunist resistance fighter; third, it aims to raise public awareness through educational activities; and, finally, it is a research institute that studies the history of totalitarian regimes or, rather, their repressive aspects. Some of these functions, Kopeček argues, complement one another, such as the archive and historical research, while others are necessarily at odds, e.g. academic research and the promotion of a politically motivated anticommunist historical memory and with it also national identity.[8]

Others already saw an initial problem in the Institute's name: the word 'totalitarian', they argued, not only falsely equates the Nazi occupation with communist rule as totalitarian regimes, but is also misleading as a descriptive term for the liberalization of the 1960s and late socialism in general.[9] One of the architects of the Prague Spring, Zdeněk Jičínský, even unsuccessfully put a proposal to the Constitutional Court to abolish the Institute based on this objection.[10] His initiative spearheaded a wider debate in the press on the nature of totalitarianism, which revealed that despite the use of the term in official memory politics, there is by no means a consensus around its appropriateness. This debate was further complicated by the fact that in Czech, totalitarianism (*totalitarismus*), as an analytical term developed by Hannah Arendt and as a historiographical framework, is used interchangeably with the much fuzzier term *totalita*, which simultaneously serves as a shorthand for the entire period of communist rule.[11] Perhaps because of this linguistic ambiguity, it did not strike the founders of the Institute that the appearance of the term 'totalitarian' in ÚSTR's name exposed a methodological problem. By prescribing in its very name something that could only arise from its research – i.e. the question of whether or not the communist regime was totalitarian – ÚSTR was set up, as one commentator put it, 'as a tautology, as an examination of the totalitarian regime being totalitarian'.[12] From the outset, then, the Institute's ability to consider a plurality of interpretive frameworks was put into question.

During its first years, the most discussed activities of the Institute were 'revelations' of the supposed collaboration of several prominent public figures with the communist secret services, in an echo of the 1990s, when various memory activists took it upon themselves to publicly disclose names of alleged former StB collaborators, thus tarnishing the reputation of a number of people.[13] The most debated of these was the allegation that Franco-Czech novelist Milan Kundera had denounced a Western agent to the communist security services while a student in Prague in 1950. A newly discovered archival document suggested that the novelist had reported the presence of a stranger in his university dormitory. This piece of information caused a major stir not only in domestic but also international media, after it first appeared in an article in the current affairs weekly *Respekt* in 2008.[14] Coauthored by one of *Respekt*'s contributing editors and a researcher at ÚSTR, the article raised serious questions about how the Institute chose to disseminate its findings, especially as little effort had been made to contact Kundera himself for comment.[15] Similar critique of not approaching the individual in question for comment was levelled at the Institute in the case of the revelation that one of Václav Havel's close collaborators during the time of his election and first months as Czechoslovak President, Joska Skalník, had in fact reported information to the Secret Police.[16] Equally controversial was the claim emerging from the Institute that the Mašín brothers, members of an anticommunist resistance group, had planned to assassinate President Klement Gottwald. This was immediately denied by one of the brothers, Ctirad Mašín, in an interview for the daily *Mladá Fronta Dnes*.[17] The archival and educational work of the Institute was thus often overshadowed by such much-publicized instances of sensationalism that cast the memory of state socialism as primarily an exercise in publicly shaming perpetrators and lauding heroes, with little discussion of the spaces in between.

Alongside the state, civic initiatives also actively shaped the memory of the communist regime in public space at this time. Chapter 1 discussed a number of civic and cultural initiatives that had intervened in the memory of socialism throughout the 1990s and the early 2000s; the second half of the first decade of the new millennium saw the rise of a complex web of state-sanctioned and grassroots culture of memorialization, which actively sought to promote notions of heroism and victimhood. Among the most prominent in these efforts was the nonprofit organization Post Bellum, which since 2001 has been recording oral histories with Second World War veterans and those who in some way resisted or fell victim to the injustice of the communist regime. The organization has managed to gain a number of significant media and institutional partners who have promoted its projects, including a regular programme on Czech public radio since 2006, and, amongst numerous other activities, an online oral history archive called 'Memory of the Nation' (*Paměť národa*). Post Bellum can be seen as actively promoting a heroic discourse, which it believes is missing in the Czech public sphere – its very first oral history project was called 'Voices of Heroes' (*Hlasy hrdinů*), before being renamed Memory of the Nation.[18]

The organization's founder, Mikuláš Kroupa, admitted that although initially he had an idea of 'total heroism', he quickly discovered when gathering testimonies that he had to give up this ideal, noting that personal histories were complicated and, for instance, those who were active in the resistance movement during the Second World War behaved in less exemplary ways after the communist takeover.[19] The stance of another memorial project called Stories of Injustice (Příběhy bezpráví), organized by the largest Czech NGO People in Need (Člověk v tísni), was less equivocal. Bringing film projections and debates with eyewitnesses to schools since 2005, the language and pedagogical aims of Stories of Injustice are highly prescriptive. The project's coordinator Karel Strachota views his efforts to bring to the centre of attention the crimes of the communist regime as a corrective to Czech society attempting to 'force them out of collective memory'.[20] As one article put it, 'the most willing to remember are those who were happy in the given period. The memory of the nation is receding'.[21] The central assumption in such pronouncements is that only trauma qualifies as 'national memory' – a position compounded in the much-criticized (and hence much-discussed) Stories of Injustice educational publication *Myths about Socialist Times* (*Mýty o socialistických časech*, 2010) dealing with the final two decades of state socialism. The authors feared that the collective memory of socialism had been formed on the basis of 'nostalgically uncritical popular film production'.[22] Rejecting a plurality of memories, the book's aim was to demonstrate that 'people did not live better lives, that there was nothing at all good about Husák's socialism, and what good did happen, only happened in spite of the regime'.[23] As an antidote, they offered the familiar position of a wholesale condemnation of the previous regime. Since 2005, the daily *Lidové noviny* has given space to both Stories of Injustice and Post Bellum, publishing a series of articles every November to commemorate the 1989 Velvet Revolution and thus forging a collaboration between the two projects.

Efforts to manufacture a memory of trauma and heroic resistance were officially compounded by the passing of the 'Act on Third Resistance' in 2011 under Petr Nečas's right-of-centre government. This Act defines an anticommunist resistance fighter as anyone who carried out armed struggle against the communist regime, as well as anyone who contributed to destabilizing or overthrowing this regime through written and editorial work, including work from abroad. Certificates of membership in the resistance are granted by the Ministry of Defence after an assessment of relevant documentation by ÚSTR and the ABS, and are associated with a monetary reward and certain pension benefits.[24] The Act thus updates and grants practical impact to an earlier resolution from 1993, which stated that opposition to the communist regime was 'legitimate, just, morally justified, and is worthy of respect'.[25] It clearly prescribes a vision of heroism founded on action and represents a shift in emphasis from the previous accent on victimhood promoted by the Confederation of Political Prisoners (discussed in Chapter 1).[26]

Yet the Act revealed that there was no public consensus on the existence or legitimacy of armed resistance against the communist regime, let alone on whether it should be officially commended. The most divisive case remains that of the resistance group of the Mašín brothers, who in their subversive activities and eventual armed flight from the country in 1953 killed several people, including police officers and, even more controversially, at least one civilian.[27] This complex and ambiguous case, in which a number of questions remain unanswered, has been reconstructed in painstaking detail in Jan Novák's novel *So Far So Good* (*Zatím dobrý*).[28] Reactions in the press, opinion polls and television debates have repeatedly shown that public opinion of whether the Mašíns' activities are to be lauded or condemned remains very divided.[29] Despite this divisiveness, right-wing politicians were ready to grant the Mašíns various official accolades.[30]

From the second half of the first decade of the new millennium, the coming together of several state and nongovernmental institutions to generate a national memory increasingly represented an effort to hold together a discourse that was falling apart. In the heat of debates and personnel changes surrounding ÚSTR, Michal Uhl, a member of ÚSTR's council at the time, summarized an aspect of this memory transformation in a 2013 interview: 'The value consensus about the criminal nature of the previous regime has disintegrated. If the consensus still existed, Czech society would not be debating about ÚSTR.'[31] The brand of anticommunism that had played such a role in the public discourse of the immediate aftermath of 1989 was increasingly being challenged, not only through criticism of ÚSTR and the Third Resistance Act. Another significant factor was the emergence of new press platforms outside of the traditional centre-right dailies and weeklies. With the rise of the internet, new digital media significantly diversified the political spectrum represented in public debate. Blogging platforms attached to the online news sites of the major dailies have given voice to opinions across the political spectrum. Since 2005, a number of left-wing print and online platforms expanded the political range present in Czech media and were willing to question the dominant anticommunist discourse.[32]

Another important aspect in this process of change was the engagement of academic historians in public debate through contributions in mainstream media. Prominently among them, Michal Pullmann and Pavel Kolář presented challenges to the totalitarian paradigm not only in their scholarly work, but also in the weekend supplements of the major Czech dailies, ensuring that such alternative interpretative frameworks were the topic of debate and shifted discourse not only amongst a specialized academic readership, but also in the wider public sphere.[33] Overall, what Michael Bernhard and Jan Kubik term 'memory pluralists'[34] – i.e. actors who believe in a peaceful coexistence of competing visions of the past – gained an increasing say in the Czech public debate in this period. These developments suggest that a wholesale condemnation of the socialist past had become less salient and instead more critical approaches received exposure.

The lack of consensus around ÚSTR and around the issue of Third Resistance points to a discursive shift in the Czech public sphere, where anticommunism was no longer as convenient a tool with which to demonstrate allegiance to the new elites as it was in the 1990s. In a climate of rising contestation, official memory politics was used on the part of political elites more strongly as a legitimating mechanism for the path that Czech society took after 1989. However, this phenomenon was not limited to the Czech Republic, but rather was part of a wider trend in European memory politics. Anthropologist Kristen Ghodsee argues that the institutional activities of the Platform for European Memory and Conscience, an alliance of several dozen public and private memory organizations, have worked to establish a European-wide memory equating Nazi and communist crimes. This development, Ghodsee suggests, must be read as a reaction to the financial crises of 2008; the new European memory politics had a vested interest in discrediting emerging left-wing challenges to the model of economic austerity propagated in much of Europe at the time by suggesting that left-wing thought can ultimately lead to crimes as heinous as those committed by the Nazi regime.[35] In its Czech iteration, the totalitarian interpretation presented by the various memory institutions discussed above provided a convenient grand historical narrative: its emphasis on active resistance and simultaneous exculpation of the general population, who in this view suffered under total control, provided an expedient means of restoring national pride in a time of global economic uncertainty. How this happened on the discursive level in reaction to several interventions into the memory landscape has been the topic of public debate; what has been less discussed is how, in the same period, the cultural memory of socialism has been slowly restructured by changes in representational strategies.

The Dramatic Turn

Alongside the change in public discourse, representations, whether literary or cinematic, saw a shift away from retro and comedy, and towards different generic repertoires that cast the past as tragedy and trauma. No longer did these representations move towards easy reconciliation, but instead staged stark moral conflicts. More often than the ironic distance of comedy, they recounted the past through pathos.[36] The preoccupations of the new wave of representations gathered around three core themes that echoed the debates around ÚSTR and Third Resistance. I will not attempt to review here all the representations of socialism that arose at this time; my aim is to outline several distinctive trends contributing towards what I call a 'dramatic turn'.

First, historical documents, rather than personal memory, as providing access to the past became a feature not only of institutional discourse, but also representational strategies in this period. In parallel to discussions of the appropriateness of the StB archives as a means of shedding light on historical events, which had once again been reanimated with the transfer of the ABS under ÚSTR, 'the archive' emerged as a motif and metaphor in fictional accounts. Arguably this move signals an increased sense of distance from the past – it is only through letters and files rather than their own memories that audiences can now, with the increasing time gap since the demise of the previous regime, access the past. The shift of the late 2000s suggests that memory is less reliable. While the small stories of retro-comedy narratives were able to recount personal tales without additional means of authentication, the new turn requires historical validation of its vision of the past. Despite numerous scholarly exposures of the problematic claim to veracity secret police archives present, archives as repositories of truth 'continue to occupy an almost sacred place in the public imagination'.[37] The archive thus plays a double role here of, on the one hand, a mechanism of verification, but, on the other hand, it functions as a device that testifies to the complexity and confusion about this past in both representation and public discourse.

Second, related to the archival move in its concern with evidence is the discourse of authenticity that representations of the past generated via both textual and contextual means. As Astrid Erll points out, representations of the past reference not only historical events, but often also a previous canon of representations. As such, rather than historical accuracy, 'authenticity' is achieved by creating images of the past that 'resonate with cultural memory'.[38] Aside from archival documents, invoking other extratextual realities (the most obvious being the 'based on a true story' rubric) is an additional mechanism of constructing 'authentic' depictions of history. Visual representations also employ a reserved visual language attempting to connote a more serious engagement with the past. Whereas comedies with a strong retro-pastiche aesthetic such as *The Rebels* (*Rebelové*, dir. Filip Renč, 2001), discussed in the previous chapter, made little pretence of realism, it was precisely the realistic aspirations of the dramatic wave of films and series that became another means of authenticating historical narratives and manufacturing a recognizable verisimilitude of the period.

The third element completing the newfound concerns of representational culture is an intersection with the search for heroes witnessed in public debates. Stories about the socialist past no longer find their locus in the 'cosy dens' of everyday occurrences where gestures of petty heroism or *stiob* acted as a convenient outlet for expressing dissatisfaction with a vaguely defined 'Other' in the form of representatives of the regime. Instead, representations increasingly cast the socialist past as grand narrative, portraying large-scale historical events, moments of trauma and heroic actions that broke out of the small-scale resistance of the everyday.

The shift was initially evident particularly in literature. In the second half of the 2000s, novels depicting the socialist period often played out in a genre that could be described as 'intimate tragedy' – the focus, as with comedies, remained on the private and on the family, but these spheres were encroached upon by traumatic historical events. Several texts were published at roughly the same time as the new trend in memorialization took off and gained institutional validation through the award of a range of literary prizes,[39] which serves as an indication of the topics that the cultural elite was interested in promoting. A sign that said elite is small but influential is given by the accumulation of acclaimed titles concerning the state socialist past published by the Brno-based publishing house Host (Guest), which has a strong record of bringing out young contemporary Czech authors. What unites this body of literature is the archive as the key means of accessing, while also often obscuring, the past. The newfound concern of literary production thus resonated with the ways in which information emerging from ÚSTR's archives revealed, but at the same time further tangled, the histories surrounding individuals such as the Mašín brothers or Milan Kundera.

This trend was not limited to Czech literature. The passage of time since 1989 and the slow slipping away of the socialist past from living communicative memory into a more institutionalized cultural memory saw Slovak writers also reaching for validation of historical narratives through archival documents, the best example perhaps being Peter Krištúfek's *Dom hluchého* (*The House of the Deaf*, 2012). This monumental novel maps the history of one family from the 1930s to the present, interspersed with would-be historical documents. Other authors have adopted the wider features of this 'dramatic turn', if not necessarily the mechanism of archival authentication. Viliam Klimáček's 2011 novel *Horúce leto 68* (*The Hot Summer of '68*) is, according to literary scholar Dobrota Pucherová, 'a paradigmatic example of the construction of collective trauma'[40] via literary means, by staging a stark moral tale where good (dissidents and those who express opposition to the regime) and bad (communists, secret police collaborators, 'Asiatic' Soviets) remain clear-cut categories, with no room for compromise or reconciliation, unlike the earlier Czech comedies.

A precursor to this new wave of literature was the aforementioned novel *So Far So Good* by Jan Novák from 2004, an extensive work running to well over 700 pages in its first edition, capturing the story of the Mašín brothers' resistance against the communist regime. The novel is far from the anecdotal sketches of Šabach and Viewegh, instead resembling in its attention to detail the work of an academic historian. However, the book that truly inaugurated the 'archival trend' in depictions of the socialist past was Jiří

Hájíček's *Rustic Baroque* (*Selský baroko*, 2005). In this text, set in the present, archivist and genealogist Pavel Straňanský returns to the traumatic history of the 1950s and the forced collectivization of Czechoslovak agriculture. He is commissioned to find a denunciation letter written by one-time village beauty Rozálie Zandlová, which had been used as a pretext by local authorities to create a case against several successful farmers. Thanks to this ploy, the latter were labelled 'kulaks' and forced to leave their village. *Rustic Baroque* is a novel of the unspoken – Hájíček resorts to a framing narrative in which we follow the silent and meditative Straňanský as he uncovers snippets of the past to form a jigsaw puzzle that can never be fully reconstructed. The text builds a contrast around Straňanský's trustworthy laptop, which holds his own archive of collected data, and faulty human memory that cannot or does not want to remember how events had really unfolded. In the end, the opening up of the past does not lead to greater understanding or redemption; the letter that Straňanský searches for is used to discredit an opponent by a local politician. The only use of the past is a political instrumentalization in the present.

Similarly to *Rustic Baroque*, the archive or the letter – textual traces of the past – emerge in Tomáš Zmeškal's *Love Letter in Cuneiform* (*Milostný dopis klínovým písmem*, 2008), Jan Balabán's *Ask Dad* (*Zeptej se táty*, 2010) and Kateřina Tučková's *The Goddesses of Žítková* (*Žítkovské bohyně*, 2012) to disrupt or change the lives of the characters in the present. In these novels, the past is no longer an object of amusing memories of childhood or adolescence, the main structuring mechanism of comic and nostalgic portrayals of the past. The subject position of the protagonists and the reader is that of an adult, and moreover an adult who is willing to reflect critically upon the past. While the child's perspective allowed authors to adopt a deliberately naïve view of political events and focus instead on private joys and 'small' histories, here the firmly adult, mature perspective is prepared to face trauma. Even Věra Nosková's *We Take What Comes* (*Bereme, co je*, 2005), though a straightforward memoir that eschews a double timeframe of past and present, recounts its heroine's childhood years from a perspective that ascribes to the child an adult distance and political awareness: 'Now I'm ten, I know many things about life and falsehood',[41] she notes in a precocious manner reminiscent of Kvido in Michal Viewegh's *Bliss Was It in Bohemia*. But where the latter child protagonist was only murkily aware of the political realities that affected his parents' lives, Nosková's heroine Pavla can read the situation from the outset and already in the opening of the novel passes harsh judgement on her grandfather, whom she considers a 'a so-called honest communist or rather communist-idiot'.[42]

Practically all of these works either implicitly or explicitly value the present perspective from which they are written as superior to the past they deal with: in *The Goddesses of Žítková*, ethnographer Dora is grateful that she no longer has to accommodate her work to the empty political demands and meaningless materialist phrases that the pre-1989 period asked for; in Jiří Hájíček's *Fish Blood* (*Rybí krev*, 2012), the characters place high hopes in the new democratic political representation to address environmental concerns in their region. Yet the judgement passed on the socialist period is not unequivocal. The motivations of the characters are complex, and clear heroes or role models appear only seldom. For instance, Josef, the hero of Zmeškal's *Love Letter in Cuneiform*, does not fit into any of the established vocabularies that circulated in public debates at this time; he is a former political prisoner, but is unwilling to think of himself as a victim or hero: 'He had never thought of himself as a victim. Not him. The idea of being a victim didn't fit with him or his profession. He had always thought of himself as having had an accident, an unpleasant political accident with lasting consequences, but the thought that he might be a victim had never crossed his mind.'[43] However, it is always much clearer who the villains are. Both *Love Letter* and *The Goddesses of Žítková* demonize the figure of the StB officer, a trope that also comes up frequently in film production. In *We Take What Comes*, the heroine's hated parents are at fault for being Communist Party members. Official representatives of power are thus clearly condemned, but positive examples are harder to come by. The period is depicted as producing some form of character flaw in most protagonists.

The turn away from comedy is even more apparent in cinema in a series of successful and critically acclaimed films.[44] Two film portrayals of the socialist past, both cast as personal tragedy, appeared in 2009: the tale of a morally compromised former dissident, *Kawasaki's Rose* (*Kawasakiho růže*, dir. Jan Hřebejk, 2009) and the StB drama *Pouta* (*Walking Too Fast*, dir. Radim Špaček, 2010). These pictures were followed by three films that recounted socialism as moral drama, pitching clean-cut heroes against communist villains in *In the Shadow* (*Ve stínu*, dir. David Ondříček, 2012), the HBO miniseries *Burning Bush* (*Hořící keř*, dir. Agnieszka Holland, 2013) and *Fair Play* (dir. Andrea Sedláčková, 2014). These films can be seen as a reaction to the dominant representational mode of socialism as retro-comedy and instead make use of different generic conventions. *Walking Too Fast*, which deals with the dark practices of the StB in an atmosphere of general moral decay of the 1980s, is set up as a psychological thriller. The mendacious practices of the StB in the 1950s are also the subject of *In the Shadow*, which is stylized as a neo-noir detective film. *Burning Bush* tackles the changing social and political circumstances after the Soviet occupation of Czechoslovakia as a courtroom drama, recounting the story of lawyer Dagmar Burešová who takes on a high-ranking Party official. Finally, *Fair Play* and *Kawasaki's Rose* are both personal and family dramas in which difficult moral choices complicate the lives of the characters. These generic repertoires evoke fear as a dominant mood, but also the desire to depict Czechoslovak history as grand narrative with a large societal trajectory.

Searching for Heroes

The notion of the hero as mediated by the archival document is taken up explicitly in *Kawasaki's Rose*. In the manner of several literary examples, events from the socialist past are framed by a present-day narrative. The film echoes the themes central to the debates around ÚSTR and Third Resistance: the psychiatrist and former dissident Pavel Josek is meant to receive a 'Memory of the Nation Prize' in a prescient move on the part of the filmmakers (the organization Post Bellum began to award eponymous prizes in 2010, a year after the film's release). The central plot revolves around the appearance of an StB file, which documents that prior to his dissident activities, Josek had informed on his future wife's boyfriend in order to rid himself of his rival. The archive thus emerges, as in *The Goddesses of Žítková* and *Rustic Baroque*, as an intrusion of the past that affects protagonists in the present.

The main topic of the film clearly resonated with contemporary 'agent scandals'; revelations about Milan Kundera and Joska Skalník's possible involvement with the secret police had circulated in the press only shortly before the film's premiere and became part of the journalistic discourse around the picture.[45] Indeed, as Sune Bechmann Pedersen has observed, the filmmakers consciously drew inspiration from the Kundera affair for their story. For instance, the real-life Western agent Kundera allegedly denounced ended up emigrating to Gothenburg in Sweden after 1968. Likewise, the man whom Josek informs on in *Kawasaki's Rose* was forced to emigrate by the secret police and starts a new life in Gothenburg.[46]

Kawasaki's Rose directly thematizes and explores memory; the film does not contain any flashbacks and the past emerges only in text or in the spoken word. Who can be considered a hero and what counts as failure is problematized, but what remains clear, like in some of the literary production discussed above, is the identity of the villain. The StB officer who stepped into the lives of the young Josek and his rival, forcing the latter to emigrate, is portrayed as a demonic, sadistic man who maintains a cool, professional detachment from his past activities. In the final scene, depicting the former officer surrounded by loving family and friends celebrating his birthday, Hřebejk comments on the lack of public condemnation and ostracization of those who had inflicted the power of the state's repressive apparatus on others.

The character is representative of a larger development of the figure of the secret policeman in Czech cinema. This comes in opposition to the largely passive characters of comedies, whose individual agency was limited to a few fleeting private gestures. In Jan Svěrák's Oscar-winning 1996 film *Kolya* (*Kolja*), the StB officers who interrogate the protagonist, Louka, are mostly pathetic and at times comic characters whom Louka more or less outwits; while the 'good cop' doesn't get Louka's jokes, the 'bad cop' turns out to be clumsy rather than threatening when he gets his hand stuck to a roll of sellotape. But in the films of the dramatic wave such as *Walking Too Fast*, *Kawasaki's Rose*, *In the Shadow*, *Burning Bush* and *Fair Play*, the figures of StB officers are far from the inept characters of *Kolya*; rather, like *Walking Too Fast*'s main protagonist, the antihero Antonín Rusnák, they are cruel and despicable, even sadistic.

In this context, the Slovak, Czech and Polish coproduction *The Informer* (*Eštébák*, dir. Juraj Nvota, 2012) would seem to complicate the above-described pattern. The character of Adam, a radio communications specialist, who joins the StB out of helplessness rather than conviction, stands in direct opposition to the figure of the evil secret police officer – and, indeed, the prevalent discourse on victims and perpetrators – and would seem to integrate representatives of the repressive apparatus into the legitimate collective memory of the period. The film was, however, a box office flop, though it fared slightly better in Slovakia,[47] and is perhaps noteworthy amongst the Czech corpus of representations of socialism for its linguistic realism featuring both Czech and Slovak actors speaking their respective languages (or indeed mixing the two). Despite its based-on-a-true-story origins found in the archive of the Slovak Institute of National Memory,[48] the picture entirely failed to create an enduring image of how the previous regime is remembered. It received poor reviews, complaining mainly of logical gaps in the screenplay that only brought confusion as to the characters' motivations in this would-be psychological thriller.[49] Although *Walking Too Fast* was hailed as the Czech answer to the German Oscar-winning Stasi drama *The Lives of Others* (*Das Leben der Anderen*, dir. Florian Henckel von Donnersmarck, 2006), *The Informer* evinces greater similarities to the German film in terms of its central conceit of the secret-police-officer-turned-good-man who tries to protect his victims. However, the benign character of Adam is fully compensated by his ruthless cold-blooded superior, Major Dravec. The archive once again emerges as key in the form of a recording found by Adam, which holds compromising information on Dravec. Together with the Major's ambitious colleague, Stb officers embody the evil of the regime.

The latter is a typical move: the dramatic wave shifts the enemy 'within', where evil rests with specific characters. This marks a difference from comedies in which the 'regime' was often someone else, an absent Other hovering in the background. Representatives of power were quite often an object of laughter, while 'evil' remained vague and depersonalized. By employing the archive as a means of historical authentication, these narratives play out their conflicts in strongly moral terms, where perpetrators and victims are clearly identified. But not even written documents can necessarily provide moral clarity about the past. For instance, *Kawasaki's Rose* uses the archive as a mechanism to simultaneously authenticate the past and question its veracity, in a similar way to the public debates that cited the StB archive as both a tool of shedding light on the past and misusing it. Is Josek ultimately a villain or someone who deserves our sympathy for displaying weakness at one point? *Kawasaki's Rose* does not guide the viewer towards a clear answer. Similarly, scandals such as the one around Milan Kundera showed how difficult it is to establish any kind of 'verified' narrative about the past based on archival documents; indeed, the question of Kundera's alleged collaboration was never satisfactorily resolved. The paradox of the archive is thus that, despite its promises of clear evidence, it often just adds more troubling layers to an already complicated picture.

Literary works are able to use reprints of archival documents – whether real or fictional – as a further means of authentication. Reproductions of the fictional StB file of the heroine's aunt in *The Goddesses of Žítková* allow the reader to follow how the communist authorities built a case against the aunt's practice as a healer, which they construed as 'anti-state activities'. These excerpts, complete with graphic layout resembling typewritten documents, are interspersed throughout the text. Similarly, films have resorted to inserting archival footage into their narratives and thus generate authenticity through colour schemes resembling those employed by filmmakers during the time represented. For example, Agnieszka Holland's mini-series *Burning Bush*, which recounts the aftermath of the self-immolation of student Jan Palach in January 1969, occasionally inserts black-and-white footage into a story otherwise shot in colour as a means of self-authentication.

Indeed, the use of archival footage as a historical anchor was present already in the Czech Television serial production *Tell Me a Story* (*Vyprávěj*, dir. Biser Arichtev, 2009–13), discussed in the previous chapter. The series framed each episode in several minutes of clips from the archives of Czechoslovak Television, most often reminding viewers of period products or popular culture; at the end of the first round of archival footage, the scene would fade from black-and-white into full colour, signalling the beginning of the fictional narrative. Within the genre of a retro soap opera, these archival documents served to draw attention to the stylized portrayal of the past, while the project of *Burning Bush* is to match its visuals as closely as possible with period footage. But the visual identity of the mini-series does not make it inherently more authentic than *Tell Me a Story*; authenticity is a constructed category negotiated between the filmmakers and the audience.[50] In the case of *Burning Bush*, the story's basis in true historical events and real personages is the most obvious authenticating mechanism;⁵¹ in addition, it chimed in with the changing discursive context, which saw a greater interest in grand narratives, heroism and trauma, as opposed to making light of the past.

This brings me to the second main feature of this corpus of 'dramatic' portrayals of the past, namely their negotiation of perceived authenticity through their visual design. A precursor to such dramatic portrayals was the depiction of the invasion of August 1968 in comedies such as *The Rebels* or *Cosy Dens* (*Pelíšky*, dir. Jan Hřebejk, 1999). As Chapter 5 recounted, the unexpected arrival of Warsaw Pact troops brought about a sudden shift in tone in these films. Dispensing with bright colours and jokes, these films instead attempted to wrestle an emotional response from audiences through visually restrained, but all the more poignant images of loss and injustice, invoking tragedy, which dispenses with the easy resolution of comedy. This mode of emplotment necessarily brings about a number of cultural valences, 'seriousness' and 'veracity' being two of the principal connotations of tragic narratives. In terms of their emotional repertoire, rather than ironic distance, they play on sincerity. If we reach for a comparison with Germany, the discourse around Florian Henckel von Donnersmarck's *The Lives of Others* offers similarities. Despite objections from historians as to the historical detail present in the film, the director actively promoted the picture as a depiction of 'how things really were' in his view, in contrast to allegedly 'sentimental' and 'trivializing' depictions.⁵² In this sense, dramatic films display an impulse to preserve something 'true' about history that they see comedy as presumably not capable of. Indeed, in the Czech context, scholars have tended to be dismissive of comedy as a vehicle for portraying the period, usually on the grounds that comedy is deemed to be less appropriate and dignified to deal with historical topics, despite the fact that the cultural legitimacy of comedy remains high.⁵³

Agnieszka Holland, the Polish director of *Burning Bush*, who had herself studied at FAMU, Prague's acclaimed film school, in the 1960s and witnessed the Prague Spring there, explicitly confirmed a need for gravity as a factor contributing to the stylistic project of the mini-series:

> The young people who developed the project – the writer and the young producers – had been thinking that I was the only person who could do it because I experienced it. And at the same time I was an outsider and so I could look at the history without a sort of Czech complex. And by Czech complex they meant the aversion to talking seriously about the country's problems. You know, 'Let's make it funny'. And the young people behind this film had grown tired of a culture that was turning everything into some kind of joke. They saw that in some ways their parents and themselves were the victims of this silence. So they wanted to reconstruct or express their roots more seriously – and re-discover their roots for themselves.⁵⁴

Here, Holland clearly sets *Burning Bush* directly in opposition to the comedic portrayals of socialism that had become standard within Czech cultural production. Reviewers of the films of the dramatic turn also praised the 'serious' tackling of historical subjects.[55] This set of films takes as its subject matter not the everyday lives of ordinary characters, but exceptional narratives of oppression, injustice, heroism and direct confrontation with the regime.

The 'seriousness' conveyed by the choice of cinematic genre is usually corroborated by a muted colour palette in greys and browns, as opposed to the bursting colours that characterized films like *The Rebels*. The trope of grey Normalization, discussed in Chapter 4, emerges in *Walking Too Fast* and *Fair Play*, both set in the 1980s, and indeed encompasses the whole socialist period, including the 1950s in *In the Shadow* and the late 1960s in *Burning Bush*. In an interview, *In the Shadow*'s director David Ondříček explained this in the language of historical authenticity: 'The costumes and props almost completely lacked warm colours, because the period lacked them too.'[56] Visually, the film uses the highly stylized generic conventions of the neo-noir. The main character, detective Hakl, in Ivan Trojan's elegant portrayal, never goes out without his fedora and trench coat; despite living in a modest courtyard flat, his wife is always immaculately styled. What could thus be interpreted as a retro style, understood as a particular attention to period detail, is here a representation of the vestiges of a First Republic elegance that the characters hold on to in the immediate postwar period, the attractiveness of their outfits shrouded in the darkened colour scheme (Figure 6.1). Just as I argued in the previous chapter that in *Tell Me a Story*, the implicit object of nostalgia is not so much socialism as the interwar Republic, here too it is what survived

Figure 6.1 *Ve stínu* (*In the Shadow*), David Ondříček (director, screenwriter) and Marek Epstein, Misha Votruba (screenwriters), 2012. © Image Lucky Man Films.

of the First Republic that forms the film's aesthetic attraction. The supposed authenticity of the décor is further evoked through the shabby exteriors, depicting a Prague falling into disrepair after years of war and early socialism. The distinction to be made between the visual style of *In the Shadow* and retro is that the former is not double-edged, aimed at updating period looks to contemporary taste. The look of *In the Shadow* is undoubtedly attractive, but also decidedly dated: the fashions and styles of the film are not packaged to be consumed by a contemporary viewer, but to be enjoyed at a distance.

Third, the choice of genre contributes to a particular vision of heroism. Where the episodic structure of retro-comedies gave rise to self-enclosed moments of petty heroism, grand and sustained narratives require large or genuine heroic acts. Such portrayals have their predecessors in Jiří Stránský's novels *A Land Gone Wild* (*Zdivočelá země*, 1991) and *The Auction* (*Aukce*, 1997), and their subsequent television adaptation, discussed in Chapter 2, which present an all but flawless hero in the form of pilot and 'cowboy' Antonín Maděra, whose robust masculinity ultimately helps him survive hardship. *In the Shadow*, *Burning Bush* and, to an extent, *Fair Play* also consciously present heroic role models.

Petty heroic acts consisted of confronting authority indirectly (think of Kraus in *Cosy Dens* shouting obscenities at communists from his balcony) or in the form of a prank (such as the heroes of *The Identity Card* shaking an officiating policeman's hand with a crack to his knuckles when picking up their identity cards). In the new dramatic turn, heroes are ready to stand up to authority face to face. In *Burning Bush*, lawyer Dagmar Burešová wages a personal battle with a high-profile party official as she defends the family of Jan Palach; in *In the Shadow*, detective Hakl decides to fight for justice when he sees a case he has been working on has been politically manipulated; in *Fair Play*, athlete Anna refuses to take part in the Olympic Games despite having qualified, because she 'simply will not represent this system',[57] as she tells her trainer and a Party representative in a scene shot in dramatic close-up.

In the Shadow director David Ondříček described detective Hakl as a '[morally] clean hero', a type that does not appear frequently in Czech cultural representations.[58] Part of the discourse around *In the Shadow* and *Burning Bush* consisted of a comparison of Czech and Polish traditions of heroism. Agnieszka Holland called Jan Palach 'a rather Polish hero';[59] she corroborated this idea with the cultural stereotype that the Czechs have a much more tortured and self-conscious relationship to their heroes than the Poles, who celebrate theirs wholeheartedly. Ondříček agreed with this distinction, suggesting that 'in Poland, the Mašín brothers would have been declared national heroes long ago, while we are still musing about the opportuneness of assassinating Heydrich'.[60] Clearly, these filmmakers aimed to introduce a corrective to what they perceived as an insufficiently heroic narrative in Czech culture.

It is here that these narratives resonate most with the new discourse on resistance and heroism in the public sphere: these are heroes who in their own way also qualify as anticommunist resistance fighters and are not afraid to state this explicitly. Nevertheless, if the heroism of retro was petty and destined to failure, the results of the 'genuine' heroism of dramatic narratives are also not guaranteed. In *In the Shadow*, this message is brought home particularly transparently in the words with which detective Hakl attempts to reassure his small son about an 'invincible monster' he is fighting: 'If we fight it often enough, it will get tired and weak. And perhaps then someone will beat it someday.'[61] The vision of heroism in which these films partake is founded on the notion of sacrifice: both Burešová and Hakl engage in fights that they know are meaningful but futile; in *Fair Play*, Anna's mother accepts being sentenced to a term in prison for copying illegal materials rather than becoming an StB informer, thus sacrificing her daughter's career as a professional athlete.

Such an image of the hero resonates with what scholars working on Czech national identity have identified as a cult of victimhood in the Czech historical imaginary.[62] As journalist Zbyněk Petráček points out, the heroes of anticommunist resistance are figures like army general Heliodor Píka or politician Milada Horáková, i.e. people who were unjustly persecuted and executed in show trials (in 1949 and 1950 respectively), rather than those who actively fought back, like the much-disputed Mašín brothers.[63] The Third Resistance narrative, Petráček further suggests, turns both groups into heroes by co-opting the victims of the communist regime into the category of resistance fighters. But despite institutional attempts to promote an image of active or even armed resistance, this effort remains fraught and is still awaiting its cinematic depiction.

The films of the dramatic turn imply a memory of socialism predicated on trauma, a move that we also saw in educational initiatives such as Stories of Injustice or earlier in the discourse of the Confederation of Political Prisoners. Whereas the emotional repertoire of trauma was virtually absent from comedies, which subverted potentially threatening moments through humour, the dramatic turn links the causes of collective trauma to clear, embodied sources: the sadistic StB officer in *Kawasaki's Rose*; likewise the StB, who wish to frame a crime on members of the Jewish community in *In the Shadow*; and the trainer and doctor of Anna in *Fair Play*, who collude to give her risky illegal drugs in order to increase her performance. Such a clear demarcation of the responsibility for wrongdoing implies that if culprits can be identified, this should in theory enable justice or redemption, an assumption also present in the initial idea of opening the StB archives.

In portraying grand narratives with genuine heroes, films of the dramatic wave also have an inherent pedagogy. This is not an unprecedented move: rudiments of such ambitions in relation to the past could already be witnessed in the discourse around Irena Dousková discussed in Chapter 4, but an educational approach to the past in representation appeared even earlier in the 1990s in *A Land Gone Wild*. The films of the late 2000s and early 2010s build on such an edifying project. In particular, *In the Shadow* and *Burning Bush* were directly used for didactic purposes: the former film was promoted as part of the National Museum's educational initiative 'I zlo může být pozlátko' ('Evil Too Can Glitter'), and the director of the Museum was quoted as saying that the film corresponds with the initiative's antitotalitarian project.[64] *Burning Bush* has become part of the Stories of Injustice project, which developed a series of teaching materials relating to the film, available on the project's website.[65] Such efforts represent one of the most prominent intersections of representational culture with ongoing efforts in the public sphere, as these films were employed as educational tools to warn about the totalitarian nature of the communist regime.

Linked to this educational project is the desire of these pictures to become 'memory films' that shape the way in which the past is remembered. Memory films impact their social context, partaking through financial backing and marketing strategies in 'plurimedially constructed processes of negotiation', as Astrid Erll and Stephanie Wodianka argue.[66] Efforts to plant these films in wider social contexts, such as didactic initiatives, can be seen as precisely such processes of negotiation. It is in these attempts to create representations of the past that are deemed accurate enough to be used as educational tools that such representations posit their vision as the 'correct' interpretation of modern Czechoslovak history. Through their educational ambition, narratives of authenticity can be seen as self-proclaimed guardians of a democratic national memory. The First Republic is thus presented as an implicit object of nostalgia not only on an aesthetic but also a political level. It is in the interwar period where true Czech values are to be found: the 'good cop' Hakl was trained before the Second World War and his strong moral compass is a legacy of that time. Likewise, lawyer Dagmar Burešová's similarly upright position and graciousness of manner and style in *Burning Bush* obliquely point to her coming from a 'good' First Republic family background.

Herein also lies the principal difference in the political projects of retro and the dramatic turn. Retro relegates 'the system' to the background, creating an essentially nonparticipatory image of socialism, where the disagreement of protagonists with the ruling communist ideology is taken for granted; yet through the deflating use of humour, their acts of resistance remain petty and ineffectual, but their failure is also ultimately forgiven. Although the aesthetic veneer of retro masks an implicit binary framework of 'us' and 'them', with protagonists existing within a political system for which they never take coresponsibility, the generic conventions of comedy often play on human weakness and leave space for self-reflection and even self-criticism. Films of the dramatic turn, on the other hand, do not leave space for such self-reflexivity. They take themselves seriously in their attempt at 'restoring' an authentic vision of the past. Although it was also present in retro representations, here the implicit political object of restoration can be found even more strongly in the interwar First Republic with its perceived democratic tradition and ideals.

Towards a Plural Memory

The subject of this book has mainly been mainstream representations of socialism – films with a wide circulation in cinemas and on DVD, bestselling books or books that have been awarded literary prizes and TV serials with high ratings, which have all come together to shape the memory of the socialist past in the Czech Republic. But not all attempts at depicting socialism that arose after 1989, whether on screen or though the written word, fit the typology of retro comedies or the 'dramatic turn'. Over the years, a host of documentary films and art-house productions beyond the mainstream offered alternative modes of grappling with the pre-1989 past. Some of these productions innovatively elided and overcame the two competing tendencies of portraying the past via small petty gestures and grand heroic narratives. Drawing on these traditions, the made-for-television docudrama *Czech Century* (*České století*, dir. Robert Sedláček, 2013–14) moved beyond the narrative structures this book has focused on and challenged established modes of representing the past in the Czech context. If many of the discussed representations prescribed specific political interpretations of the past, *Czech Century* goes to show that representations can produce an open, multifaceted memory that complicates and questions, rather than simplifies, understandings of the past.

The public broadcaster, Czech Television, aired the initial five episodes of *Czech Century*, the joint project of screenwriter, publicist and public historian Pavel Kosatík and documentary and feature film director Robert Sedláček, in the autumn of 2013. The remaining four instalments premiered a year later. The series, which in spite of its inaccurate name reconstructs key moments of Czechoslovak history in the twentieth century, focused mainly on the highest levels of political representation. The filmmakers used their authorial licence to imagine and stage a number of behind-the-scenes and private dialogues that are not documented in any sources. Yet despite its preoccupation with men in the highest echelons of power, the series shuns the more recent search for grand narratives. *Czech Century* was criticized for a number of reasons – for its excessive use of the undynamic 'talking heads' format, the series' casting choices, its gender dynamics and a 'confusing' structure.[67] However, what is significant here are not the perceived shortcomings of the programme, but the discussion it sparked about the representation of historical figures.

Commentator Ondřej Štindl wrote that 'Czech Television can congratulate itself that it managed to produce a work that is somehow alive, perhaps even provocative'[68] and, together with others, praised the fact that the series triggered a genuine debate.[69] Yet it should also be noted that in the case of *Czech Century*, the debate was restricted to a small circle within an already circumscribed public sphere. The series presupposed a large degree of historical knowledge on the part of the audience and as such was aimed at a specialized segment of the public with particular levels of education or experience. Despite this fact, it premiered in prime time on Czech Television's First Channel, suggesting that the public broadcaster placed high hopes in this flagship project.

The ensuing debate was significant for cutting across a number of levels: it engaged not only journalists and commentators, but also eyewitnesses and even some of the historical actors portrayed in the series, in particular in relation to the episodes dealing with the more recent events of the Velvet Revolution and the economic transformation. Among those who felt compelled to comment on the accuracy of their own portrayals, as well as on the series' historical veracity in general, were former dissident and Havel's close collaborator Alexandr Vondra, first post-1989 Prime Minister Petr Pithart and Oskar Krejčí, advisor to the last communist Prime Minister Ladislav Adamec.[70]

The series itself makes no attempts at objectivity and presents clear historical arguments – for instance, Czechoslovak communism is understood as a Soviet import; the musical underground directly inspired Charter 77; November 1989 was not a revolution, but a deal between 'enlightened' communists and the Civic Forum, etc. But the interpretation of events garnered less critical attention than the portrayal of particular personages in this character-driven drama. In this, the series radically differed from the retro mode that often devised situations and character plots only in order to showcase particular aspects of the historical setting. Kosatík and Sedláček dispense with dense sets full of period markers; through focusing primarily on personalities, they set out to demythologize and deheroicize key figures. The filmmakers thus adopted a classic strategy of defamiliarization to provoke discussion: historical actors neither perform petty gestures nor attempt genuinely heroic endeavours, but are exposed as people with a number of flaws and weaknesses who engage in banal and everyday activities. We witness the second Czechoslovak President Edvard Beneš in the shower, Communist Party leaders urinating, the reformers of the Prague Spring debating in their underwear in a Moscow hotel, Václav Havel in the sauna and one of the architects of the economic transformation gutting a fish in his swimming costume. The motif of nudity emerges repeatedly to remind the audience not only of the vulnerability but also of the ordinariness of these men of power. The fact that the series was populated almost exclusively by male characters was often remarked upon by critics,[71] yet at the same time, it strips away some of the narratives and challenges the modes of thinking audiences may have inherited about these 'great men' in such scenes.

Probably the most debated of these everyday moments, which also points to the common expectations about the depiction of respected male figures, was the philosopher Jan Patočka expounding on the meaning of Charter 77 while opening a can of pâté. Critics questioned whether it behoves the thinker to engage in the banal act of opening a can and 'spreading pâté onto bread like a lumberjack in a forest',[72] and found the scene contrived (on the grounds that opening the can takes an unnaturally long time), undignified and belittling of Patočka's thought.[73] Such reactions demonstrate that, if nothing else, the authors were successful in generating unexpected and provocative images of well-known figures. The most controversial in this respect was the portrayal of Havel, whom some commentators felt to be a 'pitiable wimp'[74] in the series: Havel's own agency is downplayed as he is often found reacting to the impulses of others rather than presenting his own agenda. As the broadcast of the episodes featuring Havel roughly coincided with the third anniversary of his death, it also generated a broader discussion of the former dissident's and president's legacy. Should Havel, a figure already memorialized in a number of successful documentaries,[75] be remembered in the way *Czech Century* portrays him? Those who had known Havel personally offered their comments in the press.[76]

The refusal to ascribe heroism to figures like Havel was often remarked upon and it is a feature that the filmmakers themselves highlighted.[77] Film critic Tomáš Baldýnský suggested that the effectiveness of *Czech Century* is diminished by the fact that Czech culture lacks 'conformist works against which they [Sedláček and Kosatík] could define their own non-conformity'.[78] Baldýnský draws attention to the absence of a national canon of grand heroic narratives about the socialist past and 1989 in particular. Arguably, this is precisely the space that films of the dramatic turn have attempted to fill, though Baldýnský's comment in 2014 underscored the fact that their aspiration to becoming received memory films still required more sedimentation or had simply not been successful at that point. Sedláček quoted *Burning Bush* in particular as a portrayal of the past that avoids any kind of ambiguity, which he aimed to counter with his project.[79]

What was novel about the discussion around *Czech Century* was on the one hand the wide spectrum of opinions that accompanied the series – ranging from approval to complete disagreement – and also the consistent recognition in the media that the way in which events and personages were depicted reflected the personal interpretation of the filmmakers. In an ironic comment, Sedláček proclaimed in an interview: 'I am the Pujmanová of capitalism.'[80] He thus referred to the canonical communist writer Marie Pujmanová, who died in 1958, after becoming one of the new regime's main propagators of the socialist realist aesthetic programme. Sedláček noted that 'we are now filming history in service of the current regime. I'm afraid that I'm not enough of a genius to be able to overcome the prejudices of my time'.[81] This understanding on the part of the filmmakers of how difficult it is to escape historical interpretation through the prism of present political values moved the debate to a new level.

Sedláček and Kosatík acknowledged that their reading of the twentieth century would ultimately appear, despite their historical awareness, to posit the present political constellation as its only possible outcome. The way to combat this inherent problem of retrospective historical retelling is to make the resulting representation open to a plurality of readings: as Kosatík remarked in an interview, 'national memory, or whatever we should call it, has a tendency towards simplification. People are black and white in it, some are good, others are bad … In my opinion it is an unproductive attitude, which needs to be returned closer to the truth by complicating it'.[82] By avoiding the established patterns of both a self-congratulatory or victimizing narrative, the series made no effort to take up the role of a memory film that would present a cohesive, national mythology. In this sense, as one reviewer remarked, *Czech Century* successfully fulfilled its mission as public broadcasting by enabling a multiplicity of interpretations of the past to emerge.[83]

The fact that *Czech Century* offered portrayals of recent historical events that are open to challenge and criticism makes it a site of productive contestation of the past in which history is not used to promote the memory of any particular group. While the impact of this project on popular memory was limited (each episode of the series was watched by 350,000–650,000 viewers, which amounted to an approximately 8–16 per cent share of television audiences),[84] the liveliness of the debate around it does demonstrate that representations can actively intervene in memory processes and, instead of positing a single vision of the past, can serve to question it. *Czech Century* was thus one of the manifestations of the increasing dynamism of the Czech memory landscape in the 2010s, which oscillated between a preoccupation with public collective remembrance, but also increasing criticism of the forms taken by official memory politics.

The changes in representational strategies discussed in this chapter thus need to be understood in the context of a transforming public discourse about the socialist past. With the gradual challenge to the dominant post-1989 anticommunist story and the greater plurality of opinion in the public sphere, state actors and cultural elites saw a more pressing need to present strong model narratives about the past. A similar trend can be observed in popular culture. Alongside a preoccupation with the archival document, which has at times helped to problematize categories of heroism and collaboration, particularly in literature, large-scale film production embarked on an expanded quest for authenticity and heroes in narratives about socialism. At the same time, the changing climate allowed for the development of critical representations like *Czech Century*.

While public discourse tended to revolve around sensationalist 'agent scandals', the StB officer emerged as the real culprit in representations, be it in *Kawasaki's Rose, Love Letter in Cuneiform* or *Walking Too Fast*. These new narratives sketched a polarized moral map of socialism, in which evil StB officers were pitched against heroes who are not afraid to confront state power directly. The official efforts to promote an active memory of resistance and narratives featuring characters that embodied evil both used ethical categories to construct exemplary tales. This intensified preoccupation with heroes, villains and morality from the mid 2000s onwards can thus be interpreted as an ever-increasing effort at manufacturing a nationally inflected historical memory – a move that is not unique to the Czech Republic. Indeed, questions of nationalism and national identity – like in much of Europe and the United States – gained increasing prominence in political discourse towards the end of the period studied in this book, leading to the constant negotiation of the relationship to the past that had defined the era of postsocialism becoming less salient. This chapter has shown the longer genesis of this development in both memory politics and cultural production.

Notes

1. Parts of this chapter have previously appeared in V. Pehe, 'Authenticating the Past: Archives, Secret Police, and Heroism in Contemporary Czech Representations of Socialism', in M. Blaive (ed.), *Perceptions of Society in Communist Europe: Regime Archives and Popular Opinion* (London: Bloomsbury Academic, 2018), 207–22.
2. For more on the genesis of the Institute and its situation in the wider context of postsocialist 'memory institutes', see T. Sniegon, 'Implementing Post-communist National Memory in the Czech Republic and Slovakia', *European Studies* 30(1) (2013), 97–124.

3. For more on the Prague Declaration, see K. Ghodsee, 'Tale of "Two Totalitarianisms": The Crisis of Capitalism and the Historical Memory of Communism', *History of the Present* 4(2) (2014), 115–42.
4. 'I teď je vidět, jak se tetelíš nad tím, že na tebe někdo něco donášel. Myslíš si, že seš tím pro ostatní trochu zajímavější.' P. Šabach, *Občanský průkaz* (Prague and Litomyšl: Paseka, 2006), 165.
5. Among these rank the punk-rock comedy *Don't Stop* (dir. Richard Řeřicha, 2012) and the television film *Wisdom Teeth* (*Osmy*, dir. Jiří Strach, 2014) about an accidental signing of Charter 77.
6. P. Žáček, *Boje o minulost. Deset let vyrovnávání se s komunistickou minulostí – pokus o předběžnou bilanci* (Brno: Barrister and Principal, 2000).
7. P. Zídek, 'Druhá bitva o ústav' ['Second Battle for the Institute'], *Lidové noviny*, 3 November 2007, 4.
8. M. Kopeček, 'ÚSTR lépe a vědecky: Ale jak?' ['A Better and More Scholarly ÚSTR: But How?'], *Lidové noviny*, 8 April 2013, 13.
9. See V. Drchal, 'Češi pochybují o roce 1968' ['Czechs Have Doubts about 1968'], *Lidové noviny*, 18 August 2008, 1.
10. Drv, 'ČSSD chválí komunistický režim před rokem 1989' ['ČSSD Praise Communist Regime before 1989'], *Lidové noviny*, 28 December 2007, 1.
11. See M. Blaive, '"Hidden Transcripts" and Microhistory as a Comparative Tool: Two Case Studies in Communist Czechoslovakia', *East Central Europe* 40(1–2) (2013), 74–96.
12. M. Hekrdla, 'ÚSTR v době ústrků' ['ÚSTR in a Time of Machinations'], *Týden*, 2 April 2013, 61.
13. For an overview of various 'collaboration scandals', see M. Blaive, 'Zpřístupnění archivů komunistické tajné policie: případ České republiky – od Zdeny Salivarové k Milanu Kunderovi', *Souvislosti: 'Kauza Kundera' rok poté* 20(4) (2009), 158–73.
14. A. Hradilek and P. Třešňák, 'Udání Milana Kundery' ['The Denunciation of Milan Kundera'], *Respekt* 19(42) (2008), 38–45.
15. For more on the Kundera case, see J. Přibán, 'The Kundera Case and the Neurotic Collective Memory of Postcommunism', *Verfassungsblog*, 12 January 2018. Retrieved 23 August 2019 from https://verfassungsblog.de/the-kundera-case-and-the-neurotic-collective-memory-of-postcommunism. See also the special issue of *Souvislosti: 'Kauza Kundera' rok poté* 20(4) (2009), 140–80.
16. P. Eichler, 'Dialog o Ústavu?' ['Dialogue about the Institute?'], *Literární noviny*, 3 November 2008, 3; drv, 'Hlasy za odvolání Žáčka sílí: Přidal se i Havel' ['More Voices Call for Žáček's Removal: Havel Has Joined Them'], *Lidové noviny*, 20 November 2009, 1.
17. L. Navara, 'Atentát na Gottwalda? Pouhé úvahy, říká Mašín' ['A Plan to Assassinate Gottwald? Mere Contemplation, Says Mašín'], *iDnes.cz*, 5 April 2008. Retrieved 23 August 2019 from http://zpravy.idnes.cz/atentat-na-gottwalda-pouhe-uvahy-rika-masin-feq /domaci.aspx?c=A080405_114528_domaci_jan.
18. M. Kozumplík, 'Mikuláš Kroupa: Hrdinové nejsou', *Instinkt* 7(45) (2008), 68–69.
19. Ibid., 68.
20. K. Strachota, 'Výslech' ['Interrogation'], *Lidové noviny*, 9 Septmebr 2007, 11.
21. L. Martinková, 'Novodobá historie děti zajímá' ['Children Are Interested in Contemporary History'], *Lidové noviny*, 6 December 2011, 19.
22. K. Strachota, 'Nebylo naší ambicí vydat odbornou práci' ['It Was Not Our Ambition to Publish a Scholarly Work'], *Lidové noviny*, 11 November 2010, 11.
23. A. Drda, J. Mlejnek and S. Škoda, *Mýty o socialistických časech* (Prague: Člověk v tísni, 2010), 5.

24. L. Navara and J. Gazdík, 'Byli jste hrdinové: První odbojáři to uslyší už (až) dnes' ['You Were Heroes: The First Resistance Fighters Will Hear it Already (Only) Today'], *Mladá fronta Dnes*, 10 April 2012, 4.
25. Act 198/1993 Coll. Available on the Chamber of Deputies of the Parliament of the Czech Republic website. Retrieved 23 August 2019 from http://www.psp.cz/sqw/sbirka.sqw?cz=198&r=1993.
26. For more on the activities of the KPV and their claims to a memory of victimhood, see Chapter 6 of F. Mayer, *Les Tchèques et leur communisme: Mémoire et identités politiques* (Paris: Editions de l'Ecole des hautes études en sciences sociales, 2004), 167–94.
27. For a comprehensive overview of the Mašín case and accompanying debates, see J. Švéda, *Mašínovský mýtus: ideologie v české literatuře a kultuře* (Příbram: Pistorius and Olšanská, 2012).
28. J. Novák, *Zatím dobrý: Mašínovi a největší příběh studené války* (Brno: Petrov, 2004).
29. During this period, a 2011 poll conducted for Czech Television showed that only 15 per cent of respondents considered the Mašín brothers' actions 'heroic', 27 per cent perceived them as 'unjustifiable criminal acts', while 41 per cent were undecided. Statistics cited in Švéda, *Mašínovský mýtus*, 224. See also N. Adamičková and M. Königová, 'Třetí odboj: Mašínové rozdělili sněmovnu' ['Third Resistence: Mašín Brothers Divided Parliament'], *Právo*, 11 June 2011, 4.
30. Premier Mirek Topolánek had declared the Mašín brothers 'heroes' in 2007 and granted them special recognition in the form of a 'Prime Minister's Plaque' in 2008, while the Defence Minister honoured the Mašíns' sister in 2009. The death of Milan Paumer, member of the Mašíns' resistance group, in 2010 directly accelerated the passing of the Act on Third Resistance.
31. M. Švehla, 'Ke slovu musí přijít levicoví historici' ['Left-Wing Historians Must Be Heard'], *Respekt*, 14 April 2013, 38–43.
32. These include the mid 2000s incarnation of *Literární noviny* (*Literary News*) before some of its editorial staff went on to found the online daily *Deník Referendum* (*Referendum Daily*) in 2009. Further examples are the initially weekly and later biweekly critical magazine *A2* (since 2005) and later its online daily platform *A2larm* (since 2013). The online periodical *Britské listy* (*British Papers*), already active since 1999, can also be counted into this group.
33. Many of Pullmann and Kolář's essays are now usefully collected in their edited volume *Co byla Normalizace?* (Prague: Nakladadelsvtví Lidové noviny; ÚSTR, 2017). The fact this 'revisionist' book was published in ÚSTR is itself symbolic of a changing and pluralizing discourse.
34. M. Bernhard and J. Kubik, 'A Theory of the Politics of Memory', in M. Bernhard and J. Kubik (eds), *Twenty Years after Communism* (Oxford: Oxford University Press, 2014), 7–30 (12–13).
35. Ghodsee, 'Tale of "Two Totalitarianisms"', 117.
36. In this sense, these representations correspond with pathos as one of the characteristics of low mimetic tragedy in Northrop Frye's *Anatomy of Criticism* (Princeton: Princeton University Press, 1971).
37. M. Todorova, 'Introduction: The Process of Remembering Communism', in M. Todorova (ed.), *Remembering Communism: Genres of Representation* (New York: Social Science Research Council, 2010), 9–34 (23).
38. A. Erll, 'Literature, Film, and the Mediality of Cultural Memory', in A. Erll and A. Nünning (eds), *Cultural Memory Studies: An International and Interdisciplinary Handbook* (Berlin: Walter de Gruyter, 2008), 389–98 (389).

39. Among these prose works are J. Novák, *Zatím dobrý* (Brno: Petrov, 2004), which won the Magnesia Litera prize in 2005; J. Hájíček, *Selský baroko* (Brno: Host, 2005), received the Magnesia Litera prize in 2006; V. Nosková, *Bereme, co je* (Prague: Abonent ND, 2005), was nominated for the Magnesia Litera prize; V. Nosková, *Obsazeno* (Prague: MozART, 2007), was nominated for the Josef Škvorecký prize; T. Zmeškal *Milostný dopis klínovým písmem* (Prague: Torst, 2008), won the Josef Škvorecký prize in 2009; J. Balabán, *Zeptej se táty* (Brno: Host, 2010), received the Magnesia Litera prize in 2010; K. Tučková, *Žítkovské bohyně* (Brno: Host, 2012), won the Josef Škvorecký prize in 2012; J. Hájíček, *Rybí krev* (Brno: Host, 2012), received the Magnesia Litera prize in 2013.
40. D. Pucherová, 'Trauma a pamäť augusta 1968 v súčasnom slovenskom románe', *World Literature Studies* 6(2) (2014), 64–77 (66).
41. 'Teď je mi deset, o životě a falši leccos vím.' V. Nosková, *Bereme, co je* (Prague: Abonent ND, 2005), 60.
42. '… takzvaný poctivý komunista neboli komunista blbec.' Ibid., 10.
43. 'On, a oběť? To nešlo dohromady ani s ním, ani s jeho profesí. Vždy o sobě smýšlel jako o člověku, který měl takřka nehodu, nepříjemnou politickou nehodu, po které byly trvalé následky, ale že by byl oběť, to ho nikdy nenapadlo.' T. Zmeškal, *Milostný dopis klínovým písmem* (Prague: Torst, 2008), 173. Trans. A. Zucker, *Love Letter in Cuneiform* (New Haven: Yale University Press, 2016), 150.
44. *Walking Too Fast* was critically acclaimed despite its poor performance in cinemas – it did not make it into the top fifty films in terms of audience figures in 2010, but received the country's main annual film award, the Czech Lion, for best picture. *Kawasaki's Rose* and *In the Shadow* were both commercially successful for domestic films with over 150,000 tickets sold in both cases. Holland's *Hořící keř* aired on HBO as a three-part mini series; its film version also won a number of Czech Lion awards. *Fair Play* was not a major commercial success, but made it into the top fifty most-watched films in 2014.
45. V. Rynda, 'Lidé se "škraloupem" s tím musejí ven' ['People with a "Blot" on Their Reputation Must Come out'], *Lidové noviny*, 30 December 2009, 7.
46. S. Bechman Pedersen, *Reel Socialism: Making Sense of History in Czech and German Cinema since 1989* (Lund: Lund University/Media-Tryck, 2015), 245.
47. The film did not make it into the fifty most-watched films in 2012 in the Czech Republic; in Slovakia, it was the most-watched picture for two weekends after its opening, but even so was only seen by about 10,000 viewers.
48. Interview with Juraj Nvota, Czech Television website. Retrieved 23 August 2019 from https://www.ceskatelevize.cz/porady/10331553019-konfident/21151212062/10640-juraj-nvota.
49. See, for example, J. Gregor, 'Recenze: Příliš sympatickému Konfidentovi chybí odvaha' ['Review: Too Likeable Informer Lacks Courage'], *aktualne.cz*, 11 July 2012. Retrieved 23 August 2019 from https://magazin.aktualne.cz/kultura/film/recenze-prilis-sympatickemu-konfidentovi-chybi-odvaha/r~i:article:751132/?redirected=1543657565; or D. Bernát, 'Recenzia: Eštebák s rozpakmi' ['Review: The Uneasy Informer'], *Pravda.sk*, 23 April 2018. Retrieved 23 August 2019 from https://kultura.pravda.sk/film-a-televizia/clanok/58727-recenzia-estebak-s-rozpakmi.
50. For more on authenticity in historical film, see C. Classen, 'Balanced Truth: Steven Spielberg's Schindler's List among History, Memory, and Popular Culture', trans. K. Wächter, *History and Theory* 48(2) (2009), 77–102 (88).
51. K. Činátl, *Naše české minulosti, aneb, jak vzpomínáme* (Prague: Nakladatelství Lidové noviny, 2014), 138.

52. J. James, 'Coming to Terms through Cinema: The Lives of Others in Germany's Cultural Landscape of Memory', *Journal of the Society for the Anthropology of Europe* 10(2) (2010), 29–40 (29). See also von Donnersmarck quoted in A. Enns, 'The Politics of Ostalgie: Postsocialist Nostalgia in Recent German Film', *Screen* 48(4) (2007), 475–91 (490).
53. P. Dominková, '"We Have Democracy, Don't We?" Czech Society as Reflected in Contemporary Czech Cinema', in Oksana Sarkisova and Péter Apor (eds), *Past for the Eyes: East European Representations of Communism in Cinema and Museums after 1989* (Budapest: Central European University Press, 2008), 215–44; F. Mayer, *Les Tchèques et leur communisme: Mémoire et identités politiques* (Paris: Editions de l'Ecole des hautes études en sciences sociales, 2004), in particular 266.
54. J. Sperling, 'In Conversation: Agnieszka Holland with Joshua Sperling', *The Brooklyn Rail*, 18 December 2013. Retrieved 23 August 2019 from http://www.brooklynrail.org/2013/12/film/agnieszka-holland-with-joshua-sperling.
55. D. Prejdová, 'Pocit, že za oknem prší kamení' ['The Feeling It's Raining down Stones outside the Window'], *Lidové noviny*, 4 Febraury 2010, 8; K. Steigerwald, 'Hořící keř, konec žoviálnosti' ['Hořící keř, the End of Joviality'], *Mladá fronta Dnes*, 25 January 2013, 10; I. Zemanová, 'Kawasakiho růže' ['Kawasaki's rose'], *Hospodářské noviny*, 11 December 2009, 15.
56. T. Spáčilová, 'Ano, chtěl bych Oscara' ['Yes, I Would Like an Oscar: Interview with David Ondříček'], *Reflex*, 6 September 2012, 70.
57. 'Já prostě tenhle systém reprezentovat nebudu.' *Fair Play*, 2014.
58. M. Spáčilová, 'Lampa, klobouk, dlouhý plášť: Vítejte v temném světě Ve stínu' ['Lamp, Hat, Long Overcoat: Welcome to the Dark World of Ve stínu – Interview with David Ondříček'], *Mladá fronta Dnes*, 13 September 2012, 2.
59. M. Spáčilová, 'Nemusí jít o život: Hrdina nelže, nekrade a chodí k volbám' ['It Doesn't Have to Be a Matter of Life and Death: A Hero Does Not Lie or Steal and Votes in Elections'], *Mladá fronta Dnes* ['Hořící keř' supplement], 25 January 2013, 53.
60. Spáčilová, 'Lampa, klobouk, dlouhý plášť', 2.
61. 'Když se s ní často budeme prát, tak se unaví a zeslábne. A třeba ji někdo jednou porazí.' *Ve stínu*, 2012.
62. R. Pynsent, *Questions of Identity: Czech and Slovak Ideas of Nationality and Personality* (Budapest: Central European University Press, 1994), in particular 190–210; L. Holý, *The Little Czech and the Great Czech Nation: National Identity and the Post-communist Transformation of Society* (Cambridge: Cambridge University Press, 1996), 72–73.
63. Z. Petráček, 'Od obětí k odboji' ['From Victims to Resistance'], *Lidové noviny*, 12 August 2013, 8.
64. (sen), 'Ondříčkův film Ve stínu se ohlašuje' ['Ondříček's film *In the Shadows* Announces itself'], *ČT24*, 24 August 2012. Retrieved 23 August 2019 from http://www.ceskatelevize.cz/ct24/kultura/193214-ondrickuv-film-ve-stinu-se-ohlasuje.
65. See https://www.jsns.cz/lekce/15234-60-leta-a-prazske-jaro (retrieved 23 August 2019).
66. A. Erll and S. Wodianka, 'Einleitung: Phänomenologie and Methodologie des "Erinnerungsfilms"', in A. Erll and S. Wodianka (eds), *Film und kulturelle Erinnerung: Plurimediale Konstellationen* (Berlin: Walter de Gruyter, 2008), 1–20 (2).
67. E. Zajíčková, 'České století počtvrté: Ty vole, bacha, Klémo' ['Czech Century the Fourth Time: Kléma, Mate, Watch out'], *Právo*, 18 November 2013, 21; M. Spáčilová, 'Klaus a Mečiar ukončí stát i seriál: Díky, ať si jdou' ['Klaus and Mečiar Will End Both State and Series: Thanks, Let Them Go'], *Mladá fronta Dnes*, 5 December 2014, 11; P. Zídek, 'České století jako obskurní' ['Czech Century as Obscure'], *Lidové noviny*, 20 December

2014, 24; red, 'České století: Pěkný guláš' ['Czech Century: What a Goulash'], *A2larm.cz*, 4 November 2013. Retrieved 23 August 2019 from https://a2larm.cz/2013/11/pekny-gulas/.
68. O. Štindl, 'Mocní a ztracení muži' ['Powerful and Lost Men'], *Lidové noviny*, 3 December 2013, 7.
69. Petr Zídek called *Czech Century* 'the most debated television project of the past year'. '*České století jako obskurní*' ['*Czech Century* as Obscure'], *Lidové noviny*, 20 December 2014, 24. See also E. Tabery, 'Jak to tehdy bylo' ['What Happened Back Then'], *Respekt*, 8 December 2014, 3.
70. See, e.g. V. Ševela, 'Pithart: Havla jsem na tajnou schůzku s Čalfou poslal já' ['Pithart: I Sent Havel to Secret Meeting with Čalfa'], *echo24.cz*, 3 December 2014. Retrieved 23 August 2019 from http://echo24.cz/a/i8YtY/pithart-havla-jsem-na-tajnou-schuzku-s-calfou-poslal-ja; V. Ševela, 'Z Havla udělali blbečka, říká Vondra o seriálu České století' ['They Made Havel into a Fool, Says Vondra about Czech Century'], *echo24.cz*, 2 December 2014. Retrieved 23 August 2019 from http://echo24.cz/a/wV5Lw/z-havla-udelali-blbecka-rika-vondra-o-serialu-ceske-stoleti; Alexandr Vondra and director Robert Sedláček polemicized on DVTV, 17 December 2014. Retrieved 23 August 2019 from http://video.aktualne.cz/dvtv/vondra-o-ceskem-stoleti-pri-pohledu-na-havla-mi-bylo-trapne/r~e5efe9ca855511e4833a0025900fea04.
71. Štindl, 'Mocní a ztracení muži'; J. Machalická, 'České století je jen mužská záležitost' ['Czech Century is an All-Male Affair'], *Lidové noviny*, 14 December 2013, 9; I. Hartman, 'Století rozhněvaných mužů' ['A Century of Angry Men'], *Hospodářské noviny*, 14 November 2014, 20.
72. J. Peňás, 'Kde si opatřit bony? U Havlů…' ['Where to Get Vouchers? At the Havels'…'], *Lidové noviny*, 25 November 2014, 1.
73. The weekly *Respekt* even published an article entitled 'Patočka's Can', which analysed the surprising attention this scene had provoked. J. Spurný, 'Patočkova konzerva', *Respekt*, 1 December 2014, 32.
74. See, for instance, P. Zídek, 'Havel jako ňouma' ['Havel as a Wimp'], *Lidové noviny*, 13 December 2014, 10; Ševela, 'Z Havla udělali blbečka'.
75. These include the film *Citizen Havel* (*Občan Havel*, dir. Pavel Koutecký and Miroslav Janek, 2007), which captures Havel's presidency over a number of years. The films *Citizen Václav Havel Goes on Holiday* (*Občan Václav Havel jede na dovolenou*, dir. Jan Novák and Adam Novák, 2005) and *Citizen Havel is Rolling the Empty Barrels* (*Občan Havel přikuluje*, dir. Jan Novák and Adam Novák, 2009) portray episodes from Havel's life in the 1970s and 1980s. Havel has also been the subject of numerous television and student films.
76. See M.M. Šimečka, 'Jiný Václav Havel' ['A Different Václav Havel'], *Respekt*, 8 December 2012, 14; M. Švehla, 'Jak to bylo doopravdy' ['How it Really Was'], *Respekt*, 8 December 2012, 23.
77. Pavel Kosatík noted in an interview that 'for me, there is no such thing as an ideal hero'. P. Andreas, 'Co je to být Čechem?' ['What Does It Mean to be Czech?'], *A2*, 19 June 2013, 21.
78. T. Baldýnský, 'Pravda vítězí' ['Truth Wins'], *Lidové noviny*, 3 December 2014, 20.
79. J. Bělíček and J. Fiala, 'Režisér Sedláček: Jsem Pujmanová kapitalismu' ['Director Sedláček: I am the Pujmanová of Capitalism'], *A2larm.cz*, 22 December 2014. Retrieved 23 August 2019 from https://a2larm.cz/2014/12/reziser-sedlacek-jsem-pujmanova-kapitalismu/.
80. Ibid.

81. O. Suchan, 'Havla jsem hledal nejdéle' ['The Search for Havel Took the Longest'], *Lidové noviny*, 19 April 2014, 2.
82. Andreas, 'Co je to být Čechem?', 21.
83. K. Fila, 'Havel pro každého' ['Havel for Everyone'], *Respekt*, 24 November 2014, 92.
84. Data available on MediaGuru.cz: mav, 'České století vidělo poprvé 630 tisíc diváků' ['First Episode of Czech Century Seen by 630,000 viewers'], *Mediaguru.cz*, 28 November 2013. Retrieved 23 August 2019 from https://www.mediaguru.cz/2013/10/ceske-stoleti-videlo-poprve-pres-600-tisic-divaku.

Conclusion

SOCIALISM REMEMBERED

In a memorable scene from Jan Hřebejk's 2003 film *Pupendo*, which was hailed as an eagerly awaited sequel to the massively successful *Cosy Dens* (*Pelíšky*, dir. Jan Hřebejk, 1999),[1] two friends argue about who is a bigger hero. On one side stands out-of-favour sculptor Mára, who has given up on his art, and floats through the early 1980s fairly contentedly in a grey zone of semi-dissent, supporting himself with small commercial commissions. Facing him is opportunist school headmaster Míla Břečka, who would also like to resist the system, but fears to do so overtly. Having been commissioned to install a mosaic of spring motifs in the school where Břečka teaches, Mára challenges the headmaster to write a 'message to future generations', which he will then hide in the mosaic. Knowing that no one will ever read this message and that his act of resistance is destined to remain completely private and secret, Břečka suddenly becomes outspoken. 'Not all commies are the same. Some people enter [the Party] to soften it from the inside, mate, some sacrifice themselves!',[2] he tells Mára boisterously. As a result of Mára's egging on, Břečka writes a note stating that 'Communism is crap and Bolsheviks are swine' and adds that 'headmaster Míla Břečka was forced to feign loyalty in the interests of thousands of children although internally he was always in opposition',[3] which he then hands over to Mára, who cements it into a crack in the wall.

The scene captures several key elements of the Czech memory of state socialism that this book has analysed. Mára and Břečka commit acts of minor resistance to demonstrate their anticommunist credentials, knowing that their gestures have limited reach and remain, ultimately, insignificant. They serve to secure the protagonists' peace of mind and feeling of self-worth in a repressive regime rather than posing a real challenge to the ruling power. I have termed this mechanism 'petty heroism' and have traced its presence in a range of comedies about the socialist past. This genre dominated the memory of socialism in popular culture until well into the first decade of the new millennium, when it was supplanted by a 'dramatic turn' that cast the previous regime as trauma and saw characters attempt large-scale heroic acts.

The memory of the past expressed by petty heroism is cosy and comfortable: for characters who perceive themselves as not implicated in the system, communists are always the Other, someone else. In the scene above, Břečka, who is a member of the Communist Party, also externalizes communism – he is a 'better' kind of communist, exculpated through his insignificant gesture. In this instance, we laugh at his hypocrisy, which is later compounded by his panic when building works threaten to dislodge the mosaic, thus risking the discovery of the message. Reeling off all the possible damaging consequences to Mára, Břečka convinces the sculptor to immediately go and remove the paper, and then proceeds to swallow it for good measure. While Břečka's backtracking on his 'heroism' is an object of ridicule here, anticommunism is the default position from which life under the previous regime is narrated. Opposition to communist ideology and its implementation as real existing socialism is a given through the character of the stoic Mára, who unlike the ambitious headmaster has little to lose. The film leads the viewer to sympathize with Mára's resistance, shining a kindly light on the somewhat romantic vision of the everyday state of opposition he lives in, but simultaneously, it shows understanding for Břečka's moral compromises.

Despite this political orientation of the film that clearly values the communist regime negatively, the wistful musical accompaniment, soft colours and side plot detailing the joys and woes of adolescence would all suggest a nostalgic tone in relation to the 1980s. The production design betrays a fascination with the aesthetics of the period, but this is not at odds with a condemnation of its politics. I have used the term 'retro' to capture this dynamic. Unlike nostalgia, which looks back to better times, retro draws on a somewhat complacent congratulatory narrative of 'knowing better'. This 'velvet retro' turns back to state socialism from the retrospective vantage point of having successfully overthrown the dictatorial regime through the events of the Velvet Revolution – a result achieved, such comedies implied, precisely through minor acts of everyday resistance.

As the condition known as postsocialism in the former Eastern Bloc is increasingly being historicized, memory processes of coming to terms with the past require re-examination. The task of this book was thus to tell the history of Czech postsocialism as seen through the prism of the evolving relationship to the past negotiated by cultural producers in their work and by media and institutions in public discourse. How did Czechs live through the forty years of Communist Party dictatorship and who is to be commended for their actions during this period? These were the implicit questions addressed in literature, film and television representations of the past. I argued that the memory of state socialism was initially shaped by a certain tension: while on the one hand, public discourse posited a radical break with the past, on the other hand, popular novels and film comedies offered a more forgiving and conciliatory view of the communist regime, creating an image of a nation that may not have stood up heroically to injustice, but collectively resisted with small gestures of opposition. With the passage of time, representations too became more radical, in an effort to pass moral judgement on perpetrators and seek role models for good behaviour, while public discourse became diversified with new media voices and political actors calling for a more complex and pluralized approach to the past.

One of the starting premises of this book was that collective memory in cultural artefacts can only be understood if it is examined simultaneously with public discourses on the past and official memory politics. I thus looked at the role of anticommunism as the main overarching narrative of the new era in Czech political and media discourse after 1989 and traced how it made its way both implicitly and explicitly into literary, cinematic and television representations of state socialism. Political interpretations of the past, I argued, coalesce most clearly around ideas of heroism. How the category of hero is understood is closely tied to the political project of building national identity; it is thus an instance that illustrates particularly clearly how uses of the past play into present political discourses. Petty heroism, present mainly in comedies, did not offer obvious role models for behaviour, but rather created an inclusive image of widely shared resistance against the communist regime, thus also obscuring any meaningful engagement with the regime's consensual aspects. By contrast, the turn towards new genres of representation, such as psychological or courtroom drama or neo-noir, which took off as a prominent force in portraying the past after the turn of the millennium, focused not on everyday narratives, but on tales of exceptionalism. Resistance was no longer widely distributed amongst the general population, which was instead seen as oppressed by a totalitarian regime. While comedy strove to accommodate a broad spectrum of Czech society into the legitimate memory of state socialism, narratives of trauma attempted to delegitimize and cast out perpetrators from the shared stories of the past.

On a further level, the preceding chapters questioned whether nostalgia, so widely discussed in the German and post-Yugoslav cases, is still an adequate framework to understand the memory processes described above. The Czech case opens up a range of themes central to the memory of socialism that give us alternative ways of thinking through how this period has been remembered to the nostalgia paradigm. In contrast to other national contexts, I have demonstrated that Czech cultural representations of state socialism in fact display relatively little sentimental longing for the past. Instead, nostalgia takes an unlikely object in the Czech case – that of nostalgia for resistance against the regime and for bringing it down with small, private gestures. While the literature on *Ostalgie* traced a longing for the promise of a more just society in both everyday consumer practices and in literary and cinematic representations, and searched for the redeeming features of life in the GDR, the thrust towards resistance in Czech retrospective representations of state socialism stands in opposition to such established ideas about postsocialist nostalgia.

Czech representations do not dispense with nostalgia altogether; they do present a sentimental longing for aspects of the past, but this longing is rarely directed towards an assessment of the previous regime as superior to the present. If nostalgia is at stake, then it lies in the idea of a resistant way of life, enabled by a repressive system in which the difference between good and evil was easy to navigate. Through their narrative structure, popular works of literature, film and television extend an invitation to their audiences to be implicitly included into the community of 'us' – those who were always opposed to 'them', the communists. Nostalgia and a totalitarian conception of the past thus sit comfortably side by side, I have argued, where it is possible to sentimentally look back upon rebellion against a regime that is seen as holding its population tightly in check. If there is a yearning for a return to the past, this lies not in the period of state socialism, but in the myth of the interwar First Republic, which representations of socialism posit as the site of true, democratic Czech values, while the period of communist rule is seen as an aberration in the trajectory of Czech history. Nostalgia is a mechanism of overcoming loss; the loss here is not life under the previous regime and the comforts it may have afforded, such as a sense of community, social security and a vision of building a better future, as German *Ostalgie* films such as *Good Bye, Lenin!* (dir. Wolfgang Becker, 2003) or *Kleinruppin Forever* (dir. Carsten Fiebeler, 2004) suggested. Instead, the implicit lost object that representations attempt to recover is a perceived democratic national identity. In public discourse, the rhetoric of anticommunism often externalized the causes of this loss, portraying communism as a 'Soviet import'. Through 'othering' representatives of power, cultural producers too created stories that offered a picture of the communist regime as imposed on the population by someone else, but certainly not the protagonists, who through their small gestures of would-be heroism demonstrated their allegiance to democratic values.

The wider implication here is that a revision of nostalgia as a positive valuation of the past may be a productive way of rethinking some of the memory paradigms associated with postsocialist nostalgia throughout the region. Certainly, as we saw, representations that present an indulgent retrospective view of the rebellious exploits of adolescents testing the limits of a repressive regime are not unique to the Czech context. Such narratives are present in the German *Ostalgie* canon and elsewhere; however, the fact nostalgia turns to the regime's repressive aspects as a facilitator of resistance is a phenomenon that deserves further exploration. Czech stories about socialism, whether told as comedy or tragedy, ultimately searched for dignified ways of living through an authoritarian regime. Scholars working on Germany have also written about *Ostalgie* as a quest for returning dignity to East Germans to whom it had been denied, but cultural memory can also attempt to shape how dignity should be understood, presenting normative actions and ways of life to be commended or condemned.

At the same time, writers and filmmakers also obviously took great enjoyment in depicting the past. I have theorized retro as a designation for an appreciation of the aesthetics of state socialist design, fashion, music, hairstyles, etc., which simultaneously rejects the previous regime's politics and authoritarian nature. It picks and chooses elements from the past attractive for contemporary audiences and approaches them with tongue-in-cheek irony. But retro, I have tried to show, is more than just a postmodern version of nostalgia or the seeming malaise of meaninglessness and ahistoricity that Fredric Jameson lamented in his influential discussion of the 'nostalgia film'.[4] It would also be a mistake to interpret it as mere apolitical aestheticism. Instead, retro offers a clear value judgement. It presents an opposite temporal dynamic to the longing for a better past associated with the vocabularies of nostalgia. It dwells comfortably in the knowledge that state socialism has been overcome and in the present liberal democratic order, neither communist ideology nor the lived experience of the previous regime presents a threat. In retro's view, the past is organized teleologically to culminate in the end point of the present order.

From this position, elements of the past are available for playful reuse, including in commercial form. Mocking the past with ironic symbolism, or, by contrast, redeeming certain products as quality, sells – and not only in the postsocialist space. Retro waves of previous decades coming back into fashion are a familiar phenomenon across all of Western culture. But retro as a specific memory mode and temporal dynamic that I have conceptualized on the example of postsocialist Czech Republic is by no means limited to the former Eastern Bloc. As we have seen on the example of the TV series *Mad Men*, retro as a regime of memory reinforcing the idea of a superior present while pillaging the past for aesthetic enjoyment is also present in Western popular culture. Retro thus challenges the collapse of state socialism as a decisive memory break that allows for a specific 'post-socialist' memory to develop;

instead, it bridges the divide between the perceived specificity of East and West, and questions the usefulness of a specifically postsocialist nostalgia. As a mechanism that uses the past to affirm the present, it has wide applicability and demonstrates that memory processes in the former Eastern Bloc are embedded in a global network of cultural exchange. In its amalgamation of both sentimental enjoyment of the aesthetics of the past and a clearly distancing, ironic attitude towards the era's political realities, retro offers a possibility of integrating binary typologies of nostalgia, such as Svetlana Boym's much-quoted distinction between the 'restorative' and 'reflective', which pit longing for a return to the past and more reflective, postmodern forms against each other.

Although I have argued that the messages in cultural representations were not at odds with public discourse that sought to denounce the previous regime, such a picture is necessarily complicated if we take into account audience responses and consumer practices. In Chapter 3, I outlined how viewers and listeners defended their right to enjoy socialist popular culture through the rescreening of the TV series *The Thirty Cases of Major Zeman* and the music of Karel Gott, even as commentators in the press called for a radical caesura with the culture of the past. Just like in the case of socialist-era brands that have reinvented themselves for the postsocialist market, as discussed in Chapter 5, consumers accommodate these artefacts of the past into the present through associating them with seemingly 'extra-ideological' categories such as quality and tradition. Such responses represent what Irena Reifová terms a 'demand for continuity', which takes pleasure in the right to migrate in memory across the break of 1989.[5] They suggest a cleavage between the communicative memory shared by those who experienced the period and the institutionalized cultural memory 'from above', when especially in the years immediately following regime change, public discourse was concerned with demonizing the communist regime.[6] This aspect of the collective memory of state socialism comes closer to the antihegemonic dimension that many scholars attribute to *Ostalgie* and suggests that elite memory projects were antagonistic rather than consensual. However, this book's main focus was on the textual level of representations of the past. I have shown that cultural producers also operate within the constraints of public discourse: often the messages in representations implicitly coincided with or reacted to public debates, especially when it came to their anticommunist timbre and conceptions of what it means to be a hero. But such an approach is admittedly limited to narrow elite discourses. A gap that remains to be filled across the postsocialist region is integrating the study of the politics of representations of the past with their reception by broader audiences – an ambitious undertaking on any scale, but one that would undoubtedly bring variegated and complex results.

Looking at the wider political and social context in which representations are embedded showed that cultural producers were more than willing to support the anticommunist consensus not only in their creative work, but also in the form of collective political action, such as the initiative 'One Does Not Speak to Communists' of 2003. Such actions demonstrated that cultural elites shared many of their political convictions with influential media commentators and political actors, shaping a Manichean memory discourse of 'good' liberal democracy versus an 'evil' communist regime. This book traced how changes in the discourse of anticommunism and official memory politics correlated with the transformation of representational strategies over time. The institutional efforts to mainly break with the past could not obscure communicative memory: new media voices and historians became increasingly interested in complicating the understanding of citizens' everyday experiences under state socialism. I suggested that just as anticommunism as the grand narrative of the postsocialist era started coming under fire in the first decade of the new millennium, as a reaction, elite mnemonic actors attempted to fortify a memory of heroic anticommunist resistance, shifting from previous accents on identifying victims to searching for heroes. Simultaneously, literature and film also took up a quest for heroes, moving the focus from everyday gestures of resistance to portraying clear-cut acts of heroism, demonstrating how cultural producers either implicitly or consciously interacted with changing discursive paradigms about the past. Czech memory processes were also embedded in wider pan-European efforts to institutionalize a memory of communism and Nazism as equally totalitarian regimes in the second half of the first decade of the new millennium. Representations of state socialism no longer attempted to suspend trauma through laughter, but instead sought to pinpoint the perpetrators of collective suffering. However, such an approach did not lead to a consensus about the past; Chapter 6 detailed how various memory battles swept Czech public discourse in the new millennium.

Yet this is not to say that as the period under investigation in this book drew to a close, the memory processes relating to state socialism have been exhausted. The thirtieth anniversary of the fall of the communist regime has once again reanimated discussions about the past. The media are not willing to let go the subject of how the legacies of state socialism should be approached and who should be allowed to speak about the past, even if it no longer functions as a useful battleground for politicians. But the variety of positions vying for legitimacy shows that the debate about the nature of the communist regime has indeed become pluralized. Cultural production too continues to search for new ways of speaking about state socialism. Only in 2017, Czech Television broadcast two series that touched on the recent past. Both used innovative generic and thematic conventions that had not previously been tested on the topic of the previous regime and that fitted neither the 'retro' nor the 'dramatic turn' categories that had dominated the first quarter-century after 1989 described in this book. The historical-fantasy series *The World under One's Head* (*Svět pod hlavou*, dir. Radim Špaček and Marek Najbrt, 2017) transposed the concept of the successful BBC series *Life on Mars* to industrial Northern Bohemia of the 1980s, involving both crime and, more surprisingly, time travel. The documentary series *Stories of the Twentieth Century* (*Příběhy dvacátého století*, Czech Television, 2017), based on the eponymous radio show, had witnesses openly speak about persecution, but also open collaboration with the communist regime in candid testimonies previously unseen on Czech screens.

The changing political landscape has also become increasingly less concerned with notions of exemplary behaviour under state socialism, demonstrated by the massive political success of billionaire entrepreneur Andrej Babiš. Although allegations of his possible collaboration with the secret police before 1989 remain unresolved, this has been no obstacle to Babiš, who is simply not interested in staging conflicts about the past as a political strategy. It was precisely such a strategy that was one of the defining features of postsocialism, a periodization that through its 'post' prefix constantly reminded us of the need to view the present in relation to the communist regime. That is why this conclusion is entitled 'Socialism Remembered', using the past participle, to mark that remembering the pre-1989 period in the ways discussed in this book is gradually slipping, or has already slipped into the realm of the past.

Notes

1. The film was the most-watched picture in cinemas in 2003 and even beat the second instalment of Peter Jackson's *Lord of the Rings* trilogy, which was a major international box office success at the time. See statistics of the Union of Film Distributors for 2003. Retrieved 23 August 2019 from http://www.ufd.cz/prehledy-statistiky/top-50-rocni-vysledky?page=1.
2. 'Není komouš jako komouš. Někdo tam vstoupí, aby to změkčoval zevnitř, vole, někdo se obětuje!' *Pupendo*, 2003.
3. 'Komunismus je svinstvo a bolševici jsou svině.' 'Ředitel školy, Míla Brčcka, byl nucen v zájmu tisíců dětí předstírat loajalitu, ačkoliv vnitřně byl vždycky proti.' *Pupendo*, 2003.
4. F. Jameson, *Postmodernism, or, the Cultural Logic of Late Capitalism* (New York: Verso, 1991), 16–25.
5. I. Reifová, 'The Pleasure of Continuity: Re-reading Postsocialist Nostalgia', *International Journal of Cultural Studies* 21(6) (2018), 587–602.
6. See J. Assmann, 'Communicative and Cultural Memory', in A. Erll and A. Nünning (eds), *Cultural Memory Studies: An International and Interdisciplinary Handbook* (Berlin: Walter de Gruyter, 2008), 109–18.

Bibliography

Printed Sources

Abbe, T. *Ostalgie: Zum Umgang mit der DDR-Vergangenheit in den 1990er Jahren.* Erfurt: Landeszentrale für Politische Bildung, 2005.

Adorno T., and M. Horkheimer. *The Dialectic of Enlightenment*, trans. John Cumming. London: Verso, 1997.

Angé, O., and D. Berliner (eds). *Anthropology and Nostalgia.* New York: Berghahn Books, 2015.

Arendt, H. *Původ totalitarismu I–III*, trans. Jana Fraňková. Prague: OIKOYMENH, 1996.

Assmann, A. *Der lange Schatten der Vergangenheit: Erinnerungskultur und Geschichtspolitik.* Munich: C.H. Beck, 2006.

Assmann, J. 'Collective Memory and Cultural Identity', trans. John Czaplicka. *New German Critique* 65 (1995), 125–33.

———. 'Communicative and Cultural Memory', in A. Erll and A. Nünning (eds), *Cultural Memory Studies: An International and Interdisciplinary Handbook.* Berlin: Walter de Gruyter, 2008, 109–18.

Bach, J. '"The Taste Remains": Consumption, (N)ostalgia, and the Production of East Germany'. *Public Culture* 14(3) (2002), 545–56.

Baker, S.E. *Retro Style: Class, Gender and Design in the Home.* London: Bloomsbury, 2013.

Bal, M. *Quoting Caravaggio: Contemporary Art, Preposterous History.* Chicago: University of Chicago Press, 1999.

Balabán, J. *Zeptej se táty.* Brno: Host, 2010.

Baláž, A. *Len jedna jar.* Bratislava: Marenčin PT, 2013.

Baudrillard, J. 'History: A Retro Scenario', in *Simulacra and Simulations*, trans. S. Faria Glaser. Ann Arbor: University of Michigan Press, 1994, 43–48.

Beasley-Murray, T. 'Ruins and Representations of 1989: Exception, Normality, Revolution', in D. Gafijczuk and D. Sayer (eds), *The Inhabited Ruins of Central Europe: Re-imagining Space, History, and Memory.* London: Palgrave Macmillan, 2013, 16–39.

Bechmann Pedersen, S. *Reel Socialism: Making Sense of History in Czech and German Cinema since 1989.* Lund: Lund University/Media-Tryck, 2015.

Bělohradský, V. 'Antipolitika v Čechách: Příspěvek ke gramatice kýče', in P. Fiala and F. Mikš (eds), *Česká konzervativní a liberální politika.* Brno: CDK, 2000, 33–59.

Berdahl, D. '"(N)Ostalgie" for the Present: Memory, Longing, and East German Things'. *Ethnos* 64(2) (1999), 192–211.

Bernhard, M., and J. Kubik. 'A Theory of the Politics of Memory', in M. Bernhard and J. Kubik (eds), *Twenty Years after Communism.* Oxford: Oxford University Press, 2014, 7–30.

Bílek, P.A. 'Předmluva', in P.A. Bílek (ed.), *James Bond a Major Zeman: Ideologizující vzorce vyprávění*. Příbram: Pistorius and Olšanská, 2007, 7–9.

Blacker, U., A. Etkind and J. Fedor (eds), *Memory and Theory in Eastern Europe*. Basingstoke: Palgrave Macmillan, 2013.

Blaive, M. 'Zpřístupnění archivů komunistické tajné police: případ České republiky – od Zdeny Salivarové k Milanu Kunderovi'. *Souvislosti: 'Kauza Kundera' rok poté* 20(4) (2009), 158–73.

———. '"Hidden Transcripts" and Microhistory as a Comparative Tool: Two Case Studies in Communist Czechoslovakia'. *East Central Europe* 40(1–2) (2013), 74–96.

Blum, M. 'Remaking the East German Past: Ostalgie, Identity, and Material Culture'. *Journal of Popular Culture* 24(3) (2000), 229–53.

Bockman, J., and G. Eyal. 'Eastern Europe as a Laboratory for Economic Knowledge: The Transnational Roots of Neoliberalism'. *American Journal of Sociology* 108(2) (2002), 310–52.

Bolton, J. *Worlds of Dissent: Charter 77, the Plastic People of the Universe, and Czech Culture under Communism*. Cambridge, MA: Harvard University Press, 2012.

Boyer, D. 'Ostalgie and the Politics of the Future in Eastern Germany'. *Public Culture* 18(2) (2006), 361–81.

Boym, S. *The Future of Nostalgia*. New York: Basic Books, 2001.

Bren, P. *The Greengrocer and His TV: The Culture of Communism after the 1968 Prague Spring*. Ithaca: Cornell University Press, 2010.

Bugge, P. 'Longing or Belonging? Czech Perceptions of Europe in the Inter-war Years and Today'. *Yearbook of European Studies* 11 (1999), 111–29.

Carpentier Reifová, I., K. Gillarová and R. Hladík. 'The Way We Applauded: How Popular Culture Stimulates Collective Memory of the Socialist Past in Czechoslovakia: The Case of the Television Serial *Vyprávěj* and its Viewers', in A. Imre, T. Havens and K. Lustyik (eds), *Popular Television in Eastern Europe During and Since Socialism*. New York: Routledge, 2013, 199–221.

Činátl, K. 'Časy normalizace', in P.A. Bílek and B. Činátlová (eds), *Tesilová kavalérie: popkulturní obrazy normalizace*. Příbram: Pistorius and Olšanská, 2010.

———. *Naše české minulosti*. Prague: Nakladatelství Lidové noviny, 2014.

Classen, C. 'Balanced Truth: Steven Spielberg's *Schindler's List* among History, Memory, and Popular Culture', trans. K. Wächter. *History and Theory* 48(2) (2009), 77–102.

Cook, P. *Screening the Past: Memory and Nostalgia in Cinema*. New York: Routledge, 2005.

Cooke, P. 'Performing "Ostalgie": Leander Haussmann's *Sonnenallee*'. *German Life and Letters* 56(2) (2003), 156–67.

———. *Representing East Germany since Unification: From Colonization to Nostalgia*. New York: Berg, 2005.

Čulík, J. *Jací jsme: Česká společnost v hraném filmu devadesátých a nultých let*. Brno: Host, 2007.

———. *A Society in Distress: The Image of the Czech Republic in Contemporary Czech Feature Film*. Eastbourne: Sussex Academic Press, 2013.

De Groot, J. '"Perpetually Dividing and Suturing the Past and Present": *Mad Men* and the Illusions of History'. *Rethinking History* 15(2) (2011), 269–85.

Dimou, A., M. Todorova and S. Troebst (eds). *Remembering Communism: Private and Public Recollections of Lived Experience in Southeast Europe*. Budapest: Central European University Press, 2014.

Dominková, P. '"We Have Democracy, Don't We?" Czech Society as Reflected in Contemporary Czech Cinema', in O. Sarkisova and P. Apor (eds), *Past for the Eyes: East European Representations of Communism in Cinema and Museums after 1989*. Budapest: Central European University Press, 2008, 215–44.

Dousková, I. *Hrdý Budžes*. Prague: Hynek, 1998.
———. *Oněgin byl Rusák*. Brno: Druhé město, 2006.
———. *B. Proudew*, trans. M. Clarke. Brno: Pálava Publishing, 2016.
———. *Onegin was a Rusky*, trans. M. Clarke. Brno: Pálava Publishing, 2018.
Dyer, R. *Pastiche*. New York: Routledge, 2007.
Enns, A. 'The Politics of Ostalgie: Post-socialist Nostalgia in Recent German Film'. *Screen* 48(4) (2007), 475–91.
Erll, A. 'Literature, Film, and the Mediality of Cultural Memory', in A. Erll and A. Nünning (eds), *Cultural Memory Studies: An International and Interdisciplinary Handbook*. Berlin: Walter de Gruyter, 2008, 389–98.
Erll, A., and S. Wodianka, 'Einleitung: Phänomenologie and Methodologie des "Erinnerungsfilms"', in A. Erll and S. Wodianka (eds), *Film und kulturelle Erinnerung: Plurimediale Konstellationen*. Berlin: Walter de Gruyter, 2008, 1–20.
Eyal, G. *The Origins of Postcommunist Elites: From Prague Spring to the Breakup of Czechoslovakia*. Minneapolis: University of Minnesota Press, 2003.
Feuer, J. *The Hollywood Musical*. Bloomington: Indiana University Press, 1993.
Fiala, P. et al. *Komunismus v České republice*. Brno: Masarykova univerzita, 1999.
Fiske, J. *Reading the Popular*. Boston: Unwin Hyman, 1989.
Franc, M. 'Ostalgie v Čechách', in M. Kopeček and A. Gjuričová (eds), *Kapitoly z dějin české demokracie po roce 1989*. Prague and Litomyšl: Paseka, 2008, 193–216.
———. 'Ostalgie v České republice a v SRN', in D. Kunštát and L. Mrklas (eds), *Historická reflexe minulosti aneb 'Ostalgie' v Německu a Česku*. Prague: CEVRO Institut, 2009, 7–14.
Frye, N. *Anatomy of Criticism*. Princeton: Princeton University Press, 1971.
Fulbrook, M. *Anatomy of a Dictatorship: Inside the GDR, 1949–1989*. Oxford: Oxford University Press, 1995.
Gaus, G. *Wo Deutschland liegt – Eine Ortsbestimmung*. Hamburg: Hoffmann & Campe, 1983.
Ghodsee, K. 'Tale of "Two Totalitarianisms": The Crisis of Capitalism and the Historical Memory of Communism'. *History of the Present* 4(2) (2014), 115–42.
Gjuričová, A. et al. (eds). *Rozdělení minulostí: Vytváření politických identit v České republice po roce 1989*. Prague: Prague: Ústav pro soudobé dějiny, 2012.
Gjuričová, A., and T. Zahradníček, *Návrat parlamentu: Češi a Slováci ve Federálním shromáždění 1989–1992*. Prague: Argo, 2018.
Godeanu-Kenworthy, O. 'Deconstructing Ostalgia: The National Past between Commodity and Simulacrum in Wolfgang Becker's *Good Bye Lenin!* (2003)'. *Journal of European Studies* 41(2) (2011), 161–77.
Goll, T. 'Einführung – Erinnerungskultur und Ostalgie', in T. Goll and T. Leuerer (eds), *Ostalgie als Erinnergungskultur? Symposium zu Leid und Politik in der DDR*. Baden Baden: Nomos, 2004, 9–15.
Grainge, P. *Monochrome Memories: Nostalgia and Style in Retro America*. Westport: Praeger, 2002.
Grębecka, Z. 'Między śmiechem a nostalgią – powroty do komunistycznej przeszłości', in M. Bogusławska and Z. Grębecka (eds), *Popkomunizm: Doświadczenie komunizmu a kultura popularna*. Cracow: Libron, 2010, 321–43.
Greif, M. 'You'll Love the Way It Makes You Feel'. *London Review of Books* 30(20) (2008), 15–16.
Guffey, E.E. *Retro: The Culture of Revival*. London: Reaktion Books, 2006.
Hájíček, J. *Selský baroko*. Brno: Host, 2005.
———. *Rybí krev*. Brno: Host, 2012.
Halbwachs, M. *On Collective Memory*, ed. and trans. Lewis A. Coser. Chicago: University of Chicago Press, 1992.

Hames, P. 'The Good Soldier Svejk and after: The Comic Tradition in Czech Film', in D. Holmes and A. Smith (eds), *100 Years of European Cinema: Entertainment or Ideology?* Manchester: Manchester University Press, 2000, 64–76.
Hanley, S. *The New Right in the New Europe: Czech Transformation and Right-Wing Politics, 1989–2006.* London: Routledge, 2006.
Harvey, D. *A Brief History of Neoliberalism.* Oxford: Oxford University Press, 2005.
Hašek, J. *Osudy dobrého vojáka Švejka.* Vols 1–4. Prague: Cesty, 2000.
Havel, V. 'Příběh a totalita', in *Eseje a jiné texty z let 1970–1989: Dálkový výslech.* Prague: Torst, 1999, 931–59.
Hirsch, M. *The Generation of Postmemory: Writing and Visual Culture after the Holocaust.* New York: Columbia University Press, 2012.
Hladík, R. 'Traumatické komedie: Politika paměti v českém filmu'. *Sociální studia* 1 (2010), 9–26.
———. 'Vážné, nevážné a znevážené vzpomínání v postsocialistické kinematografii', in P. Kopal (ed.), *Film a dějiny 4: Normalizace.* Prague: Casablanca and ÚSTR, 2014, 461–75.
Hoenig, B., 'Možnosti a meze jednoho paradigmatu: Teorie totalitarismu aplikovaná na státní socialismus středovýchodní Evropy'. *Soudobé dějiny* 16(4) (2009), 640–52.
Hojda, Z., and J. Pokorný. *Pomníky a zapomníky.* Prague and Litomyšl: Paseka, 1996.
Holubec, S. *Ještě nejsme za vodou: Obrazy druhých a historická paměť v období postkomunistické transformace.* Prague: Scriptorium, 2015.
Holý, L. *The Little Czech and the Great Czech Nation: National Identity and the Post-communist Transformation of Society.* Cambridge: Cambridge University Press, 1996.
Hudek, A., M. Kopeček and J. Mervart (eds). *Čechoslovakismus.* Prague: Nakladatelství Lidové noviny, 2019.
Huyssen, A. *Twilight Memories: Marking Time in a Culture of Amnesia.* New York: Routledge, 1995.
Imre, A. 'Why Should We Study Socialist Commercials?'. *VIEW Journal of European Television History and Culture* 3(2) (2012), 65–76.
Ivanova, N. 'No(w)stalgia: Retro on the (Post)-Soviet Television Screen'. *Harriman Review* 12(2–3) (1999), 25–32.
James, J. 'Coming to Terms through Cinema: *The Lives of Others* in Germany's Cultural Landscape of Memory'. *Journal of the Society for the Anthropology of Europe* 10(2) (2010), 29–40.
Jameson, F. *Postmodernism, or, the Cultural Logic of Late Capitalism.* New York: Verso, 1991.
Kalinina, E. *Mediated Post-Soviet Nostalgia.* Huddinge: Södertörn University, 2014.
Klaus, V. 'Místo prologu', in M. Remešová and D. Mácha (eds), *Karel Gott: Zlatý hlas z Prahy.* Prague: Eminent, 2009, 7–9.
Klimáček, V. *Horúce leto 68.* Bratislava: Marenčin PT, 2011.
Kohoutek, J. 'Veřejná polemika o uvedení seriálu Třicet případů majora Zemana v České televizi po roce 1989 (diskurzivní analýza českého celostátního tisku)'. MA dissertation. Masaryk University Brno, 2011.
Koubek, J., and M. Polášek. *Antikomunismus: nekonečný příběh české politiky?* Prague: Friedrich-Ebert-Stiftung, 2013.
Kolář, P. 'Čtyři "základní rozpory" východoevropského komunismu', in P. Kolář and M. Pullmann (eds), *Co byla normalizace? Studie o pozdním socialismu.* Prague: Nakladatelství Lidové noviny and Ústav pro studium totalitních režimů, 2017.
Kopal, P. (ed.). *Film a dějiny 4: Normalizace.* Prague: Casablanca and ÚSTR, 2014.
Kopeček, L. *Éra nevinnosti: Česká politika 1989–1997.* Brno: Barrister and Principal, 2010.

———. *Deformace demokracie? Opoziční smlouva a česká politika v letech 1998–2002*. Brno: Barrister and Principal, 2015.
Kopeček, M. 'In Search of "National Memory": The Politics of History, Nostalgia and the Historiography of Communism in the Czech Republic and East Central Europe', in M. Kopeček (ed.), *Past in the Making: Historical Revisionism in Central Europe after 1989*. Budapest: Central European University Press, 2007, 75–95.
———. 'Disent jako minulost, liberalismus jako projekt. Občanské hnutí – Svobodní demokraté v české polistopadové politice', in A. Gjuričová et al. (eds), *Rozděleni minulostí: Vytváření politických identit v České republice po roce 1989*. Prague: Ústav pro soudobé dějiny, 2012, 61–106.
Kopeček, M., and Gjuričová, A. (eds). *Kapitoly z dějin české demokracie po roce 1989*. Prague and Litomyšl: Paseka, 2008.
Kopeček, M., and Wciślik, P. (eds). *Thinking through Transition: Liberal Democracy, Authoritarian Pasts, and Intellectual History in East Central Europe after 1989*. Budapest: CEU Press, 2015.
Köpplová, B. and J. Jirák. 'Masová média a česká společnost 90. let 20. století: Průběh a důsledky transformace českých médií', in G. Heiss et al. (eds), *Česko a Rakousko po konci studené války: různými cestami do nové Evropy*. Ústí nad Labem: Albis International, 2008, 207–29.
Krapfl, J. *Revolution with a Human Face: Politics, Culture, and Community in Czechoslovakia, 1989–1992*. Ithaca: Cornell University Press, 2013.
Krištúfek, P. *Dom hluchého*. Bratislava: Marenčin PT, 2012.
Kundera, M. 'The Tragedy of Central Europe'. *New York Review of Books*, 6 April 1984, 33–38.
———. *The Unbearable Lightness of Being*, trans. Michael Henry Heim. London: Faber & Faber, 1995.
Landsberg, A. 'Prosthetic Memory: The Ethics and Politics of Memory in an Age of Mass Culture', in P. Grainge (ed.), *Memory and Popular Film*. Manchester: Manchester University Press, 2003.
Liehm, A. 'The New Social Contract and the Parallel Polity', in J. Leftwich Curry (ed.), *Dissent in Eastern Europe*. New York: Praeger, 1983, 172–81.
Losev, L. *On the Beneficence of Censorship: Aesopian Language in Modern Russian Literature*, trans. J. Bobko. Munich: Otto Sagner in Kommission, 1984.
Lyotard, J. *The Postmodern Condition: A Report on Knowledge*. Minneapolis: University of Minnesota Press, 1984.
Macek, V., and J. Paštéková. *Dejiny slovenskej kinematografie*. Martin: Osveta, 1997.
Mayer, F. *Les Tchèques et leur communisme: Mémoire et identités politiques*. Paris: Editions de l'Ecole des hautes études en sciences sociales, 2004.
———. 'Des musées de l'anticommunisme', in F. Rousseau (ed.), *Les présents des passés douloureux: Musées d'histoire et configurations mémorielles. Essais de muséohistoire*. Paris: Michel Houdiard Editeur, 2012, 304–25.
Meerzon, Y. 'Dancing on the X-rays: On the Theatre of Memory, Counter-memory, and Postmemory in the Post-1989 East-European Context'. *Modern Drama* 54(4) (2011), 479–510.
Moss, K. 'A Russian Munchhausen: Aesopian Translation', in A. Horton (ed.), *Inside Soviet Film Satire: Laughter with a Lash*. Cambridge: Cambridge University Press, 1993, 20–35.
Mulkay, M. *On Humour: Its Nature and Place in Modern Society*. Cambridge: Polity Press, 1988.
Nadkarni, M., and O. Shevchenko. 'The Politics of Nostalgia: A Case for Comparative Analysis of Postsocialist Practices'. *Ab Imperio* 2 (2004), 487–519.

Neller, K. *DDR-Nostalgie: Dimensionen der Orientierungen der Ostdeutschen gegenüber der ehemaligen DDR, ihre Ursachen and politischen Konnotationen*. Wiesbaden: VS Verlag für Sozialwissenschaften, 2006.

Niżnik, J. (ed.). *Twentieth-Century Wars in European Memory*. Frankfurt am Main: Peter Lang, 2013.

Nora, P. 'Between Memory and History: Les Lieux de Mémoire'. *Representations* 26 (1989), 7–24.

Nosková, V. *Bereme, co je*. Prague: Abonent ND, 2005.

———. *Obsazeno*. Prague: MozART, 2007.

Novák, J. *Zatím dobrý: Mašínovi a největší příběh studené války*. Brno: Petrov, 2004.

Orwell, G. 'Funny, But Not Vulgar', in S. Orwell and I. Angus (eds), *The Collected Essays, Journalism and Letters of George Orwell: Vol. 3, As I Please, 1943–1945*. London: Secker & Warburg, 1968, 283–88.

Otáhal, M. *Opozice, moc, společnost 1969–1989: příspěvek k dějinám 'normalizace'*. Prague: Ústav pro soudobé dějiny AV ČR, 1994.

Pająk, P. 'Czeska komedia dla początkujących (szkic z historii gatunku)', in M. Bogusławska and Z. Grębecka (eds), *Popkomunizm: Doświadczenie komunizmu a kultura popularna*. Cracow: Libron, 2010, 139–48.

Pakier, M., and J. Wawrzyniak (eds). *Memory and Change in Europe: Eastern Perspectives*. New York: Berghahn Books, 2015.

Pehe, V. 'Retro Reappropriations: Responses to *The Thirty Cases of Major Zeman* in the Czech Republic'. *VIEW Journal of European Television History and Culture* 3(5) (2014), 100–7.

———. 'The Colours of Socialism: Visual Nostalgia and Retro Aesthetics in Czech Film and Television'. *Canadian Slavonic Papers/Revue Canadienne des Slavistes* 57(3–4) (2015), 239–53.

———. 'Drobné hrdinství: Vzdor jakožto předmět nostalgie v díle Petra Šabacha a Michala Viewegha'. *Česká literatura* 63(3) (2015), 419–34.

———. 'Authenticating the Past: Archives, Secret Police, and Heroism in Contemporary Czech Representations of Socialism', in M. Blaive (ed.), *Perceptions of Society in Communist Europe: Regime Archives and Popular Opinion*. London: Bloomsbury Academic, 2018, 207–22.

Pergler, T. *Babiš: Příběh oligarchy*. Prague: Mladá fronta, 2014.

Platt, K.M.F. 'Russian Empire of Pop: Postsocialist Nostalgia and Soviet Retro at the "New Wave" Competition'. *The Russian Review* 72(3) (2013), 447–69.

Post, V. 'Putting out the Fire, or Fanning the Flames? How Regulating Secret Service Files and Personnel Affects Contestation over the Communist Past'. PhD thesis. Department of Political Science, McGill University, 2015.

Přibáň, J. 'The Kundera Case and the Neurotic Collective Memory of Postcommunism'. *Verfassungsblog*, 12 January 2018. Retrieved 25 August 2019 from https://verfassungsblog.de/the-kundera-case-and-the-neurotic-collective-memory-of-postcommunism.

Pucherová, D. 'Trauma a pamäť augusta 1968 v súčasnom slovenskom románe'. *World Literature Studies* 6(2) (2014), 64–77.

Pullmann, M. *Konec experimentu: přestavba a pád komunismu v Československu*. Prague: Scriptorum, 2011.

Pynsent, R. *Questions of Identity: Czech and Slovak Ideas of Nationality and Personality*. Budapest: Central European University Press, 1994.

Pytlík, R. *Jaroslav Hašek a Dobrý voják Švejk*. Prague: Panorama, 1983.

Rak, J. *Bývali Čechové: české historické mýty a stereotypy*. Jinočany: H and H, 1994.

Rankov, P. *Stalo sa prvého septembra (alebo inokedy)*. Bratislava: Kalligram, 2008.

Reifová, I. 'Kryty moci a úkryty před mocí: Normalizační a postkomunistický televizní seriál', in J. Končelík, B. Köpplová and I. Prázová (eds), *Konsolidace vládnutí a podnikání v České Republice a v Evropské unii II. Sociologie, prognostika a správa. Média*. Prague: Matfyz Press, 2002, 354–372.

———. 'The Pleasure of Continuity: Re-reading Postsocialist Nostalgia'. *International Journal of Cultural Studies* 21(6) (2018), 587–602.

Remešová, M., and D. Mácha. *Karel Gott: Zlatý hlas z Prahy*. Prague: Eminent, 2009.

Roberts, A. 'The Politics and Anti-politics of Nostalgia'. *East European Politics & Societies*, 16(3) (2002), 764–809.

Roubal, P. 'Anticommunism of the Future. Czech Post-dissident Neoconservatives in Post-communist Transformation', in M. Kopeček and P. Wciślik (eds), *Thinking through Transition: Liberal Democracy, Authoritarian Pasts, and Intellectual History in East Central Europe after 1989*. Budapest: CEU Press, 2015, 171–200.

Šabach, P. *Jak potopit Austrálii*. Prague and Litomyšl: Paseka 1999.

———. *Občanský průkaz*. Prague and Litomyšl: Paseka, 2006.

Samuel, R. *Theatres of Memory: Volume 1: Past and Present in Contemporary Culture*. New York: Verso, 1994.

Škvorecký, J. *The Cowards*, trans. Jeanne Němcová. Harmondsworth: Penguin, 1972.

Slačálek, O. 'Český antikomunismus jako pokus o obnovu hegemonie'. *Britské listy*, 22 June 2009. Retrieved 25 August 2019 from https://legacy.blisty.cz/art/47533.html.

Sniegon, T. 'Implementing Post-communist National Memory in the Czech Republic and Slovakia'. *European Studies* 30(1) (2013), 97–124.

Sperling, J. 'In Conversation: Agnieszka Holland with Joshua Sperling', *The Brooklyn Rail*, 18 December 2013. Retrieved 25 August 2019 from http://www.brooklynrail.org/2013/12/film/agnieszka-holland-with-joshua-sperling.

Sontag, S. *Against Interpretation*. London: Vintage, 1994.

Stern, J. *Média, psychoanalýza a jiné perverze*. Prague: Malvern, 2006.

Stoianova, V. 'The Communist Period in Postcommunist Bulgarian Cinema', in M. Todorova and Z. Gille (eds), *Post-communist Nostalgia*. New York: Berghahn Books, 2010, 373–90.

Stránský, J. *Zdivočelá země*. Prague: Nakladatelství Lidové noviny, 1991.

———. *Zdivočelá země. Aukce*. Prague: Knižní klub, 1997.

Suk, J. *Labyrintem revoluce: Aktéři, zápletky a křižovatky jedné politické krize (od listopadu 1989 do června 1990)*. Prague: Prostor, 2003.

Švéda, J. *Mašínovský mýtus: ideologie v české literatuře a kultuře*. Příbram: Pistorius and Olšanská, 2012.

Švihlíková, I. *Jak jsme se stali kolonií*. Prague: Rybka Publishers, 2015.

Szomolányi, S. *Kľukatá cesta Slovenska k demokracii*. Bratislava: Stimul 1999.

Terian, A. 'The Rhetoric of Subversion: Strategies of "Aesopian Language" in Romanian Literary Criticism under Late Communism'. *Slovo* 24(2) (2012), 75–95.

Ther, P. *Europe since 1989: A History*, trans. Charlotte Hughes-Kreutzmüller. Princeton: Princeton University Press, 2016.

Todorova, M. (ed.). *Remembering Communism: Genres of Representation*. New York: Social Science Research Council, 2010.

Todorova, M., and Z. Gille (eds). *Post-communist Nostalgia*. New York: Berghahn Books, 2010.

Trnka, S. 'Forgotten Pasts and Fearful Futures in Czechs' Remembrances of Communism'. *Focaal – Journal of Global and Historical Anthropology* 66 (2013), 36–46.

Tučková, K. *Žítkovské bohyně*. Brno: Host, 2012.

Tyl, J. 'Autorský subjekt jako osvoboditel (sebe sama)'. *Iniciály* 4(36) (1993), 25–26.
Valeš, L. 'Antikomunismus jako nová politická ideologie?', in P. Kopeček et al. (eds), *Společenskovědní aspekty fenoménu vyrovnání se s minulostí v kontextu výchovy k občanství*. Prague: Nakladatelství Epocha, 2013, 60–81.
Velikonja, M. 'Lost in Transition: Nostalgia for Socialism in Post-socialist Countries'. *East European Politics and Societies* 23(4) (2009), 535–51.
Viewegh, M. *Báječná léta pod psa*. Prague: Československý spisovatel, 1992.
———. *Výchova dívek v Čechách*. Prague: Český spisovatel, 1994.
———. *Bliss Was It in Bohemia*, trans. D. Short. London: Jantar Publishing, 2015.
White, H., *Metahistory: The Historical Imagination in Nineteenth-Century Europe*. Baltimore: Johns Hopkins University Press, 1973.
Williams, K. 'National Myths in the New Czech Liberalism', in G. Hosking and G. Schöpflin (eds), *Myths and Nationhood*. London: Hurst, 1997, 132–40.
Williams, R. *The Long Revolution*. London: Penguin, 1965.
Wirsching, A. *Der Preis der Freiheit: Geschichte Europas in unserer Zeit*. Munich: C.H. Beck, 2012.
Yurchak, A. *Everything was Forever, Until It was No More: The Last Soviet Generation*. Princeton: Princeton University Press, 2006.
———. 'Post-post-communist Sincerity: Pioneers, Cosmonauts, and Other Soviet Heroes Born Today', in T. Lahusen and P. H. Solomon, Jr. (eds), *What Is Soviet Now? Identities, Legacies, Memories*. Berlin: Lit Verlag, 2008, 257–76.
Žáček, P. *Boje o minulost: Deset let vyrovnávání se s komunistickou minulostí – pokus o předběžnou bilanci*. Brno: Barrister and Principal, 2000.
Zmeškal, T. *Milostný dopis klínovým písmem*. Prague: Torst, 2008.
Zmeškal, T. *Love Letter in Cuneiform*, trans. A. Zucker. New Haven: Yale University Press, 2016.

Film, Television and Theatre Productions

Anglické jahody (*English Strawberries*). Vladimír Drha (director), Martin Šafránek (screenwriter). Czech Republic/Slovakia/Ukraine, 2008.
Beseda k seriálu Třicet případů Majora Zemana (*Debate Accompanying the Series* The Thirty Cases of Major Zeman). Marek Straka (director). Česká televize. Czech Republic, 1999.
Bumerang (*Boomerang*). Hynek Bočan (director), Jiří Stránský (screenwriter). Czech Republic, 1996.
Černí baroni (*Black Barons*). Zdeněk Sirový (director, screenwriter), Miloslav Švadrlík (screenwriter). Czechoslovakia, 1992.
Červený kapitán (*Red Captain*). Michal Kollár (director, screenwriter), Miro Šifra and Anna Fifíková (screenwriters). Slovakia/Czech Republic/Poland, 2016.
České století (*The Czech Century*). Robert Sedláček (director), Pavel Kosatík (screenwriter). Česká televize, nine episodes. Czech Republic, 2013–14.
Das Leben der Anderen (*The Lives of Others*). Florian Henckel von Donnersmarck (director, screenwriter). Germany, 2006.
Dom solntsa (*The House of Sun*). Garik Sukachev (director, screenwriter), Nataliya Pavlovskaya and Ivan Okhlobystin (screenwriters). Russia, 2010.
Don't Stop. Richard Řeřicha (director, screenwriter). Czech Republic/Slovakia, 2012.
Eštébák (*The Informer*). Juraj Nvota (director), Ľubomír Slivka (screenwriter). Czech Republic/Slovakia/Poland, 2012.

Fair Play. Andrea Sedláčková (director, screenwriter). Czech Republic/Slovakia/ Germany, 2014.
Good Bye, Lenin! Wolfgang Becker (director, screenwriter), Bernd Lichtenberg (screenwriter). Germany, 2003.
Helden Wie Wir (*Heroes Like Us*). Sebastian Peterson (director, screenwriter), Thomas Brussig and Markus Dittrich (screenwriters). Germany, 1999.
Hořící keř (*Burning Bush*). Agnieszka Holland (director), Štěpán Hulík (screenwriter). HBO, mini-series. Czech Republic/Poland, 2013.
Inženýrská odysea (*The Engineer's Odyssey*). Evžen Sokolovský (director), Jaroslav Dietl (screenwriter). Československá televize, thirteen episodes. Czechoslovakia, 1979.
Kawasakiho růže (*Kawasaki's Rose*). Jan Hřebejk (director), Petr Jarchovský (screenwriter). Czech Republic, 2009.
Kleinruppin Forever. Carsten Fiebeler (director), Peer Klehmet and Sebastian Wehlings (screenwriters). Germany, 2004.
Kolja (Kolya). Jan Svěrák (director), Zdeněk Svěrák (screenwriter). Czech Republic, 1996.
Konec velkých prázdnin (*The End of the Long Vacation*). Miloslav Luther (director), Pavel Kohout and Jelena Mašínová (screenwriters). Česká televize, six episodes. Czech Republic, 1994.
Kousek nebe (*A Piece of Sky*). Petr Nikolaev (director), Jiří Stránský (screenwriter). Czech Republic, 2005.
Mad Men. Matthew Weiner (creator). Weiner Bros./AMC, ninety-two episodes (seven seasons). USA, 2007–2010, 2011–15.
Mladý muž a bílá velryba (*The Young Man and the White Whale*). Jaromil Jireš (director), Mária Dufková-Rudlovčáková (screenwriter). Czechoslovakia, 1978.
Občanský průkaz (*The Identity Card*). Ondřej Trojan (director), Petr Jarchovský (screenwriter). Czech Republic/Slovakia, 2010.
Operace Dunaj (*Operation Danube*). Jacek Głomb (director), Jacek Kondracki and Robert Urbański (screenwriters). Czech Republic/Poland, 2009.
Osmy (*Wisdom Teeth*). Jiří Strach (director), Marek Epstein (screenwriter). Česká televize. Czech Republic, 2014.
Pelíšky (*Cosy Dens*). Jan Hřebejk (director), Petr Jarchovský (screenwriter). Czech Republic, 1999.
Pouta (*Walking Too Fast*). Radim Špaček (director), Ondřej Štindl (screenwriter). Czech Republic/Slovakia, 2009.
Příběhy dvacátého století (*Stories of the Twentieth Century*). Viktor Portel, Radim Špaček, Petr Hátle and Janek Kroupa (directors), Adam Drda, Mikuláš Kroupa and Tomáš Netočný (screenwriters). Česká televize, sixteen episodes. Czech Republic, 2017.
Pupendo. Jan Hřebejk (director), Petr Jarchovský (screenwriter). Czech Republic, 2003.
Rebelové (*The Rebels*). Filip Renč (director), Zdeněk Zelenka (director, screenwriter). Czech Republic, 2001.
Rozpaky kuchaře Svatopluka (*The Hesitations of Chef Svatopluk*). František Filip (director, screenwriter), Jaroslav Dietl (screenwriter). Československá televize, thirteen episodes. Czechoslovakia, 1984.
Rukojemník (*The Hostage*). Juraj Nvota (director), Peter Pišťanek and Marian Urban (screenwriters). Slovakia/Czech Republic, 2014.
Šakalí léta (*Jackal Years*). Jan Hřebejk (director, screenwriter), Petr Jarchovský (screenwriter). Czech Republic, 1993.
Šedá sedmdesátá aneb Husákovo ticho (*Grey Seventies, or Husák's Quiet*). Jan Mikulášek (director, writer), Dana Viceníková (writer). Theatre on the Balustrades, Prague, 2013.

Skalpel, prosím (*Scalpel, Please*). Jiří Svoboda (director), Václav Nývlt (screenwriter). Czechoslovakia, 1985.
Sonnenallee (*Sun Alley*). Leander Haußmann (director, screenwriter), Thomas Brussig (screenwriter). Germany, 1999.
Svět pod hlavou (*The World under One's Head*). Radim Špaček and Marek Najbrt (directors), Ondřej Štindl, Robert Geisler and Benjamin Tuček (screenwriters). Česká televize, ten episodes. Czech Republic, 2017.
Stilyagi (*Hipsters*). Valery Todorovsky (director), Yury Korotkov (screenwriter). Russia, 2008.
Tankový prapor (*The Tank Battalion*). Vít Olmer (director, screenwriter), Radek John (screenwriter). Czechoslovakia, 1991.
Tito i ja (*Tito and Me*). Goran Marković (director, screenwriter). Yugoslavia, 1992.
Tlustá čára za minulostí? (*A Thick Line behind the Past?*). Debate accompanying the series *The Thirty Cases of Major Zeman*. Marek Straka (director). Česká televize. Czech Republic, 1999.
Třicet případů majora Zemana (*The Thirty Cases of Major Zeman*). Jiří Sequens (director, screenwriter). Československá televize, thirty episodes. Czechoslovakia, 1974–79.
Učiteľka (*The Teacher*). Jan Hřebejk (director), Petr Jarchovský (screenwriter). Slovakia/Czech Republic, 2016.
Uniforma (*The Uniform*). Hynek Bočan (director), Jiří Stránský (screenwriter). Česká televize. Czech Republic, 2001.
Vesničko má středisková (*My Sweet Little Village*). Jiří Menzel (director), Zdeněk Svěrák (screenwriter). Czechoslovakia, 1985.
Ve stínu (*In the Shadow*). David Ondříček (director, screenwriter), Marek Epstein and Misha Votruba (screenwriters). Czech Republic/Slovakia/Poland, 2012.
Vyprávěj. (*Tell Me a Story*). Biser Arichtev (director), Rudolf Merkner (screenwriter). Dramedy Productions/ Česká televize, 115 episodes (five seasons + bonuses). Czech Republic, 2009–13.
Wszystko, co kocham (*All That I Love*). Jacek Borcuch (director, screenwriter). Poland, 2009.
Žabák (*The Frog*). Hynek Bočan (director), Jiří Stránský (screenwriter). Česká televize. Czech Republic, 2001.
Žena za pultem (*The Woman behind the Counter*). Jaroslav Dudek (director), Jaroslav Dietl (screenwriter), Československá televise, twelve episodes. Czechoslovakia, 1977.
Zdivočelá země (*A Land Gone Wild*). Hynek Bočan (director, screenwriter), Jiří Stránský (screenwriter). Česká televize, forty-five episodes (four seasons). Czech Republic, 1997, 2001, 2008–9, 2012.
Zlatá šedesátá aneb Deník Pavla J. (*Golden Sixties, or the Diary of Pavel J.*). Jan Mikulášek (director), Pavel Juráček (writer). Theatre on the Balustrades, Prague, 2013.

INDEX

Aesopian language, 74–75
All That I Love (film, Borcuch), 51, 96
Anti-Charter, 67
anticommunism, 6, 12–3, 20, 21, 25n, 27–9, 31–3, 35–40, 46, 65–6, 68–9, 73, 79, 85–8, 93, 96–7, 111–2, 114–5, 119, 123, 125–130, 141, 147, 154–7, 159–60
    tradition of, 29–30
archive, 15, 124, 126–7, 131–3, 135–7. *See also* Security Services Archive (Czech Republic)
archival television shows, 64
authenticity, 104
    in representation, 114, 119, 131, 137–40, 142

Babiš, Andrej, 4, 161
Beneš, Edvard, 145
Black Barons (film, Sirový), 46–7, 49, 51, 54
Bočan, Hynek, 34–5, 5
    Bumerang (TV film), 34
    Frog, The (TV film), 35, 44n
    Land Gone Wild, A (TV series), 33–4, 48, 61n, 140, 142
    Uniform, The (TV film), 35, 44n
Botas (shoes), 103–6, 111, 114
Boučková, Tereza, 88
Boym, Svetlana, 8–9, 11, 74, 76, 159
Brussels Style, 1
Burning Bush (mini series, Holland), 134, 136–140, 142, 145

camp, 17, 47, 55, 60, 75–6, 108
Černý, David, 35, 38

anti-fascist resistance memorial, 38–9
    'One Does Not Speak to Communists' petition, 38
    Pink Tank, 35–8
Charter 77, 40, 67, 88–9, 91, 144–5
child's perspective, 7–8, 46, 50–1, 53, 59, 84–7, 133
Cibulka, Petr, 37
Civic Democratic Party (ODS), 31, 51
Civic Forum (OF), 30, 36, 144
Civic Movement (OH), 35, 38
comedy, 7, 11, 13–4, 20, 23n, 37, 46–51, 53, 58–9, 65–6, 70–2, 79–80, 84–5, 87–8, 90, 92–3, 97, 105, 107–8, 110, 114–9, 123–4, 130–2, 134, 136, 138–43, 155–6, 158
communism; communist regime, 8, 21n, 102, 124
    in Czechoslovakia, 2, 4, 11–2, 18, 27–30, 32–4, 36–40, 46, 53, 56, 76, 78, 84, 126–8, 133, 141–2, 155–6, 159–61
    reform communism, 13, 28, 32, 40, 112, 145
Communist Party (Czechoslovakia), 1, 3, 4, 21n, 28–9, 34, 36, 40, 47, 112, 134, 145, 155, 156
Communist Party of Bohemia and Moravia. *See* KSČM
Confederation of Political Prisoners, 18, 32–33, 71, 73 128, 141, 114, 118, 123
consumer products, 103, 108
    Czech Republic, 89, 103–7
    GDR, 17, 96, 105

Cosy Dens (film, Hřebejk), 6, 66, 70, 72–3, 76–9, 105, 114, 116, 117–8, 138, 140, 154
Czech Century (TV series), 143–7
Czech Television (public broadcaster), 4, 20, 34, 70–4, 86, 89, 107, 137, 143–144, 160

David, Michal, 65–6, 70
dissent, 12, 28, 36, 40, 88–9, 154
dissident, 5, 11, 20, 29, 30–2, 35, 38, 40, 47, 67, 69, 88–9, 92, 113, 132, 134–5, 144–5
Doležal, Bohumil, 68–9
Don't Stop (film, Řeřicha), 85, 148n
Dousková, Irena, 85–8, 96, 142
  B. Proudew, 86–7
  Onegin was a Russky, 86–8
Drda, Adam, 68, 73

Earthly Paradise for the Eyes, An (film, Pavlásková), 85, 88–9
East Germany, 7, 12, 14–7, 79, 103, 158
elites
  cultural, 19–20, 27–28, 30, 32, 38, 67–9, 132, 147, 160
  and memory, 20, 67–8, 159, 160
  political, 13, 28, 32, 36, 47, 130
End of the Long Vacation, The (TV series), 48
Engineer's Odyssey (TV series), 71
English Strawberries (film, Drha), 118–9

Fair Play (film, Sedláčková), 134, 136, 139–41
First Republic (Czechoslovakia), 15, 17, 24n, 30, 34, 40, 113, 139–40, 142–3, 157
First World War, 37, 93
Fish Blood (novel, Hájíček), 134
Forman, Miloš, 48, 90

genre, 7, 13, 35, 47–8, 54–55, 57, 67, 70, 74, 79, 85, 91–2, 97, 108, 112, 117–8, 124, 132, 137, 139–40, 155–6
German Democratic Republic. *See* GDR
GDR, 12, 14–17, 69, 97, 105, 114, 157. *See also* East Germany

Goddesses of Žítková, The (novel, Tučková), 133–5, 137
Good Bye, Lenin! (film, Becker), 14–7, 158
Gott, Karel, 66–70, 72–4, 76–7, 159
Grainge, Paul, 55, 59, 78

Havel, Václav, 27–8, 31, 35, 67, 88–90, 127, 144–5
Heroes Like Us (film, Peterson), 14
heroism, 7, 17, 21, 27, 32–3, 35, 40, 48, 57, 85, 117, 123–5, 127–30, 134–5, 138–45, 147, 154–7, 159–60
  Czech cultural tradition of, 33–34, 88, 93
  petty heroism, 20, 57–8, 78–9, 84, 89, 92–7, 117–9, 124, 131–2, 140–4, 155–6
  in Polish culture, 140
Hesitations of Chef Svatopluk, The (TV series), 71
Hipsters (film, Todorovsky), 96, 110
Hostage, The (film, Nvota), 8, 14, 50
House of the Deaf, The (novel, Krištúfek), 132
House of the Sun, The (film, Sukachev), 51, 96
Hot Summer of '68, The (novel, Klimáček), 132
Hrabal, Bohumil, 90
Hřebejk, Jan, 6, 14, 53–5, 66, 70, 72, 77–8, 85–6, 88, 105, 108, 134–5, 138, 154
humour, 7–8, 14–5, 17, 46–51, 53, 56, 58, 64, 75–6, 84–7, 92, 94, 97, 114, 117–8, 124, 141–2
Hus, Jan; Hussites, 33–4
Husák, Gustáv, 51, 68, 84, 89, 128

Identity Card, The
  film (Trojan), 85, 92, 95, 124
  novel (Šabach), 92–6, 124, 140
Informer, The (film, Nvota), 14, 136
Institute for the Study of Totalitarian Regimes, 4, 18, 39, 123. *See also* ÚSTR
In the Shadow (film, Ondříček), 134, 136, 139–42
Iron Curtain, 30, 48, 50, 53, 56, 104

irony, 5, 7–9, 11–2, 14, 17, 34, 36–7, 39, 49–53, 55, 59, 66–7, 75–76, 78, 87, 92, 95, 101–2, 104, 106, 110, 130, 134, 138, 146, 158–9

Jackal Years (film, Hřebejk), 54–6, 72, 75, 77, 108
Jameson, Fredric, 23n, 52–3, 158
Jarchovský, Petr, 53, 72, 91–2, 95
Jireš, Jaromil, 91
Just One Spring (novel, Baláž), 90

Kawasaki's Rose (film, Hřebejk), 88, 134–7, 141, 147
kitsch, 46, 55–6, 58–60, 103, 106
Klaus, Václav, 30–1, 38, 47, 50, 69, 70
Kleinruppin Forever (film, Fiebeler), 16, 157
Kofola, 103–4, 106, 111, 114
Kohout, Pavel, 89, 92
Kolya (film, Svěrák), 6, 56–9, 77–8, 85, 136
Krapfl, James, 7, 47
KSČM, 1, 28, 30–2, 37–39
Kundera, Milan, 132, 135
　Book of Laughter and Forgetting, The, 68
　Joke, The, 47
　'Kundera affair', 127, 135, 137
　Tragedy of Central Europe, The, 36
　Unbearable Lightness of Being, The, 58

Land Gone Wild, A (novel, TV series). *See* Stránský, Jiří
Lives of Others, The (film, von Donnersmarck), 136, 138
Love Letter in Cuneiform (novel, Zmeškal), 133–4, 147
Lukeš, Zdeněk, 68–9
lustration, 28, 37

Mad Men (TV series), 115, 158
Magnesia Litera prize, 150n
Markíza (TV channel), 71
Masaryk, Tomáš Garrigue, 27, 33, 113
Mašín, Ctirad and Josef, 127, 129, 132, 140–1

Mayer, Françoise, 5, 11, 33
media, 1, 3–6, 12–3, 20–1, 27–8, 31, 38, 41–2n, 65, 67, 69–70, 73, 75, 109, 112, 125, 127, 129, 146, 156, 160
　memory-making media, 19, 142
memory, 3–5, 8, 11–4, 17–21, 27, 32–4, 36, 39, 49, 65–71, 88–9, 91, 104, 107–8, 115, 117, 119, 123–33, 135–6, 141–3, 146–7, 154–60
　collective, 5, 18, 32, 35, 128, 156, 159
　communicative, 18–9, 132, 159–60
　cultural, 2, 4–7, 18–9, 27–8, 52, 65, 69, 84–5, 97, 101–2, 119, 131–2, 158–9
　memory film, 142, 145–6
　memory politics, 4, 18–20, 40, 123–6, 128, 130, 146–7, 156, 160
Menzel, Jiří, 48, 90–1
Museum of Communism (Prague), 9
musical, 53–5, 72, 107–8, 110
My Sweet Little Village (film, Menzel), 91

national identity, 7, 19, 147, 156
　Czech, 15, 28, 33–4, 126, 141, 157
　German, 14–6
Nazism, 3, 15, 39, 123
　equivalence to communism, 41, 123–4, 126, 130, 160
neoliberalism, 30–1, 42n
New Wave (Czechoslovakia), 48, 90
Normalization, 7, 28, 37–8, 40, 48–51, 67–8, 71, 84–5, 88–91, 93, 95–6, 101–2, 104, 112, 117, 124, 139
nostalgia, 1–2, 8–14, 17, 41, 49, 51–2, 54, 58–60, 65–7, 74, 76, 86–7, 94, 97, 102, 104, 106, 115, 119, 139, 142, 156–9
　for East Germany (*see* Ostalgie)
　postmodern, 9, 52–3, 101–2
　postsocialist, 8–9, 13, 20, 28, 79, 84, 103, 157–9
　for resistance, 8, 78–9, 84, 86, 94–7, 157–8
Nova (TV channel), 29, 71

'One Does Not Speak to Communists', 38, 40, 160

Operation Danube (film, Głomb), 118
Opposition Agreement, 31, 43n
Ostalgie, 7, 11–17, 51–2, 69, 79, 96–7, 103, 105, 113, 157–9

Palach, Jan, 33, 124, 137, 140
pastiche, 52, 54, 75, 77, 102, 106, 110–1, 115–6, 131
Patočka, Jan, 145
Peňás, Jiří, 54, 58, 74, 89
Piece of Sky, A, (film, Nikolaev) 35
Pink Tank. *See under* Černý, David
Pišťanek, Peter, 50
Platform for European Memory and Conscience, 130
Podebal (artistic collective), 37
Poláček, Karel, 50, 86
political prisoners, 5, 20, 29, 34–5, 40, 73, 134. *See also* Confederation of Political Prisoners
Post Bellum (organization), 127–8, 135
postmodernism, 9, 40, 49, 52–6, 59, 75–6, 101–2, 110, 116–7, 158–9
Prague Declaration on European Conscience and Communism, 124
Prague Spring, 40, 77, 84, 90, 102, 111–3, 116, 126, 138, 145
Pupendo (film, Hřebejk), 85, 154–5

Rebels, The (film, Renč), 107–114, 116–7, 131, 138–9
reception, 5–6, 9, 19–20, 25n, 36, 66, 70, 73–4, 101, 104, 111, 114, 118, 159
Red Captain (film, Kollár), 14
reform socialism. *See under* communism, communist regime
Reifová, Irena, 20, 67, 159
resistance, 3, 7–8, 12, 15, 20–1, 58, 89, 124–30, 147, 158–60. *See also* Third Resistance
  anticommunist, 3, 27, 32–5, 40, 48, 123, 141, 160
  antifascist, 38–9
  in representation, 84–5, 91–7, 115–6, 118–9, 124, 132, 142, 154–7 (*see also* petty heroism)

retro, 5, 9, 11, 14, 20, 52, 54–6, 59–60, 65, 70, 72–3, 75–7, 79, 102–4, 107–111, 114–9, 123–4, 130–1, 134, 137, 139–43, 144–5, 155, 158–9, 161
  in material culture, 104–7
  and postmodern nostalgia, 9, 17, 52–3, 75, 158–9
  TV programme, 64
  in Western culture, 52, 102–103, 115
retrochic, 54, 108
Rustic Baroque (novel, Hájíček), 133, 135

Šabach, Petr, 53, 59, 72, 78, 85–7, 91, 108, 132
  How to Sink Australia, 53
  Identity Card, The, 92–6, 124, 140
  'Jackal Years', 54
Second World War, 30, 33–5, 38–9, 52, 93, 114, 125, 127, 142
Security Services Archive (Czech Republic), 124–6, 128, 131, 137, 141
Scalpel, Please (film, Svoboda), 91
Skalník, Joska, 127, 135
Škvorecký, Josef, 47, 93
  literary prize, 150n
Slovakia, 3, 11, 13, 15, 28, 32–33, 65, 71–2, 90, 123, 132
  and 1968, 28–29, 118
  film production, 8, 13–14, 50, 136
  in representation, 15, 107–8, 113, 116
Social Democratic Party (ČSSD), 30–1, 37
So Far So Good (novel, Novák), 129, 132
Soviet Union, 27, 35–6, 40, 74, 92, 96, 102, 118, 132, 144, 157
Stasi, 15, 137
State Security (Czechoslovakia). *See* StB
Stb, 4, 37, 124, 126, 131, 134–7, 141, 147
Štindl, Ondřej, 68, 144
stiob, 92–3, 131
Stránký, Jiří, 33–5, 48, 59, 73
  Auction, The (novel), 33, 140
  Bumerang (TV film), 34
  Frog, The (TV film), 35, 44n
  Land Gone Wild, A (novel), 33, 140
  Land Gone Wild, A (TV series), 33–4, 48, 142

Piece of Sky, A (film), 35, 44n
Uniform, The (TV film), 35, 44n
Stories of the Twentieth Century, 161
students, 40, 104
    in 1989, 3
    International Students' Day, 3
    'Thank you, time to go' initiative, 43n
Sun Alley (film, Haußmann), 8, 14, 16, 51, 96
Svoboda, Jiří, 91
Švejk, 37, 48, 75, 92–3
Svěrák, Jan, 6, 52, 56, 85, 135
Svěrák, Zdeněk, 48, 56, 58
Švorcová, Jiřina, 29

Tank Battalion, The (film, Olmer), 46–7, 49, 54
Teacher, The (film, Hřebejk), 14
Tell Me a Story (TV series, Arichtev), 4, 20, 34, 40, 85, 107–13, 116–7, 137, 139
Theatre on the Balustrades, 89–90
Third Resistance, 35, 130, 135, 141
    Act on (2011), 35, 128–9
Thirty Cases of Major Zeman, The (TV series, Sequens), 66, 70–6, 79, 102, 111, 159
Tigrid, Pavel, 29–30
Tito and Me (film, Marković), 7
totalitarianism, 3, 7, 12, 21n, 29, 39–40, 88, 123, 125–6, 129–30, 142, 156–7, 160
    and *totalita*, 21n, 126
transitional justice, 6, 18, 47
trauma, 13–4, 46, 48–51, 117–9, 128, 130, 132–3, 138, 141, 155–6, 160

underground, 28, 95, 110, 112, 144
ÚSTR, 123–32, 135

Velčovský, Maxim, 106
Velvet Revolution, 2, 5, 11, 30, 47, 54, 113, 128, 155
    anniversary of, 3–4
    in representation, 56, 124, 144
Viewegh, Michal, 49, 78, 85, 133
    Bliss Was It in Bohemia, 7, 49–53, 55, 85–7, 92, 133
    Bringing up Girls in Bohemia, 53
Vergangenheitsbewältigung, 3, 53, 58
Vondráčková, Helena, 66

Walking Too Fast (film, Špaček), 88, 134, 136, 139, 147
Warsaw Pact invasion of Czechoslovakia (1968), 7
    in representation, 72, 78, 107, 111, 116–9, 138
We Take What Comes (novel, Nosková), 133–4
Wisdom Teeth (TV film, Strach), 89, 148n
Woman Behind the Counter (TV series), 91
World under One's Head (TV series), 161
World War I. *See* First World War
World War II. *See* Second World War

Young Man and the White Whale, The, (film, Jireš) 91
Yugonostalgia, 12

Zeman, Miloš, 3

www.ingramcontent.com/pod-product-compliance
Lightning Source LLC
Chambersburg PA
CBHW071345080526
44587CB00017B/2968